RACIAL DISCRIMINATION AGAINST OVERSEAS INDIANS
(A CLASS ANALYSIS)

RACIAL DISCRIMINATION AGAINST OVERSEAS INDIANS
(A Class Analysis)

PRAKASH C. JAIN

CONCEPT PUBLISHING COMPANY, NEW DELHI-110059 (INDIA)

The Indian Council of Social Science Research gave the financial support towards the publication of this work. However, the responsibility for the contents of the book—facts, opinions, conclusions, etc.—is entirely that of the author and not of the ICSSR.

ISBN 81-7022-288-5

First Published 1990

Prakash Chand **Jain** (*b.* 1946)

Published by
Ashok Kumar Mittal
Concept Publishing Company
A/15-16, Commercial Block, Mohan Garden
NEW DELHI - 110059 (India)

Lasertypeset by
Microtech Advance Printing Systems (Pvt.) Ltd.
H-13, Bali Nagar,
NEW DELHI - 110015

Printed in India by
Taj Press
DELHI - 110006

Contents

List of Tables

Preface

This book is based on my Ph.D. (Sociology) thesis "Colonialism, Class and Race Relations : The Case of Overseas Indians" which was submitted to the Faculty of Graduate Studies and Research, Carleton University, Ottawa in 1985. It seeks to apply class analysis to race relations situations involving overseas Indian communities in colonial/post-colonial societies.

The study is primarily a theoretical reinterpretation of race relations situations of overseas Indian communities and as such it takes issues with some of the established theories of ethnic and race relations such as pluralism, middleman minority theory and the work of John Rex. The major objective of the study is to show that a class approach can better explain the race relations situations of overseas Indians than other theoretical approaches. It is suggested that a class analysis of race relations must take into account the ideological as well as material bases of class formation and class conflict, and the interventionist role of the state. In this connection such neo-Marxist concepts as articulation of the modes of production, relative autonomy of the superstructural elements, class fraction, and intra-class conflict were found to be useful.

It is argued that overseas Indian communities are not necessarily corporate groups and therefore their race relations *vis-a-vis* other groups cannot be analysed as monolithic situations in which "racial groups" *in toto* attempt to compete with or dominate each other. Race relations do not arise automatically because of phenotypical differences but are articulated under certain economic and socio-political conditions in a given social formation.

In this study three cases of Guyana, Malaysia and Kenya are examined, using both quantitative as well as qualitative secondary data. The three cases represent different conjunctures of class, race and colonialism with respect to the overseas Indian communities. Whereas in Guyana the Indian community was formed as a result of indentured labour migration, in Kenya it was the middle class which constituted the core of the Indian community. The Malaysian case represents the mixture of the two : estate-bound *kangani* labourers and segments of the middle classes.

I wish to thank my thesis supervisor Professor Frank Vallee, and thesis committee members–Professors Joseph Manyoni, Derek Smith, and Daiva Stasiulis of the Department of Sociology and Anthropology, and Professor V. Subramaniam of the Department of Political Science, for their useful suggestions and constructive criticism throughout the various stages of this book.

I must express my gratitude to the Canadian Commonwealth Scholarship and Fellowship Committee for awarding me a scholarship for my doctoral programme at Carleton. I also gratefully acknowledge the moral and material support I received from a number of my friends in Canada, especially, Kamlesh and Rita Dwivedi, Niranjan Nathwani, Phanindra Reddy, Shekhar Singh and Tejinder Walia, and Sassan Amiri. Among my colleagues and friends in New Delhi whose companionship has been a source of encouragement to me I wish to thank Dr. Girijesh Pant, Dr. Tulsiram, Dr. N. Ram, Dr. P.P. Pandey, Dr. P.K. Jayaswal, Shri B.N. Rao, and Shri M.P. Singh.

Some parts of this book have already appeared as articles in various journals. I sincerely thank the editors and publishers of the *Sociological Bulletin*, *Economic and Political Weekly*, *Journal of Contemporary Asia*, and *Global Migration of Indians* for allowing me to incorporate most of the materials from these in Chapters 1, 2, 3 and 4, and 5 respectively (see Biblography, Jain, P.C. 1988a, 1988b, 1989a, and 1989b).

Finally, this book is dedicated to the members of my extended family whose love, understanding and support have helped me pursue my academic interests. Four of them need special mention here: my wife Dr. Renu Saxena, my younger brother Dr. H.C. Jain, and my maternal uncles Shri M.L. Jain and Shri K.C. Jain.

Prakash C. Jain

26 Nov. 1989

Centre for West Asian & African Studies,
School of International Studies
Jawaharlal Nehru University
New Delhi-110067

Introduction

The Meaning of "Race" and "Ethnicity"

"Race" and "ethnicity" are highly controversial and ambiguous terms. In the case of "race" part of this ambiguity is derived from the fact that biologists and physical anthropologists use the term in the biological sense wherein human beings are classified into a certain number of "races" on the basis of phenotypical and/or genotypical variations. In the nineteenth century, various schemes of racial classification–ranging from two races (with four sub-races) to two hundred races were presented (Singer 1983: 142). Many European and North American thinkers spread the notion that some races were superior to others. A whole range of social phenomena, including the rise and fall of civilisations, was explained in these terms. In the nineteenth century, this kind of thinking gave rise to various racist theories which claimed the superiority of the "Caucasian race"–in particular its "Aryan branch". Today, on the strength of genetics research, we know that there are no scientific grounds for classifying *homo sapiens* into "races". Instead, race is regarded as a socially defined category (Harris 1964; Miles 1982; Schermerhorn 1970; Wagley 1965). As van den Berghe (1970: 10) put it, by the term "race" is meant "a group of people who in a given society are socially defined from other groups by virtue of certain real or putative physical differences. What makes a society multi-racial is not the presence of physical differences between groups, but the attribution of social significance to such physical differences as may exist".

Like the term race, ethnicity also has a multiplicity of meanings. It has been defined by a number of criteria such as common ancestry, common nationality, shared way of life, consciousness of kind, cultural distinctiveness, etc. (Barth 1969; Glazer and Moynihan 1975; Epstein 1978; Lyon 1972). However, these criteria are not mutually exclusive; most of the definitions of ethnic groups based on these criteria abstract either the fact of cultural differences or the process of their maintenance.

Notwithstanding the various difficulties in precise conceptualisation of "race" and "ethnic group", social scientists seem to agree that both terms are similar in so far as they are social definitions. Racial distinctions are based on perceived physical differences, while ethnic differences are based on perceived cultural differences. Therefore, as Wilson (1973: 6) suggested, "classification of a particular group as either racial or ethnic is dependent on the perceptions and definitions of members of the larger society".

The above discussion of race and ethnic groups is meant to raise the question whether overseas Indian communities should be regarded as racial or ethnic categories. The answer to this question is simple. In the host societies overseas Indian communities are marked off by both their phenotypical characteristics as well as their cultural differences (religion, language, food habits, etc.). Therefore, they can be treated as racial as well as ethnic categories. However, in colonial societies, overseas Indians were often categorised in term of "race"; so for the sake of historical continuity we have retained this characterisation with the understanding that "race" is a social construct and as such has no objective reality independent of its social definition. Having defined overseas Indians as a racial category, our next step is to define a race relations situation.

Race Relations Defined

Park (1950) defined race relations as all relationships capable of producing racial conflict and racial consciousness. Similarly, another definition states that race relations "refer to interaction between groups socially defined as races at all levels of the social system, i.e., economic, political, and social" (Kinloch 1974: 10). A more refined definition which provides for race relations situation is provided by Rex (1970b: 39), who states:

> We shall speak of a race relations structure or problem, in so far as the inequalities and differentiation inherent in a social structure are related to physical and cultural criteria of an ascriptive kind and are rationalized in terms of deterministic belief systems ...

The three essential elements of the definition can be elaborated upon as follows:

1. Race relations situations are marked by such social structural features as severe competition, exploitation, coercion or oppression between groups.

2. Race relations situations are characterised by restrictions on group social mobility and/or ascriptive role allocation. These characteristics are derived from the fact that in an inter-group situation "all members of a group are regarded by virtue of possessing certain recognisable characteristics of the group, as being entitled to certain defined rights or as being assigned to certain defined roles" (Rex 1970a: 116-17). Thus at the group level individuals react to each other in classificatory and ascriptive ways rather than in terms of the criteria of achievement and universalism. In this context, discrimination can be considered as a particular case of ascriptive role allocation.

3. Ascriptive role allocation in situations of pluralism, inequality or oppression is justified in terms of some form of deterministic belief system, or ideology of cultural/racial differences (Kuper 1975; Rex 1970a, 1981). Such belief systems range from simple ethnic stereotypes and prejudices to religious-philosophical doctrines (e.g. the doctrine of *karma* in the context of the Hindu caste system), and from "somatic norm images" (Hoetink 1967) to explicit racist theories. They may or may not always be expressed as well articulated ideologies such as *apartheid* in South Africa. The major function of these belief systems is to maintain the *status quo* regarding socio-economic inequality and oppression, and to discourage the subordinate groups from attempting to change the situation or to improve their own position. Although Rex's definition is not without difficulties, as we shall see later, for the moment it is significant to note that it neither lends itself to structural or ideological reductionism, nor leads to tautological explanation of race relations as some neo-Marxist critics claim. For example, Miles (1982: 35) charges Rex with reification of "races" and argues that

> . . . by labeling a situation as one of 'race relations', one is implicitly denying that any other force can have an equal or predominant effect. . . . this approach means that if one labels the participants in a process as 'races', and their interactions as 'race relations', then one is denying either that they occupy a class position or that their class position is of significance to the situation and process.

Such a criticism is unwarranted. Rex does not deny that so-called races could not occupy other positions. His analysis of colonial societies in terms of "booty capitalism" based on slavery and forced labour (Rex 1970a) clearly suggests that race relations situations are not the simplistic results of "interaction" between "races" as Miles states. In the above definition the phrase "the inequalities and differentiation inherent in the social structure" signify the priority of structural factors in a situation of race relations. That Rex did not conceptualise social structure in terms of class, however, is another story, and concurring with Miles I would consider it to be a major drawback of the definition.

Rex's definition, though useful for identifying the race relations situations of overseas Indian communities, does not generate appropriate analytical categories. Thus the definition neither suggests the formative or operative context of the inequalities nor specifies the nature or kinds of inequalities. It is not clear whether he is referring to institutional, status group or class inequalities. In his earlier writings Rex (1970a) operationalised social structure in terms of Weberian estates or status groups; his recent works (1981; 1983) add classes and class segments as well. This shift occurs from his increasing realisation that colonial societies were integral parts of the world capitalist system. However, Rex's position is still that of an useasy synthesis of Weber and Marx. Thus, as a first corrective to the above definition, we suggest that structural inequalities and differentiation be operationalised in class terms. This point is particularly relevant for our purpose given the fact that as indentured or *kangani* labourers Indian emigrants necessarily entered in the production process as wage labourers. Thus, first and foremost, prior to their becoming objects of political and ideological reaction, the Indian emigrants occupied a class position in the emergent capitalist mode of production.

A second corrective we suggest is that the concept of "racial categorisation" be substituted for that of ascriptive role allocation. In this connection Miles (1982: 157) suggests the use of racial categorisation by which he means "an ideological process of delineation of group boundaries and of allocation of persons within these boundaries by primary reference to (supposedly) inherent and/or biological (usually phenotypical) characteristics". Racial categorisation, according to Miles, leads to class fractionalisation as racialised fractions are created within the class boundaries established by the dominant mode of production.

Thus by operationalising the concept of social structure in class terms and by introducing the concept of racial categorisation, we can fruitfully use Rex's definition for our purpose.

Operationally, race relations situations can be identified as inter-group relations involving one or more of the following: race riots, racial discrimination, racial segregation, expulsion, denial of citizenship, disenfranchisement, racially-based class exploitation, racial politics and discriminatory policies and practices on the part of the state.

The Study and its Organisation

This study is a comparative sociological analysis of race relations situations of overseas Indian communities in former colonial societies. Historically, overseas Indian communities in the British empire have been widely scattered in such diverse geographical areas as Southeast Asia, parts of Africa, and the West Indies. Countries with considerable numbers of overseas Indian communities have been Burma, Fiji, Guyana, Kenya, Malaysia, Mauritius, Singapore, South Africa, Sri Lanka, Surinam, Tanzania, Trinidad and Tobago, and Uganda (until 1972). However, the present study deals only with three case studies of Guyana, Malaysia, and Kenya, which represent all major intersections of colonialism, class, and race. The study generally encompasses the time period between the middle of the nineteenth century when Indian immigration and settlement began in these countries, and the early 1980s.

My interest in overseas Indian communities initially grew out of my general ignorance about them, which I guess shared with a great majority of my educated fellow countrymen. Not that I was completely ignorant. For example, I know, as do many Indians, that people of Indian origin lived in parts of Southeast Asia, Africa, and the West Indies. I knew that the famous novelist, V.S. Naipaul, was a Trinidadian-born Indian, that in 1972 the Indians were expelled from Uganda. Beyond such fragments of information, however, I did not have any systematic idea of the reasons for or circumstances of Indian emigration and settlement abroad and far less about the socio-economic and political conditions of these communities.

Given that I was doing doctoral studies in Canada, at first it seemed reasonable for me to focus on socio-cultural adjustment, organisational life, and the like. Soon, however, preliminary readings of the literature on overseas Indian communities and changes in my intellectual orientation led me to undertake the study presented here. For one thing, this reading drove home to me the fact that India itself and the places to which most Indians emigrated are Third World countries with colonial pasts. For another, in the literature on such Third World countries there is frequent reference to Indian migrants and some lively debate on the most fruitful ways to analyse their situations. These debates convinced me that class is the most crucial variable in race relations involving Indians in these countries and that given the paucity of studies which focus on class, I could contribute most meaningfully by doing a class-based study. What I offer, then, is a comparative study of overseas Indians using a uniform conceptual framework that captures the linkages between class and race relations in ex-colonial countries at different stages in their development.

My understanding of class and race relations in the colonial context has been very much influenced by neo-Marxist critiques of theories of Third World development as well as of race relations theories. These critiques have been applied not only to non-Marxist theories but also to orthodox Marxism, especially because of its Eurocentric bias. There has been a growing conviction among neo-Marxist scholars of colonial and post-colonial societies that race and ethnicity in these societies are no less important contradictions than those based on class. This study is an attempt to understand the complex interplay between race and class with particular reference to overseas Indian communities.

In the proposed theoretical framework developed in Chapter 2, it is argued that the emergence and perpetuation of race relations situations can be analysed as part of the process of class formation and class struggle in colonial and post-colonial societies. Classes are defined in terms of the means and relations of production, exchange, and distribution. A colonial and post-colonial economy and society is conceptualised as a peripheral capitalist social formation–peripheral to the metropolitan economy and society in the analytical sense. For our purpose, two sectors of colonial economy, i.e., plantation and mining, and trade and distribution, are examined. It was in relation to these sectors of colonial economy that overseas Indian migration and settlement took place. Thus, following the abolition of slavery in the British empire in 1833, for over a century Indians emigrated as labourers, traders and lower-grade professionals in various colonies. The historical patterns of Indian emigration and the formation of overseas Indian communities are discussed in Chapter 1. In Chapters 3, 4 and 5 the three case studies of Guyana, Malaysia, and Kenya are presented, respectively. In Chapter 6, the theoretical argument and its applications are summarised with reference to the case studies as well as to other overseas Indian communities.

1

Emigration and Formation of Overseas Indian Communities

Indians have been sojourning abroad since ancient times. There is historical evidence of Indian-influenced colonies and kingdoms in Southeast Asia, the most notable of them being the fifteenth century A.D. Sri Vijya empire in Indonesia (Wheatley 1961). Besides Southeast Asia, Indian cultural influence is also known to have existed in Afghanistan, Tibet and part of China. Indian scholars and entrepreneurs were in contact with their counterparts in Central Asia and the Hellenic world. Early Indian emigration, however, did not result in any significant permanent settlements overseas.

In contrast to ancient emigration, modern emigration from India was wholly a British creation. It began in 1834 when slavery was abolished in the British empire. Labour was needed to work on the sugar plantations in the various British colonies. Without dependable supplies of labour, survival of plantations would have been extremely difficult. Consequently, the British colonists followed the practice of Latin American and Cuban colonists who were importing Chinese indentured labour from the Portuguese settlement of Macao (Campbell 1969). Indian labourers had already been found useful in various colonies where as slaves and convicted prisoners they were employed in public works–roads, harbours, offices and jails (Sandhu 1969: 132-40; Tinker 1974: 44-46).[1]

In India, as Kingsley Davis (1968: 99) has pointed out, "pressure to emigrate has always been great enough to provide a stream of emigrants much larger than the actual stream given opportunities". Large scale Indian emigration, however, did not take place until the establishment of British Imperialism in India as well as many other parts of the world. Burma, for example, is a case in point where Indian emigration was numerically insignificant, and only seasonal in nature until the annexation of the Irrawaddy Delta and northern territory by the British East India Company in 1852 (Andrew 1933). Pearn (1946:

5) notes that in 1838 there were only 19 Indians in Rangoon. Similarly, Indian labour emigration to Malaysia, Ceylon, Mauritius and the West Indies and petty bourgeoisie emigration to East Africa had to wait for British colonial settlement in these places. Thus Indian overseas emigration is obviously the result of the workings of British colonialism both in India and abroad which is highlighted by the fact that the vast majority of Indians emigrated only to the British colonies.[2]

Until the Second World War Indians emigrated mainly as indentured labourers to Guyana, Trinidad, Surinam (then a Dutch colony), South Africa, Fiji and Mauritius and as *kangani* or *maistry* labourers to Burma, Ceylon and Malaysia.[3] The migration of traders also took place, espcially to Burma, Malaysia, Kenya, Uganda, Tanzania, South Africa and Fiji. Such migration, however, was proportionately very small and became of some political significance only in African countries. This form of emigration is known as 'free' or 'passage' emigration–the nomenclature being derived from the fact that the emigrants paid their own passage and were free in all respects.

It is estimated that between 1834 and 1937 some 30 million Indians migrated to different parts of the world, while during the same period about 24 million of them returned home, resulting in the net emigration of 6 million (Table 1.1). As the figures in Table 1.1 show, overseas Indian emigration was largely 'ephemeral' or transitory in character. During the period 1834-1900, the average annual emigration was 202,000, whereas for the period 1901-1937, it was 451,000.

The data in Table 1.1 also indicate four major periods of fluctuations in the migration patterns. The first, from 1834 to 1915, was the period of steady increase in indentured labour emigration. In the same period the increased net migration since the early 1890s represents the added migration of *kangani/maistry* labour to Burma, Ceylon and Malaysia. The second period (1915-20) highlights not only the difficult years of the First World War, but also the end of indentured emigration in 1917. In the third period (1921-30), emigration again picked up, mainly responding to the demands for labour on tea, rice, and rubber plantations in Ceylon, Burma and Malaysia respectively. The largest number of Indians returned home between 1929 and 1930, perhaps foreshadowing the coming global economic depression. During the depression and post-depression era until 1937, more Indians returned home than left. The *kangani/maistry* form of emigration was stopped by 1938. By then not only was sufficient labour available in the colonies, Indian public opinion was also opposed to Indians' emigration and their mistreatment abroad.[4] Thereafter only voluntary labour, over whom the Government of India had no control, continued to emigrate. But such migration was proportionately very small and was confined to Malaysia, and possibly Ceylon.

TABLE 1.1: **Estimated Total Migration To and From India, 1834 to 1937 ('000s)**

Year	Emigrants	Returned Migrants	Net*
1834-35	62	52	10
1836-40	188	142	46
1841-45	240	167	72
1846-50	247	189	58
1851-55	357	249	108
1956-60	618	431	187
1861-65	793	594	199
1866-70	976	778	197
1871-75	1,235	958	277
1876-80	1,505	1,233	272
1881-85	1,545	1,208	337
1886-90	1,461	1,204	256
1891-95	2,326	1,536	790
1896-1900	2,962	1,268	694
1901-05	1,428	957	471
1906-10	1,864	1,482	383
1911-15	2,483	1,868	615
1916-20	2,087	1,867	220
1921-25	2,762	2,216	547
1926-30	3,298	2,857	441
1931-35	1,940	2,093	-162
1936-37	815	755	59
Total	30,191	23,941	6,250

*Net migration refers to net emigration. The figures do not always correspond to the exact difference between the first two columns because of rounding.

Source: Davis (1968: 59).

While the expanding capitalist economy in the British empire created a great demand for labour and non-labour manpower, in India a combination of the following factors led to the Indian exodus overseas.[5]

The Distress of the Small Peasantry

The impact of British colonialism in India arose from the new land policies attuned to capitalist development by the middle of the nineteenth century. In 1765 the revenue administration of Bengal had passed into the hands of the East India Company (Mukherjee 1958). The Company had fixed the land taxes at ninety per cent of the rental in Bengal and over eighty per cent in North India, rates that were excessively burdensome to the peasantry. The distress of peasantry was further accentuated by the introduction of the *zamindari* system whereby landlords were converted from rent-collectors (for ten years on 2.5 per cent commission) into landlords in perpetuity (vide Permanent Land Settlement Act, 1793). In the Madras Presidency the land tenure system of *raitwari* was introduced in which *raits* or individual cultivators were the registered occupants of land and as such were free to mortgage, sell or gift their land subject to registered transaction. In the Madras Presidency the land revenues for the most part of the nineteenth century were even higher compared to Bengal.

Under these land tenure schemes, not only land transfer became easier, disputes over land also encouraged litigation, crime and corruption. Indebtedness forced many cultivators to sell or mortgage their land to the rich peasants or the money-lenders.[6] Consequently, the pauperisation of the marginal peasantry increased the number of landless labourers who eventually joined and ranks of overseas migrants.[7] Commenting on the agrarian conditions in the nineteenth century in India, Nehru (1960: 204) writes:

> ... For at the basis of all this exploitation lay the policy deliberately pursued by the British in India. The destruction of cottage-industries with no effort to replace them by other kinds of industry; the driving of the unemployed artisan to the village and the consequent over-pressure on land; landlordism; the plantation system; heavy taxation on land resulting in exorbitant rent, cruelly collected; the forcing of the peasant to the *bania* money-lender, from whose iron grip he never escaped; innumerable ejections from the land for inability to pay rent or revenue in time; and above all, the perpetual terrorism of policemen and tax-gatherers and landlords' agents; which almost destroyed all spirit and soul that he possessed.

Famines

Widespread and frequent famines and local scarcities throughout the nineteenth century and during 1905-1908 period were also a major factor in adding to the misery of rural populations, especially small cultivators, artisans (mainly native weavers), agricultural labourers and other depressed classes. The frequency of famines increased considerably after 1860. In the last four decades of the nineteenth century, the government's economic policies led to a decline in food production and a rise in food prices. On the other hand, during the same period the export of foodgrains increased resulting in further shortages of foodgrains. According to one economic historian (Bhatia 1967: vi):

> As for prevention of famine, the Government laid greater emphasis on railways, which served commercial interests of Great Britain, than on canals which were so necessary to increase food production. By legislative measures the government tried to restore the balance between creditor and debtor and between landlord and tenant, but it failed to industrialize the country, which was the ultimate remedy for unemployment and poverty. In the matter of food supplies, the compulsions of imperialism forced the Government to permit unrestricted export of foodgrains even during times of famine and allow their prices to be determined by the market forces of demand and supply.

The Decline of the Handicraft Industry

In the seventeenth century India was a great manufacturing power mainly because of its handicraft industry which provided employment for millions of people. The cotton industry was especially thriving, its produce exported to a number of markets in Europe and Asia. As the British cotton industry was unable to compete with its Indian counterpart, the British Government charged heavy customs duty on Indian imports into England. In 1720, Indian goods were prohibited entry into England. During the nineteenth century India imported an increasing amount of cotton goods from Britain. According to one estimate, the value of British exports in cotton goods, just over 100,000 pounds in 1813, rose to 5.2 million pounds in 1850 and 18.5 million pounds by 1896 (Charlesworth 1982: 33). This competition had a substantial negative impact on the handicraft industry in India.

Sluggish and Enclavist Industrialisation

While the handicraft industry in nineteenth century India declined, modern industrial development was late, slow, limited and enclavist. Modern industrialisation in India which began in the late nineteenth century was "fundamentally concentrated in three isolated enclaves–Bombay city, Calcutta and the West Bengal/Bihar coal belt–with strictly limited impact on one another and on other regions" (Charlesworth 1982: 37-38). The Madras Presidency, which in the nineteenth century had already become an important area of labour exodus, had no industrialisation even comparable to the scale of Bombay or Calcutta. Moreover, foreign capital which dominated the modern industries was not evenly and broadly invested. There was also a marked absence of a co-ordinated government policy regarding industrial development until 1914. Indeed, in the name of *laissez faire* the colonial government adopted a "passive state policy . . . with respect to industrial development" (Lamb 1955: 478). Perhaps more harmful to industrial development were the effects of the imperial connection which meant that until the First World War, Indian industry was denied any significant tariff protection. Thus the overall progress of industrialisation during the British *Raj* remained very slow. As late as 1931, out of a total population of 353 million, only just over 1.5 million workers were employed in modern factories (Buchanan 1966: 136). Under these circumstances, it is obvious that the manufacturing sector of the colonial economy was not capable of absorbing the surplus labour force created in the rural areas.

Other Factors

Excessive dependence on agriculture, seasonal unemployment, mass illiterarcy, and a caste-bound occupational structure were additional contributory factors in creating a class of proletarians, compelled to seek sustenance abroad. Under these circumstances, the Indian Government was readily persuaded by the imperial and other colonial governments to export Indian labourers.

PATTERNS OF INDIAN OVERSEAS EMIGRATION

Three major patterns of overseas Indian emigration can be identified on the basis of which Indian communities in the former colonial societies were formed. These were: (1) indentured labour emigration (the West Indies, South Africa, Fiji and Mauritius), (2) *kangani/maistry* labour emigration (Burma, Malaysia, Singapore and Sri Lanka), and (3) "free" or "passage" emigration or emigration of trading castes and classes (African countries south of the Sahara).[8]

Indentured Labour Emigration

Indenture was a contract by which the emigrant was bound to work for a given employer for three to five years, performing the tasks assigned to him for a specified wage. At the end of the contract the immigrant was free to re-indenture or to work elsewhere in the colony; after ten years he was entitled to a subsidised return passage. According to Kondapi (1951: 8):

> The chief features of the indenture system were five years of stereotyped state regulated labour, denial of the right to change the employer or employment, recruitment of labour units and not families, gross, disproportions of men to women, charges for recruitment by the employer and the denial of increased wages in spite of increased prices and profits. The employer was under a legal obligation to provide fixed wages, free housing, medical attendance and other amenities.

The emigration of Indian indenture labour began in 1834. During 1834 and 1839 "when emigration was privately arranged and full of abuses", 35,468 emigrants were sent mainly to Mauritius (Saha 1970: 23). In 1839 because of adverse public opinion both in India and in Britain, emigration was suspended till 1841. From 1842 onwards Indian emigration was government-regulated. The chief importing countries of Indian labour were the West Indian colonies, Fiji, South Africa, Mauritius, Malaysia and Ceylon. The indenture system was finally abolished in 1920. It is difficult to estimate the total volume of Indian indenture emigration. John Georghagen, an Immigrant Agent in Calcutta, states that 525,482 Indians migrated to French and British sugar colonies between 1842 and 1870. Challenging this estimate, Tinker (1974: 115) maintains that over a million Indian labourers went overseas to tropical plantations in the forty years before 1870, though the figure could be as high as two million. Indian indenture emigration to the Dutch colony of Surinam began in 1872 and ended in 1916; total emigration amounted to 34,304 persons in 64 ships (Speckmann 1965:

29). Tinker (1974: 95) notes that in the French island Colony of Reunion or Bourbon by 1856 there were 37,694 Indian workers. According to Sandhu (1969: 159), total Indian labour immigration into Malaya between 1844 and 1941 was 2,725,917 of which about 9.1 per cent (i.e., 250,000) were indentured.

The places of origin, caste and occupational composition, and other characteristics of Indian indenture emigration have been well documented. In the first phase beginning in 1834 the majority of emigrants were recruited in the 'hill collie' districts of Chota Nagpur division and Bankura, Birbhum and Burdwan districts of the Bengal Présidency. Soon the recruiting areas were pushed westward into the Hindi-speaking zones of Bihar and Eastern Uttar Pradesh which were also part of the then Bengal Presidency. From the early 1870s till the end of the indenture emigration, Eastern U.P. remained the leading recruiting area in Northern India (Saha 1970: 29-30). In South India the Tamil-speaking areas of Trichinopoly, Madura, Ramnad, Salem and Tanjore and the Telugu-speaking areas of Vizagapatnam and Ganjam were the main recruiting districts. In Bombay Presidency Ahmadnagar district was the main area of recruitment (Tinker 1974: 40). Of the three presidencies Calcutta stands first in volume of recruitment and embarkation and, Madras second.

On the basis of an analysis of Calcutta emigration reports, Saha (1970: 34) concludes that the ratio of Hindus and Muslims appears to represent the all-India ratio of the two communities, i.e. 86 : 14. Among Hindus 16 per cent belonged to higher castes, 32 per cent to agriculturist intermediate castes and the rest to lower castes and 'untouchables'.[9] From the southern zone around Madras, mostly *pariahs* or untouchables with a considerable number of *Sudras* and a few Muslims emigrated.

Following their permanent settlement in the West Indies, Fiji and Mauritius, Indian indentured labour contributed to the creation of what M.G. Smith (1965) and others prefer to call "plural society". Given the circumstances of their indentured immigration and generally lowly working and living conditions and the fact that they replaced the ex-slave labour on the plantations, Indians were accorded the lowest status in these societies. Indentured labour migration to Guyana, one of the three cases considered in this study, is briefly discussed below.

Guyana was the first British colony in the West Indies to receive Indian indentured labourers who began to arrive in 1838. Between 1838 and 1917, the year in which the indenture system was stopped, approximately 240,000 were imported into Guyana. However, in 1917 there were only 138,000 Indians in the colony. Following the influenza epidemic of 1918-19 and the large-scale repatriation to India in 1920, their population declined to an all-time low of 124,000 in this century. There was unprecedented natural growth in the Indian population after the Second World War and by the mid-1960s the Indians constituted over half of the total population of Guyana (Nath 1970: 229-32). In 1980 the population of Guyana was estimated at 850,000 and of these 450,000 were of Indian origin.

Typical of the mode of recruitment of Indian indentured labour, the immigrant population was predominantly male and young (Smith 1959). The vast majority of immigrants (85.6%) were from the then United Provinces of Agrah and Oudh (now Uttar Pradesh) and from Bihar of North India. Less than five per cent of the immigrants were recruited in South India. The rest came from other parts of India and Nepal (Smith 1959).

Kangani/Maistry Labour Emigration

The *kangani* system of recruitment prevailed in relation to Ceylon and Malaya and the *maistry* system in the case of Burma whereby labourers from famine stricken South Indian districts were exported to coffee, tea, rubber and rice plantations. The word *kangani* is the anglicised form of the Tamil word *kankani* meaning overseer and foremen. "Under this system, an employer requiring labour sent a *kangani* (himself an Indian immigrant) to India, giving him an advance for expenses and the man returned with the coolies and in due course repaid the advance" (Jain 1970: 199). According to Kondapi (1951: 29), a gang of 25-30 coolies worked under one *kangani*. All gangs on an estate worked under a head *kangani* who acted as an intermediary between an estate superintendent and the labour force in regard to the payment of wages, etc.

The *maistry* system was more or less similar to the *kangani* system except that the former was characterised by a "gradation of middlemen-employers (the labour contractor, the head *maistry*, the charge *maistry*, the gang *maistry*) and the innumerable illegal deductions by them all from the wages of workers, besides regularised under-employment" (Kondapi 1951: 40).

The *kangani-maistry* system of recruitment differed from the indentured system in two important respects:

(1) unlike the indentured labourers, the *kangani-maistry* recruits were legally free having no contract or fixed period of service, and
(2) more often than not the *kangani-maistry* recruitment was kinship and family based as opposed to the 'individual' recruitment of indentured labourers.[10]

Historically, Indian migration to Malaysia began with the movement of indentured labourers to sugar plantations as early as the 1780s and extended until 1910. This was replaced by the *kangani* system (from the last quarter of the nineteenth century to 1938) which recruited labourers for coffee, rubber, and oil-palm plantations. Throughout this period voluntary labour immigration, especially after 1938, continued.

The total Indian immigration into Malaya during the British rule (1786-1957) was 4,250,000 persons. Much of this movement, however, was transitory and about 3,000,000 persons returned to India during the same period, and about 750,000 people died due to diseases, exhaustion, malnutrition, etc. (Sandhu 1969: 157-69). The immigrants were largely Hindus (about 80%), the remainder being Muslims, Christians, and Sikhs. The regional-linguistic composition of the immigrants was dominated by Tamils, followed by Malayalese, Telugus and the North Indians. According to Sandhu (1969: 97), the proportion of each labour immigration type between 1844 and 1941 was as follows: indentured 9.1 per cent, *kangani* 43.7 per cent, assisted voluntary 10.7 per cent, non-assisted 29.9 per cent, and others 6.6 per cent.

Non-labour Indian immigrants in Malaya consisted of professionals and clericals, salesmen, pedlars, petty entrepreneurs, shopkeepers and vendors. Until 1957, the non-labour immigration constituted about one-third of the total immigration into Malaya. The major Indian commercial communities in Malaysia were Chettiar Hindus and Malabar and Coromandel coast Muslims.

"Passage" or "Free" Emigration

The third form of Indian emigration within the British empire was 'passage' or 'free' emigration, or the emigration of trading castes and classes. Passage emigration was predominant to the East African countries of Kenya, Tanzania, and Uganda, where Gujaratis and Panjabis immigrated largely during and after the Second World War.[11]

Indian immigration in East Africa followed the 'opening up' of East Africa by the British and other European powers.[12] The completion of the Uganda railway offered new economic opportunities in the hinter-land as well as along the railway route. Indians soon established themselves as *dukawalas* (shopkeepers). In the towns they monopolised trade and commercial activities. According to Tandberg (1963), Indians were merchants in native produce, carters and teamsters, small contractors, money-lenders, quarry-masters, dealers in lime, sand, stone and domestic firewood, barbers, saddlers, bootmakers, nurserymen, tailors, etc. Some of these businessmen were highly successful and quite a few of them rose to prominence.

Early Indian immigrants resented the Imperial Government's policy of exclusively reserving the fertile and climatically hospitable upland area in Kenya for Europeans whose population in 1914 was 5,438. Through a number of associations, Europeans exerted pressure on both local and imperial governments in order to bar Indians from owning land in Nairobi and other towns.

Passage immigration continued until *uhuru* (a Swahili word meaning "freedom"–used as an African nationalist motto) in the early sixties. Indian immigration patterns into East Africa have been marked by the regional-linguistic, kinship, consanguineous and affinal ties which accounts for the predominance up to this day of Gujaratis and Kutchis from Western India and to a lesser extent Panjabis from Northern Indian (Bharti 1972: 11).

No reliable data are available regarding the total volume of Indian migration to East Africa. However, different census reports throw some light on the growth of Indian communities in East Africa. Kuczynski (1949: 101) wrote that there were 40,000 Indians in 1901, 30,000 in 1911, 50,000 in 1921 and 92,000 in 1931. During the War their number increased considerably and in 1944 British East Africa had 150,000 Indians. According to Morris (1968: 13), there were 190,000 Indians in 1950, of whom fifty-seven per cent were Hindus and forty-three per cent were Muslims.

Since the mid-sixties, however, a negligible volume of immigration and growing political uncertainties in East Africa have caused the Asian minorities to decline. Following the expulsion of Asians from Uganda and problems elsewhere, the Asian population in East Africa was reduced to an estimated total of 248,000 in 1972; 170,000 in Kenya, 77,000 in Tanzania, and 1,700 in Uganda. The estimate of Asians in East Africa for the mid-1980s was as follows:

Kenya 80,000; Tanzania 50,000; Uganda about 500.

In sum, this brief survey of overseas Indian emigration highlights the socio-economic conditions and the class-structure of colonial India in fostering substantial pressures for Indian emigration. Under British colonialism, Indian agriculture continued to stagnate, the handicraft industry declined, and an already poor country was subjected to excessive economic drain which retarded indigenous capital formation and thereby the growth of any significant industrialisation (Gadgil 1971; Marx 1943).

Indian labour and non-labour emigration vitally fulfilled the economic needs of British colonialism. Indian emigrants, however, were welcome only in subservient economic roles–roles which the natives as well as the white colonialists could not perform. Whenever Indians tried to compete with whites, as in trading activities, attempts were made to block their progress. It was for this reason that labour immigration was encouraged, while passage immigration was usually resented. Similarly, the racial antagonism and repression directed against Indian labourers, while severe, did not result in policies of expulsion and repatriation. These policies were generally reserved for the members of Indian petty bourgeoisie, who were regarded as more of an economic threat by their indigenous and European counterparts. Notwithstanding declarations to the contrary, Indians were treated as "separate and unequal". One indicator of this situation was the fact that in 1920-21, when the indenture system of labour emigration was put to an end, "Indians could enter most British colonies, but the entry to most of the Dominions was closed" (Tinker 1976: 37). The U.S. was similarly closed to the Indian emigrants.[13]

NOTES

1. About Indian convicts in Mauritius Charles Darwin, on his voyage round the world, observed in 1837: "Convicts from India are banished here for life; of them at present there are about eight hundred who are employed in various public works. . . . These convicts are generally quiet and well conducted; from their outward conduct, their cleanliness, and faithful observance of their strange religious enactments, it was impossible to look at these men with the same eyes as our wreched convicts in New South Wales" (quoted in Tinker 1974: 45-46). This description of convicts is in sharp contrast to the usual description of coolies presented by planters, missionaries and officials.
2. As a result of the growth of the tea industry in Assam, internal migration was also stimulated from the 1860s onwards. In fact this internal migration to

Assam was much larger than the overseas emigration under indenture. According to one estimate, in the period between 1870 and 1900 about 700,000 to 750,000 recruits went to Assam to work on the tea estates on a seasonal or long-term basis (Tinker 1974: 50). This kind of migration continued into the twentieth century. "In 1931 there were 900,000 of the coolie class employed in the estates and 500,000 outside" (Latham 1981: 134-35). Although internal migration was larger compared to indentured emigration, it was insignificant compared to the volume of emigration outside the country, or to the population as a whole (Kumar 1965: 133).

3. *Kangani/maistry* contracts were of short-term duration, usually of thirty days. The contracts were generally verbal rather than written. These names are derived from the Tamil word *kankani* meaning ganger who was both recruiter and field foreman.
4. In arousing public opinion in India about the mistreatment of overseas Indians, Gandhi's role was particularly important. He had lived in South Africa for 21 years (1893-1914) and fought for the civil rights of Indians.
5. There were tremendous regional and/or local variations in India in terms of pre-colonial socio-economic conditions and subsequent colonial formations. Therefore, generalisations regarding the following factors are highly tentative and simplistic.
6. In addition to traditional *bania* money-lenders, the rich peasantry was also involved in banking and money-lending. This aspect of the economic stratification of nineteenth century peasantry in India was little recognised until recently (see Charlesworth 1982: 28-30).
7. Landless labourers were not necessarily the creation of British colonialism in India. They existed even in pre-British India and generally belonged to lower castes (Breman 1974; Kumar 1965).
8. In addition to these, "brain-drain", or voluntary emigration of highly skilled manpower to the metropolitan countries of Europe, North America and Oceania, and contract labour emigration to the West Asian countries are two major post-colonial patterns of Indian emigration abroad (see Jain 1982).
9. In a similar analysis of Indian Emigration to Fiji, between 1879 and 1916, Gillion (1956: 152) computes the following distribution of caste and communities: Hindus 85.3 per cent (Brahmins and other high castes 16.1 per cent; Agricultural castes 31.3 per cent; Artisan castes 6.7 per cent; low castes and outcastes 31.2%); Muslims 14.6 per cent; Christians 0.1 per cent. In the case of Fiji the indenture system was known as the *girmitiya* and the labourers as *girmitiyas*. *Girmitiyas* means "the ones who came on an agreement (i.e. indenture), the word "agreement" being rendered as *girmit* in Indian popular speech" (Lal 1983).
10. The nineteenth century emigration to Burma was an exception in which case emigrants were generally single males (Kumar 1965: 138).
11. East Africa too had its share of Indian indentured labour. According to one estimate, mainly between 1896 and 1902, about 32,000 workers were exported to East Africa in connection with the construction of the Uganda railways, of whom all but 6,724 were either repatriated, invalidated or had died (Mangat 1969: 39). See also Gregory (1971).

12. "In 1885 thirteen European countries and the United States of America signed a group of treaties known as the Congo Basin Treaties to regulate territorial rights and commercial development in the whole of East and Central Africa. In the following year the British and German Governments signed additional treaties which limited the sovereignty of the sultan of Zanzibar to the islands of Zanzibar, Pemba, Lamu, Mafia, and a narrow coastal strip on the mainland. The territory corresponding to Kenya today was designated a British 'Sphere of Influence' and Tanganyika was given to the Germans. The status of Uganda was left undecided until 1890, when by agreement, this too was included in the British sphere" (Morris 1968: 6).
13. The famous *Komagata Maru* incident at the Vancouver harbour in 1914, and the unseemly behaviour of the immigration officials towards the Nobel-laureate Rabindranath Tagore at the Canada-U.S. border which resulted in his protest and cancellation of his lecture tour of the U.S. in 1929 very well illustrate the then prevailing racial attitude towards Indians in North America.

2

Class and Race Relations: A Conceptual Framework

As briefly pointed out in the previous chapter Indian migrants in the British colonies were subjected to various kinds of racial discriminations. This happened in spite of the fact that the British official policy was one of racial equality. Thus as early as 1858 when the British assumed direct rule of India, Queen Victoria made the following proclamation:

> There shall not be, in the eyes of the law, any distinction of colour, origin, language or creed. But protection of law, in letter and substance, shall be extended to all alike.

Such an assertion was repeated time and again in different contexts. For example, the Imperial Conference of 1921 was told by the then Secretary of State for the Colonies, Winston Churchill:

> The British Empire could have only one ideal on this matter . . . no barrier of race, colour, or creed preventing any man by merit from reaching any station if he were fitted therefor. I am unable to adopt any lesser statement or principle in regard to the Crown colonies (Command Paper No. 1747, London, Aug 1921, pp. 8 and 34-39).

Notwithstanding such official claims of racial equality the actual British policy and practice in this regard was just the opposite. Indians in India as well as other colonies were never considered even remotely equal to the people of European origin. Mahatma Gandhi's fight for racial equality in South Africa until the First World War and subsequently the emergence of the "Indian Question" in East Africa adequately highlight some of the major dimensions of the problem. The notion of racial superiority on the part of the Britons did not escape the attention of Pandit Jawaharlal Nehru when he wrote:

> The British are an insular race, and long success and prosperity has made them look down on almost all others. For them, as some one has said, '*Les nègres commencent à Calais*'. But that is too general a statement. Perhaps the British upper-class division of the world would be somewhat as follows: (1) Britain–a long gap, and then (2) The British Dominions (white populations only) and America (Anglo-Saxon only) and not dagoes, wops, etc.), (3) Western Europe, (4) Rest of Europe, (5) South America (Latin races), a long gap, and then (6) the brown, yellow and black races of Asia and Africa, all hunched up more or less together. How far we of the last of these classes are from the heights where our rulers live (Nehru 1962: 500).

Nehru's statement is significant not only from the point of view of the factual British view of global racial stratification but more importantly from the point of view of its conceptual implications. Obviously, Nehru underlined the need to look at the problem of British racial insularity and its repurcussions in terms of British imperialism ("long success and prosperity"). It is perhaps fair to argue that according to him the causes of racial discrimination should be located not merely in the racist or such ideology but also in the functioning of the political economy of a given social formation. This more or less is our conceptual perspective too which is discussed in details in this chapter.

The chapter is divided into three sections. Section I provides a review of major established theories regarding race relations situations of overseas Indians. Sections II and III deal with the conceptual framework and methodology of the present study.

I. A CLASS CRITIQUE OF ESTABLISHED THEORIES

Overseas Indian communities are not only scattered in diverse geographical areas, they are equally diverse in terms of their socio-economic and political status. It is perhaps as much due to this reason as paradigmatic differences in social sciences that fragmentary, diverse and even contradictory conceptual frameworks have been presented regarding their race relations situations. Three such theoretical orientations, viz., theories of pluralism, middleman minority theory and the work of Rex, are briefly reviewed here. Pointing out their shortcomings an attempt is made to construct a political economy and class-based conceptual framework which, in the author's view, more systematically explains the race relations situations of overseas Indians in various colonial/post-colonial societies.

Theories of Pluralism

Sociological studies of overseas Indian communities in the colonial/post-colonial context generally use one or another variant of the theory of pluralism. In its current form the theory of pluralism has been developed by M.G. Smith (1965, 1969, 1974) who was influenced by the works of Furnivall (1944, 1948) and Malinowski (1945).[1] The cornerstone of Smith's theory is his focus on the mode of incorporation of institutionally diverse collectivities and their unequal or differential status. Smith argues that colonial societies are pluralistic in terms of their organisation and composition and therefore the standard theories of normative or functional integration in homogeneous societies are not applicable to them.

According to Smith, colonial societies are characterised by structural pluralism which entails a differential distribution, either through legal or extra-legal practice, of "civil and political rights and the economic, social, and other opportunities that these permit or enjoin" (Smith 1969: 338). Discussing race and stratification in the Caribbean, he writes that "in Guyana, Surinam and Trinidad, Negroes and East Indians were incorporated as mutually exclusive segments of equivalent status by their common but mutually distinct subordination to the ruling whites" (1974: 338).

For Smith, incorporation is essentially a political act; a society is held together by authority and regulation of one segment over others. Thus from the pluralist perspective, the question of inter-group conflict is a matter of political dominance of one group over the others. Smith's theory of pluralism has been applied in a preliminary way by Hilda Kuper in the African context. She argues that the Asians in Africa are "strangers" in plural societies and that their racial distinctions are rigidly maintained at the level of political incorporation. Asians in Africa are not a corporate group; corporate status is rather thrust upon them by the "host":

> In a society where power is arbitrarily ascribed, it is convenient for the dominant group to treat Asians as if they were a corporate group, and to reinforce this by separate laws, separate schools and

> so on; at times it may be convenient for Asians, despite their internal differentiation, to accept this fiction and form Asian organisations to negotiate with the representatives of the dominant group (Kuper 1969: 251).

A variant of pluralism is found in Tinker's study of overseas Indian communities. The problem of political integration appears to be Tinker's primary concern, and his conclusion is that "it is the dominant population–which determines how the Asian immigrants and their children emerge" (Tinker 1977: ix).

The plural society thesis has been criticised on several counts. The major criticisms are discussed below:

(1) The plural society approach defines society by its cultural and institutional characteristics (e.g. socio-cultural segments, primary institutional diversity, etc.) and thus ignores or deals inadequately with similarities among the segments and the ways in which socio-economic processes enmesh these segments with one another in the total society. In a study of Indians in East Africa, Morris (1956: 208) rightly observes that this approach "concentrates only on cultural differences, which in themselves are not really more than insignia". In doing so, he argues, "the underlying structural similarities are almost certain to be overlooked." In the opinion of Banton (1967: 291),

> It does not seem helpful to put emphasis upon the character of community's institutions at the cost of the structure of relations in which the various communities are involved, for it is this structure that brings them into particular forms of conflict and cooperation.

(2) A critique along the same general lines but with specific reference to the Caribbean context has been advanced by Hall (1977). He points out that while the 'plural society' model concentrates our attention on segmental cultural and institutional diversity, it does not account for the mechanisms of class power, legitimation and domination. This structure of legitimation, almost indentically present in all Caribbean societies, in which a small upper class controls access to power and reward is, according to Hall, historically derived from 'slave plantation society'. It was the slave plantation society, with its typical features of the 'separate worlds' of masters and slaves, to which the structure of legitimation as well as socio-cultural pluralism owe their existence. "Every subsequent development or stage represents . . .

a modification and transformation, but not a structural break, with this generative model" (Hall 1977: 160). In the generative model, the two socio-cultural worlds do not form plural segments of parallel but distinct cultures, but differentiated parts of a single socio-economic system. Thus there exists a complex "differentiated unity" specific to each social formation which requires analysis. Seen from this perspective, it becomes obvious that the plural society model conceives the questions of power and conflict in "too limited and segmentary a fashion" (Hall 1977: 158), and without regard to the "unity" of slave-plantation, colonial or post-colonial society.

(3) The conceptualisation of the state poses another problem in theories of pluralism. The pluralism literature rightly emphasises the importance of state and political domination in society. The pluralists, however, treat the state as the independent variable. According to Leo Kuper (1975: 17-18), "the state precedes and constitutes society; it is the state that is primary and imposes some measure of ordered relations on otherwise hostile or dissociated groups". Such a conception is obviously contrary to the Marxist conception of the state, which is understood as dependent, however indirectly, on changing material conditions. We share the Marxist view of the state as a relatively autonomous institutional ensemble whose policies and practices are influenced by the articulated interests, demands and conflicts among the dominant and subordinate classes in a given social formation. It is by virtue of this interventionist role that the state has repercussions on race relations situations.

(4) The plural society approach emphasises the importance of political dominance in race relations but at the expense of economic dominance and exploitation. In pluralism, "economic class formations (are considered) as largely irrelevant to the analysis of social and political structures" (Hall 1980: 309). Pluralists who do call attention to economic class formation relegate it to a minor role, arguing that ethnic/racial solidarities are stronger than those based on economic class. For instance, Leo Kuper (1975: 235-52) contends that in plural societies class solidarity across ethnic/racial lines rarely appears and that Marxist concepts of class do not fit situations in plural societies. However, Kuper's notion of class is too simplistic and harks back to an outdated "orthodox" Marxism. In this orthodox view there is little allowance made for intra-class variation and ethnic/racial divisions are reduced to economic or class relations in a mechanical way. The Neo-Marxist approach, in rejecting this view, is well-stated by Hall

(1977: 177-78) who rightly pointed out:

> . . . there has never been, in sophisticated Marxist analysis, any simple and predetermined necessity that class solidarity always does and must appear, for this would be to make 'consciousness' automatically coincident with objective economic position, and structure-superstructural relations simple and transparent. The distinction between 'classes in themselves' and 'classes for themselves' is pivotal to the analysis: and the whole domain of ideology and of political-class practices (not to mention the more difficult concept of 'false consciousness') intervenes to effect crucial and massive displacements. The theory of automatic class solidarities and of transparency of structure-superstructure relations is mechanistic in the extreme. If there is no predictable 'class solidarity', then there are certainly no 'ethnic' or 'cultural' solidarities either.

The pluralist understanding of Marxist class analysis is obviously based on the teleological reading of Marx which necessitates, among other things, the class solidarity across ethnic/racial lines.

The plural society approach was valuable in showing how societies are maintained primarily by dominance of some status groups (in our case ethnic/racial groups) over others rather than by a moral consensus; and in stressing the role of race and ethnicity in mobilizing people for political action. However, a serious shortcoming in the work of pluralists has been the lack of a systematic and sophisticated analysis of the material bases of these societies and how the class relations deriving from these material bases contribute to the shaping of race relations.

Middleman Minority Theories

In Africa Indians constitute what have been termed "middleman minorities" or "marginal trading communities". It has been observed that middleman minorities are often found in complex, stratified, agrarian societies characterised by a status gap or marked division between elites and masses.[2] Another feature of these communities is their economic status and role: "they occupy an intermediate rather than low-status position. They tend to concentrate in certain occupations, notably trade and commerce . . ." (Bonacich 1973: 583).

Why do middleman minorities come into conflict with other groups within the host society? Blalock argues that middleman minorities in peasant-feudal societies serve as buffer groups or as pawns in the power struggle between the two major classes—elite and peasant. "In times of prosperty and reduced class-conflict the middleman finds himself relatively secure under the protection of the elite group. In times of stress, however, he becomes a natural scapegoat." (1967: 79-84).

In contrast, Bonacich (1973) argues that sojourning is the key variable in the "middleman minority" situation. Sojourning generates thriftiness among immigrants as it also leads them to select liquidable occupations, i.e. occupations which do not tie them to the territory for long periods. Among non-economic consequences of sojourning the most important one is the high degree of internal solidarity. Other traits typical to these communities, according to Bonacich, are: a resistance to out-marriage, residential self-segregation, establishment of separate schools, resistance to assimilation, and minimal involvement in local politics. All these traits generate host society hostility which in turn reinforces their sojourning attitude and group solidarity. The cycle is self-perpetuating and the group becomes a permanent minority. Both versions of the middleman minority theory suffer from the following shortcomings:

(1) The conceptualisation of the colonial societies in which middleman minorities are found is inadequate. For example, Blalock's conceptualisation of such societies in terms of peasant-feudal societies ignores the whole context of emergent colonial capitalism and its dynamics in response to which the middleman minorities immigrated in the colonial societies in the first place.

(2) Attempts of class analyses in the theory are overly simplistic. The classes appear to be undifferentiated: elites, masses and the middleman minority in the Blalock's version, and business, labour, clientele, and the middleman minority in the Bonacich version. Moreover, in Bonacich's more recent attempt (1980) to incorporate middleman minorities into a class framework, intra-class conflict is hardly a factor, not only within the minority itself but also among the majority. The latter are shown as united in their hostility against the middleman minority because of the latter's economic success, "strangeness" and some elements of irrational behaviour on the part of the host society.

(3) In a major review of various middleman minority theories,

Zenner (1980) has rightly pointed out that the theory is not well grounded in ethnographic and historical details and that in the light of the current knowledge of such communities it can serve only as a hypothesis. The major difficulty with the middleman minority theory, for our purpose, is that it has never been rigorously applied to race relations situations in East Africa. In its earlier version, Bonacich (1973) formulated the theory in relation to a number of so-called "middleman minorities" in diverse periods of time and situations (for example, Japanese-American laundry businessmen in San Francisco in 1903; Jews in Stanford, Connecticut in 1938; and Chinese in Cambodia in 1962-63).

In an attempt to present a more systemic class analysis, we therefore would argue for a definition of a middleman minority in terms of a racially/ethnically distinguishable fraction of the petty bourgeoisie in peripheral capitalist society, whose privileged class position and interests are contradictory to those of its various class counterparts as well as to subordinate classes. Conceptualised in this manner, it becomes possible to demonstrate that the race relations situation of the middleman minority is derived not from its ethnic characteristics but from the class conflict inherent in the society.

One general difficulty with both the pluralist and middleman minority theories of race relations is that insufficient attention is given to the initial source of race relations situations, i.e. colonialism and its impact on the class structure of colonial societies.[3] Bonacich, for example, highlights Indians' supposed preference for liquidable occupations but neglects to mention the fact that the imperial policy did not allow them to own land for agricultural purposes with the result that Indians remained confined to trade and commercial activities. Similarly, in Guyana what Despres (1967) calls the problem of integration at the national level (which is essentially the problem of class relations) emerged from the fact that under colonialism Indians suffered the fate of a split labour market, and were denied educational opportunities in rural areas (where their concentration was heavy) thereby affecting their life chances. In short, a comprehensive, systematic study of overseas Indians based on a uniform conceptual framework needs to be done. Towards this end, a conceptual framework is presented in the following section which is specifically concerned with the colonial social formations and the race relations situations therein.

Some Formulations by Rex

Before we venture to suggest an outline of an appropriate theoretical framework for the analysis of race relations situations of overseas Indian communities it would be useful to briefly present here a few formations by John Rex whose work on race relations is difficult to classify in either of the two above discussed theories. Although Rex's work is primarily informed by Weber, he gives more than passing attention to class. His stress on colonialism as a key factor in the emergence of race relations situations is also shared by neo-Marxists.

The colonial social formations, according to Rex, differed from their Western counterparts in that the former were developed within the parameters of colonial conquest with the result that in such societies capitalist development generated not only the forces of class struggle but also the "race war" (Rex 1970a: 262). Rex places a great deal of emphasis on this fundamental differentiating feature between the metropolitan and colonial social formations and argues that the "adventurer" or "booty" capitalists in the colonies had the capacity to command the use of coercive violence during and after the colonial conquest, and that labour institution in colonies was not classical free labour and the resultant relationship between dominant capital and subordinate labour thus constitute one possible, though ideal typical, situation of race relations.

Other situations of race relations arise from further complexities of colonial social formation: in different points of time there emerged not only various forms of free and part-free labour (e.g. free slaves, time-expired indentured, dependent peasants), but also other social strata (e.g. colonial administrators, white settlers, missionary clergy, "middlemen minorities"). Consequently, the system of colonial stratification and thereby race relations situation became complex:

> Some of these groups are opposed to one another as classes in a Marxian sense. All of them, however, form relatively closed groups with their own distinctive cultural traits and social organization. The over-all effect is of too much overlap and inter-penetration to justify us in calling it a caste system, but too much closure of avenues of mobility for us to call it a system of social stratification. It is much too complex, involving overlapping modes of production, for it to be described as a situation of class struggle in the Marxian sense (Rex 1978: 30).

Therefore, as Hall (1980) points out, Rex takes a "Marx plus Weber" theoretical position in order to explain race relations situations. This he does by departing from simple Marxism in a two-fold sense:

> First . . . that at the level of relationships to the means of production there are more possible positions and potentialities for class formation than simply European Marxism seems to allow; and second, that over and above the actual means of production, there are a number of social functions and positions and that these functions are appropriated by closed groups which, thereafter, have their own interests and their own power position *vis-a-vis* society as a whole (Rex 1978: 23-24).

In other words, in a colonial situation various groups, classes and segments are "differentially related to a number of different modes of production and being united by their separate ethnicities as well as by class consciousness" (Rex 1981: 17). In this morphology of colonial society those who are powerfully placed explain and rationalise the system in terms of an ideology of origins of some sort. This, according to Rex, applies to race relations situations in post-colonial societies as well, in which case the processes of political independence and intensification of class struggle become additionally complicating factors.

Rex's "Marx plus Weber" synthesis, however, suffers from one major drawback in that his conceptualisation of race relations situations involve two different types of social groupings, i.e. classes and "closed groups". As a corrective to this problem, we would argue that race relations can be explained in terms of class analysis, provided that (1) each racial group identified in terms of the class position of the bulk of its members (i.e. whether it is essentially in a relation of exploitation, mediation or exclusion), and (2) it is recognised that the economic interests of a racially divided class are not necessarily homogeneous: "a social class, or fraction or stratum of a class, may take up a class position that does not correspond to its interests, which are defined by the class determination that fixes the horizon of the class struggle" (Poulantzas 1975: 15).

Whereas the first corrective corrects the error of treating racial/ethnic groups as homogeneous in their class composition, the second corrective allows us to analyse the different economic interests of a racially fractured class (i.e., Rex's "closed groups which . . . have their own interests and their own power positions *vis-a-vis* society as a whole"). In connection with the second corrective, Burawoy (1974: 528) argues that in a racially structured society

> the economic interests [of a fraction of a class] are determined not only by class interest but also by the existing institutional framework and ideology, that is, by relation to the superstructure as well as to the means of production. Thus, where the superstructure is not a direct reflection of the class structure but distinguishes it on the basis of racial categories, then the economic interests of racial groups within the same class may differ.

In short, a class theory of race relations may immensely benefit from the use of the concept of class fraction as elaborated upon in the contemporary neo-Marxist literature.

II. A CLASS ANALYSIS OF RACE RELATIONS

Class theories of race relations are an emergent phenomenon. In their present formulations they have been greatly influenced by neo-Marxist critiques of the theories of development and underdevelopment. These critiques have been applied not only to non-Marxist theories (e.g. modernisation, dependency, world system, pluralism, etc.) but also to orthodox Marxism, especially because of its Eurocentric bias. The major thrust of the emergent neo-Marxist approach to race relations, which is itself locked in internal debate, has been not only to expose the fallacy of the primordialism thesis of race relations, but also more positively to show how certain types of race relations situations are better explained in terms of their underlying class dynamics.

As already pointed out, since its emergence after the Second World War in response to the increasing inadequacy of orthodox Marxism, the neo-Marxist perspective has been mainly concerned with issues of economic development and underdevelopment in capitalist societies (Foster-Carter 1973). However, its usefulness for the study of race relations has also increasingly been recognised in a number of recent studies (e.g. Hall 1980; Hua 1983; Lim Mah Hui 1980; Rodney 1981; Stasiulis 1980; Stenson 1980; Wolpe 1972). Unlike orthodox Marxist formulations that dismiss racial categories and racist phenomena (prejudice, discrimination, ideology, etc.) as epiphenomenal to class or seek to explain them in terms of a ruling class conspiracy, the neo-Marxist perspective attempts to analyse how race or ethnicity becomes an active structuring principle of a social formation. The approach attempts to specify those conditions "which make racial distinctions socially pertinent, historically active" (Hall 1980: 337). More concretely, it seeks to understand how the development of capitalism and consequently class formation and class conflict preserve, undermine, extend or reinforce racial divisions. By understanding the developing class relations in concrete situations, we can understand the specificity and dynamics of race relations.

To reiterate, within this broader paradigm our major objective is to show how the race relations situations of overseas Indian communities have been shaped by class dynamics specific to various colonial/post-colonial societies. In this connection it is of utmost significance to realise that instead of characterising the colonial/post-colonial societies as "slave-plantation", agricultural or "peasant-feudal", it is theoretically fruitful to conceptualise them as "peripheral" capitalist economies and societies. Historically, such societies have been marked by the articulation of both capitalist and pre-capitalist modes of production in the manner that the former invariably dominated and "distorted" the latter.[4] Such a conceptualisation allows us to identify the class positions and class interests of various racial groups and the resultant situations of class and race relations. The fuller exposition of this conceptual framework is presented in the following three major headings:

(a) the creation of a peripheral economy,
(b) class formation and race relations in the colonial societies, and
(c) post-colonial derivatives and race relations.

The Creation of a Peripheral Economy

Colonial and post-colonial social formations[5] have been characterised by their "peripheral" economies–peripheral not merely geographically but more importantly in terms of their positions in the world economy. One of the most important characteristics of a peripheral economy is that it is not "autocentric" (Amin 1974 Vol.I: 228). The internal market in such an economy is underdeveloped, while the external dependence is exaggerated. Production is geared for profit through international trade rather than for the needs of the local population. And capitalist social relations are incompletely formed.

Besides trade, which we shall be discussing a little later, the typical colonial economy in Asia, Africa and the Caribbean (with which we are concerned here) was based on plantation and/or mining enterprises. These were exclusively owned by a section of the metropolitan bourgeoisie, or in some cases (e.g., Kenya) by European settlers. The colonial government's land policies were geared to encourage and make profitable such enterprises through granting long leases on land to the European entrepreuneurs and through the imposition of a new land tenure system, that invariably resulted in the rise of a proletarian class to work on plantations and in mining. In addition to making land available for plantations and mining purposes, the colonial government also provided subsidised immigrant labour, necessary infrastructural facilities, including technical expertise and a state apparatus to maintain law and order.

One of the most important features of the colonial enterprises was their organisation around the forced labour systems. Forced labour systems took various forms in the British empire: Amerindian and Negro slavery in the Caribbean (Williams 1961); Indian indentured or contract labour in the Caribbean, Mauritius, Fiji and South Africa (Tinker 1974); Indian *kangani* and *maistry* labour in Burma, Ceylon and Malaysia (Kondapi 1951; Sandhu 1969); and African 'compound' and 'reserve' labour in South Africa (Horowitz 1967; Wolpe 1972). Forced labour was recruited through a variety of strategies, all necessitating intervention by the colonial state apparatus: heavy taxation, land distribution through the transformation of the land tenure system, and infrastructural projects, especially railways (Taylor 1979: 208-12).

The major advantages of forced labour were its relative cheapness and docility. In some cases the unfree labour was found to be relatively less productive but as Taylor rightly points out, ". . . this was offset by extremely long working hours, low ground-rents, a high availability of land, and relatively cheap raw material" (1979: 131). On the whole, contrary to Max Weber's suggestion that unfree labour, especially slavery, was incompatible with the rational calculability of capitalism, it can be argued that unfree labour provided an efficient economic system. The evolution of progressively less coercive and thereby more flexibile forms of labour systems since slavery suggests the dynamic, efficient and economical nature of these colonial labour processes.

As pointed out earlier, the colonial economy was based not only on the European owned plantation and mining enterprises, but perhaps far more significantly on the oligopoly of the import-export trade, shipping and banking–all designed to serve the imperial interests. In order to extract maximum profits from the trade monopoly the imperial government in conjunction with its colonial counterparts heavily invested in such infrastructural developments as railways, roads and communication networks, and irrigation facilities. According to one estimate, in the 50 years preceding the First World War, 69 per cent of the total British international investment went to the provision of social overhead capital, including 41 per cent on railways. "A further 12 per cent . . . went to mining and extractive industries, but less than 4 per cent was channelled into manufacturing. The remaining 15 per cent went into miscellaneous outlets, of which plantations must have been important" (Latham 1978: 55). Consequently, there was considerable stimulation of external trade in countries of Asia and Africa, which exported mostly agricultural products and other raw materials to Britain and imported manufactured goods in return.

The overall effects of such preferred investment was that the colonial economies could not be diversified towards self-sufficiency and 'autocentrism'. Profitable production and export remained confined to one or two items. In Guyana, for example, throughout the colonial period, sugar and sugar products were the single most important export items. Even after independence, sugar, bauxite and rice continue to comprise three quarters of the total export-value (Nath 1970: 263). In Kenya, in 1930, 72 per cent of the total export-value was derived from three major agricultural products–coffee, sisal and maize (Wolff 1974: 137). Similarly, since the colonial days, Malaysian exports have been mainly based on rubber and tin. In India as late as its independence in 1947, over three quarters of the foreign capital was invested in such areas as jute, tea, mining and shipping. Thus the development of enclavist economies was characteristic of most of the colonial societies. Additionally, in most of the colonies, industrialisation was either discouraged or remained minimal, thus further accentuating their dependent and peripheral economic character.

Class Formation and Race Relations Situations in Colonial Societies

Class formation in colonial societies was dependent on the nature of production and the degree of penetration of the capitalist mode of production in different sectors of these economies.[6] In mainly plantation and/or mining economies, classes crystallised around these forms of production. At least until the First World War such societies remained polarised between the plantation and mining ruling class on the one hand, and the working class on the other. Earlier we mentioned two important features of colonial plantation and mining enterprises: their more or less exclusive ownership by the European bourgeoisie and/or expatriates, and their organisation around coercive labour systems. As the coercive labour systems mostly involved non-white populations–native or immigrant–the relations of production in these sectors of colonial economy directly contributed to the emergence of a class structure which coincided with racial divisions.[7] The term plantocracy perhaps best sums up this 'racial' class structure and its dynamics, in which the ruling planting and mining class also had the support of top plantation management, colonial administration and judiciary officials, missionaries, church-controlled educators and merchant capital interests.[8]

Throughout the nineteenth century and at least until the First World War, the plantocracy reigned supreme in plantation societies. In Guyana, for example, the planters dominated in the Court of Policy, which formulated all local laws and ordinances and in the Combined Court, which voted the salaries of all government officials, including the judges. Similarly, planters' interests were dominant in the College of Electors which was based on extremely narrow franchise with property and literacy qualifications. "In the articulation of their interests, planters were assisted by a declining but still valuable West Indian presence in the British Parliament in the latter part of the nineteenth century" (Rodney 1981: 122). Although in the final analysis there was no fundamental conflict between the planters and the imperial state, when occasions of antagonism obtained on certain policy matters, the former were usually successful in overriding the opposition of the Governor and the Colonial Office.

It was on the strength of such political power that the planters were able to create a surplus labour force–first slaves and then indentured coolies–to work for their profitable enterprises. Even in the depression during the mid-1890s Indian immigration to Guyana did not decline This continued immigration after the 1880s depressed the wages of Africans as well as Indians (Nath 1970: 87) and was an important reason for racial antagonism between these groups in Guyana.

The dynamics of the racial class structure in plantation societies are related to the character of the plantation as a "total institution" in which the social and industrial life of the workers were completely regimented (Smith 1967). The working conditions were extremely harsh and desertion often meant conviction under immigration and labour laws. The figures in Table 2.1 for the year 1907 show how extensively the criminal courts were used to enforce the rights of employers against their labourers in which Guyana was the worst offender.

TABLE 2.1: **Conviction of Indentured Labourers under Labour Laws in Various British Colonies, 1907**

	Number of Indentured Labour	Number of Convictions	Percentage Convicts
B. Guina	9,784	2,019	20
Fiji	10,181	2,019	20
Trinidad	11,506	1,869	16
Jamaica	2,832	237	8
Mauritius	47,000	1,492	3

Source: Rodney (1981: 41).

The indentured labourers therefore lived and worked under conditions approaching slavery. Indians avoided basic education provided on the plantations by the missionary schools for fear that they would be converted to Christianity. They therefore had little chance of occupational mobility off the estate. Although working class struggle often took the form of strikes and occasional riots over the issues of wage-cuts and excessive behaviour of the estate officials, the trade union movement was nowhere evident at least until the early 1920s. On the contrary, the working class remained divided along racial or ethnic lines for two important reasons: *first*, the existence of a "split labour market" or wage disparities between Africans and Indians (Bonacich 1972),[9] and *second*, the differential freedom and legal rights of different class fractions. In the case of the Indian workers in the British colonies the two factors were superimposed on each other: Indians were not only the lowest paid workers; as indentured labourers their social status was low even in the eyes of former slaves.

The so-called "middleman minorities"–indigenous or immigrant–owed their existence and strength to the commodity export sector of the colonial economy.

> The expansion of the home market, the export of agricultural commodities and goods from the national capitalist sector, and the distribution of imported commodities, all provide a basis for a rapid increase in the circulation of commodities, for an economic strengthening of the role of the merchant class (Taylor 1979: 226).

Two regions to which Indians immigrated in significant numbers as petty bourgeoisie and played a role in the colonial economy were South Africa and East Africa. But here they soon began to face competition from their European counterparts, a precursor to antagonistic relations in Africa. The Europeans and the Indians adopted various tactics of undercutting each other. Whereas Europeans generally relied on the favours of the colonial government in terms of tax-relief, licensing, credits, etc., Indians turned to their own ethnic resources and habits such as working long hours, using business premises as residential units, hiring Indians as shop assistants, selling goods for low profits, and aspiring to lower living standards. Indians were generally successful in undercutting European business. Consequently European resentment against Indians found expression in the exclusionary policy on the one hand, and the spread of racial prejudices and stereotypes on the other. Indian coolie immigrants were generally the source of these racial stereotypes, which were indiscriminately used against Indian traders.

The exclusionary policy was justified on the ground that the Indian trading interests were contradictory to the native as well as to European interests and that the natives ought to be protected from such unfair competition. Competition in trading practices was not, however, the only factor behind the exclusionary policy. Europeans wanted to keep intact the structure of privilege they had built around themselves, which included political dominance, a discriminatory legal system, and preferential social services–all geared to their economic interests (Rothchild 1973: 62-102). Additionally, the Indians' claim to equality and electoral representation was seen as a threat to the goal of self-government for the settlers who were outnumbered by the Indians from the very beginning.

The exclusionary policy against Indians in general and Indian traders in particular can aptly be summed up in the British attitude toward Indians as "separate and unequal" (Tinker 1976). While Indian labourers were welcomed to the British colonies, Indian traders were denied equal treatment *vis-a-vis* European settlers regarding immigration, land ownership, electoral representation, and trading licensing. Thus during most of the colonial period in Kenya and South Africa, these issues in addition to the segregation policy remained at the core of the so-called "Indian question". Similarly, in the Federated Malay States, Chinese as well as Indians were denied equal citizenship rights *vis-a-vis* Malays. Those who protested the government's policy were subjected to deportation (Arasaratnam 1970). In South Africa, until 1960 Indians were accustomed to being treated as aliens and efforts were made to repatriate them.

In the inter-War period, as the colonial economy expanded and diversified and educational facilities improved, the natives in the colonies began to join the ranks of the middle classes as merchants and traders, teachers, clerks, lawyers, doctors and other professionals (Brett 1973; Roff 1967). Although Indians certainly benefited from economic development in the colonies in terms of the increased business and other employment opportunities, thanks to the colonial policy of restriction and segregation, their position as a middle class segment and particularly as the petty bourgeoisie basically remained unaltered. In contrast, the European petty bourgeoisie transformed itself into a grand bourgeoisie. This changing class composition of colonial societies was to define and determine the situation of race relations in the post-colonial period.

After the Second World War and especially following India's independence, the Indian Government regarded overseas Indians as foreign nationals.[10] Indian claims to equality *vis-a-vis* Europeans in different colonies had been already quashed by the imperial as well as various colonial governments (Tinker 1976). Now they had lost the support of the Indian Government as well. Simultaneously, overseas Indians were faced with emergent nationalism in different colonies.

The political role of overseas Indians in the national independence movements in various colonies was generally dependent on their demographic strength as well as their class situation. Thus in colonies where they were in the majority or near-majority (e.g., Fiji, Guyana, Mauritius, Trinidad), the Indians played an active part in politics with a hope that they would be able to share political power after independence. In colonies where Indians constituted a tiny minority (e.g., the East African countries), their role was extremely limited and ambivalent (Tandon 1965). Perhaps the main reason for this was that spurning colonialism was against the interests of the Indian petty bourgeoisie which dominated the Indian community. In the post-independence period, this political ambivalence, interpreted as "cocktail integration" (Bhatia 1973) on the part of Indians, was used against them as an ideological element in the intra-class conflict between the Indian petty bourgeoisie and its African counterpart.

Post-Colonial Derivatives and Race Relations Situations

Post-colonial formations[11] do not necessarily represent breaks in their metropolitan links. This is particularly true at the economic level where the national bourgeoisie has entered into an alliance with the imperial firms or multinational corporations for continued capital accumulation. This reality in many current Third World countries is often described as "neo-colonialism" or "dependent neo-colonialism" (Nkrumah 1968; Leys 1975). The stage for an alliance of national-foreign capital was set during the national independence movement and subsequent power transfer. Independence was granted to that party or a coalition of parties in the colonies which stood for preserving the metropolitan economic interests intact. In the context of Kenya, for example, it is observed:

> The transition from colonialism to neo-colonialism was a planned one, aimed at preserving the greater part of the monopolistic colonial economic structure in the interests of large-scale commercial, financial and estate capital by coming to terms with those leaders in the nationalist movement–a majority–who represented the new petty-bourgeois strata which had been formed throughout most of Kenya under colonialism (Leys 1975: 254).

In colonies where the situation was likely to deviate from this course, the imperial state opted for constitutional and/or military interventions –generally on the pretext of halting the spread of communism. Thus in Guyana when the suspension of the constitution could not bring forth the leadership and the party preferred by the metropolitan interests, the electoral system of proportional representation was imposed on the eve of independence to achieve the same results (Smith 1971: 416-18). In

Malaysia the conservative Alliance Party which was given independence was shaped and strengthened during the political reconstruction carried out by the British in the face of the Communist threat.

Partly because of this colonial legacy and partly because of the current reality of the monopoly capitalist world economy, the post-colonial economies have been experiencing tremendous difficulties in the successful completion of capitalist industrialisation. In the economics of the less-developed countries the role of the multinational corporations is not only central, it is growing rapidly. But as the multinationals work by the logic of profit maximisation and by policies suitable to the imperialist states, the economic growth and industrialisation of the less developed countries is distorted. Although transnational capital is located in regions with an abundance of cheap labour, the long-term tendency is to foster capital-intensive rather than labour-intensive technology which generates unemployment in the less developed countries. It also has a tendency to dominate local capital; the latter tends to concentrate in the more labour-intensive but technologically least advanced and least profitable sectors of the economy. Moreover the less-developed countries have to be dependent on the import of foreign technology and know-how and market connections.

Even when economic development, based on the role of multi-national corporations, results in somewhat increased industrialisation and standard of living, the social cost of such a development are undesirable. The foreign-capital-induced rapid industrialisation has been found to result in rapid rural-urban migration, massive unemployment and underemployment, growing income inequalities between different classes and class segments, and a sense of loss of traditional values and national pride. Moreover, the need for imperialist interests to use coercion in continuing their exploitative economic relations in the post-colonial states often renders impossible the emergence of liberal democracies. Post-colonial regimes therefore become more and more repressive in order to maintain the national-foreign capital alliance.[12] State-sponsored policies and programmes are used to legitimise the regime or to win popular support. *Apartheid* in South Africa, Africanisation in East African countries, the Black Power Movement in the Caribbean and *bhumiputerisation* in Malaysia (preference for the sons of the soil, i.e., Malays, in economic and educational matters) are some of the examples of state-sponsored ideologies through which the ruling class consolidates its power-base and its economic interests.[13] Instead of removing contradictions from post-colonial societies, such policies usually generate further contradictions in terms of working class repression and/or racial and ethnic conflict.

Within the parameters of post-colonial formations, the race relations situations of overseas Indian communities have the same generic source as in the colonial period, that is, their labour status in the plantation economies and their powerless petty bourgeoisie status in other societies.

The race relations situations of Indians in post-colonial societies based mainly on export-led plantation and mining economies arise from the fact that such economies, in spite of some changes, tend to foster a rigid socio-economic structure that inhibits balanced economic growth. According to Beckford (1972: 216-17), foreign ownership of plantations which drains the supply of investible funds from other sectors of the economy creates a situation in which the planters and associated classes enjoy excessive power that is exercised more in the interest of the small dominant class than in that of the society as a whole.

Additionally, rapid population growth and labour displacement from plantations as a result of increased mechanisation have caused estate work-forces to migrate to urban areas and join the ranks of the unemployed and underemployed. The resultant competition for scarce resources between different ethnic/racial groups in urban areas becomes the major source of communal tensions. In Guyana the race riots in the early 1960s between Indians and blacks occurred precisely for these reasons. Similarly, in Malaysia the 1969 race riots between the economically dominant Chinese and impoverished though politically dominant Malays followed a similar course. As far as Indian rubber estate workers in Malaysia were concerned, they suffered from racial as well as class exploitation. "For them, Alliance rule (which represents mainly the rule of Malay bourgeoisie) meant the maintenance of the colonial economic structure, draconian labour laws, insufficient jobs and low wages" (Stenson 1980: 199).

Race relations situations of the "middleman minority" type, earlier conceptualised as a petty bourgeois class segment, can be explained in terms of the intra-class conflict in the petty bourgeoisie (Bonacich 1980: 15). Already entrenched in the economy since the colonial days, the 'alien' petty bourgeoisie provide tough competition to the economically still weak but politically now dominant native petty bourgeoisie. The latter therefore can compete more successfully in the political and ideological field than in the economic. The "middleman minority" is seen as one of the last vestiges of colonialism. Its economic and political role in colonial period is questioned. Its ethnic solidarity and separateness is interpreted as its unwillingness to integrate in the national mainstream. These factors as well as the contradictions of the post-colonial economy whereby the benefits of economic development accrue only to the rich, while the masses—especially unorganised workers, small peasantry and urban lumpenproletariat—continue to remain economically disadvantaged, compel the ruling class to adopt certain discriminatory economic policies (e.g., licensing) directed against the middleman minority.

This intra-class conflict within the petty bourgeoisie and its consequences for the emergence of race relations is well illustrated in the following comparative account of hostility against Indonesian Chinese and East African Indians:

> But significantly it was not until 1900 that the Chinese in Indonesia became victims of racial tensions. Why was it so? One theory has it that it was then that the indigenous Indonesian petty bourgeoisie were beginning to emerge, and they found that their best strategy to power and wealth was to incite mass riots against the Chinese tradesman in order to make way for themselves. This theory is reinforced by the experience of the Asians in East Africa. The first major anti-Asian trade boycott took place in Uganda in 1959, and it was led by aspiring Buganda businessman, Augustine Kamya. Predictably it was the emerging Baganda petty bourgeoisie that benefited from the boycott, for in the seven months that it lasted, they took over small trading centres and transport services from Asians.... Typically, the petty bourgeoisie was rising up on the backs of the workers and the peasants (Tandon 1973: 15).

In the case of Uganda this intra-class conflict between the native and foreign petty bourgeois class segments eventually resulted in the expulsion of all the 50,000 Indians in 1972. In the post-independence period, Indians in Kenya were also subjected to similar pressures of Africanisation, except of course the extreme measure of expulsion. Following the passage of the 1967 Immigration and Trades Licensing

Acts, the Indians were required to give way to Africans in the civil services and commercial activities (Ghai and Ghai 1971). Consequently, the Indians, devoid of political power, resisted Africanisation by increasingly resorting to tactics that would amount to "economic sabotage" These tactics included the illegal transfer of assets abroad, bribery and corruption and self-emigration. According to Kenya Census figures, between 1962 and 1979 the Indian population declined mainly by emigration by about 100,000. That most of these emigrants, like the Ugandan refusees, migrated to Britain and other Western countries belies the notion that the Indians in East Africa were "sojourners" or that they had extraordinary attachment to India. The fact of the matter is that the majority of the so-called "middleman minority" Indians belong to the commercial petty and/or compradore bourgeoisie and as such their behaviour is dictated more by their class interest than by their supposed ethnic/racial predisposition.

To sum up, unlike pluralism and the middleman minority theory which emphasise cultural and political determinism as key factors in race relations situations of overseas Indians, the class approach more fully illuminates the ideological as well as economic sources of antagonism against them. Such an approach takes into account the wider parameters of race relations situations, namely, colonialism and capitalism which provided the conditions for both the emigration of Indians and their incorporation into the colonial social formations as segments of the proletariat and/or petty bourgeoisie.

III. A METHODOLOGICAL NOTE

We have proposed a historical and comparative analysis of the race relations situations of overseas Indian communities in colonial and post-colonial societies. The major colonial societies to which Indians emigrated during the colonial period and in which they currently constitute sizeable communities are: Sri Lanka (2.7 million), Malaysia (1.3 million), South Africa (900,000), Mauritius (650,000), Trinidad and Tobago (504,000), Guyana (400,000), Burma (350,000), Fiji (320,000), Surinam (180,000) , Kenya (80,000) and Tanzania (50,000). The socio-economic and political contexts for the settlement of Indians are obviously highly diversified.

In an attempt to make sense of such diversified communities, Tinker (1977) presented the following classification of overseas Indian communities:

(1) "Permanently second class cititzen"–South Africa, Sri Lanka, Rhodesia.
(2) "Independent but still colonised"–Trinidad and Tobago, Fiji, Guyana, Mauritius.
(3) "An auxiliary minority"–Malaysia, East Africa.
(4) "The departure signal"–Burma, Uganda.
(5) "The hope of integration"–Britain, U.S.A., Canada.

Tinker's classification is based on the problem of political status or political integration of overseas Indians in their respective societies. However, it cannot be said to be satisfactory for the following reasons:

(1) contradictory dimensions of classifying criteria have been used;
(2) all categories do not display social-structural similarity;
(3) historical patterns of emigration in the formation of overseas Indian communities have been ignored.

In order to overcome some of these difficulties, therefore, we propose to take into consideration the types of overseas Indian emigration we described in Chapter 1. These emigration patterns strongly influenced the nature and formation of overseas Indian communities and defined their initial contact situations *vis-a-vis* other constituent groups in the former colonial societies. This classification is presented in Table 2.2.

In Table 2.2, we propose a three-fold classification of overseas Indians in the former colonial societies:

(i) The first category consists of overseas Indians in Mauritius, Surinam, Guyana, Fiji, Trinidad and South Africa. Indians in these countries emigrated as indentured labourers. Except in South Africa, Indians in these countries are in the majority or significant minority. Again with the exception of South Africa, all countries continue to be export-oriented plantation economies,
(ii) In the second category are overseas Indian communities in Malaysia, Sri Lanka, Singapore and Burma which were mainly formed as a result of the *kangani/maistry* form of labour emigration. Most of the Indians are either plantation workers or lower grade administrators with few professionals,
(iii) The third category consists of three East African countries–Kenya, Uganda, and Tanzania, in which Indian

communities were formed as a result of the emigration of Indian trading castes and classes. Since the colonial days Indians in these countries have constituted a town-centred petty bourgeois class in direct competition with the indigenous petty bourgeoisie.

TABLE 2.2: **Patterns of Overseas Indian Emigration**

Emigration type	Type of emigrants	Period of emigration	Country of emigration (Percentage Indian population, 1980-81)
Indentured labour	Plantation labour	1834-1920	Mauritius (67) Surinam (52) Guyana (51) Fiji (50) Trinidad (42) South Africa (3)
Kangani/ maistry labour	Plantation labour	1865-1938	Malaysia (9) Sri Lanka (18) Singapore (7) Burma (1)
'Passage' or 'free' emigration	Trading castes and classes	1902-1960	Kenya Tanzania (< 1) Uganda

One methodological advantage of our classification is that in all categories the countries with overseas Indian communities are approximately evenly distributed. This is important for our next strategy in comparative analysis, which is to select one country from each category for intensive study. In all, three case studies of Guyana, Malaysia and Kenya are proposed. The availability of data has been a major consideration in the choice of these cases. The three represent the major variations of the intersection of colonialism, class and race. Thus in Guyana, while Indian immigrants consisted exclusively of indentured labourers, in Kenya it was the petty bourgeoisie which constituted the core of the Indian community. The Malaysian case represents a mixture of the two situations.

Our study of class and race relations is placed within the neo-Marxist paradigm. As such the major objective of the study is to analyse how the processes of class formation and class struggle shape the situations of race relations of overseas Indian communities. Generally speaking, the concept of class is anchored in the mode of production–a combination of the forces and/or relations of production and exchange. Historically, colonial and post-colonial societies have been marked by the existence of both capitalist and pre-capitalist modes of production in the manner that the former dominated and 'distorted' the latter (Brett 1973; Howard 1978; Leys 1975; Petras 1978; Rodney 1981; Stasiulis 1980; Wolpe 1972). This assumption of the articulation of the modes of production underlies our characterisation of colonial/post-colonial social formations as "peripheral capitalist formations". While the dominant capitalist mode of production constitutes the foundation for the subsequent identification of the primary classes, the existence of the dependent mode of production entails the existence of additional classes. Thus, in those colonial economies where plantation agriculture was the major capitalist enterprise, the primary antagonistic classes consisted of planters on the one hand and labourers on the other. In such formations, peasantry constituted an additional and secondary class because its base, subsistence agriculture, was subservient to plantation agriculture. The existence of other classes such as the financial or industrial bourgeoisie or the petty bourgeoisie was dependent on the development of other sectors of the economy, such as, industry, trade, and services. Thus, methodologically, the identification of class positions and class interests associated with articulated modes of production is the first analytical step in the direction of an historical study of a specific social formation.

The second analytical step towards the analaysis of race relations involves the specification of the process of racial categorisation "which occurs within the parameters established by the previously determined mode of production, parameters which include the mapping out of class positions" (Miles 1982: 158). The process of racial categorisation is essentially an ideological process. The articulation of racism (which originated in Western Europe, emerged later in the United States and has undergone a lengthy historical process of articulation and reproduction) and anti-racist ideologies such as the Black Power or Africanisation are particular instances of racial categorisation. The state is the major institutional ensemble through which racial categorisation is effected. Although racial categorisation is an ideological process, it affects all three levels of a social formation: economic, political and social. "These effects can, in combination, cohere to lead to formation of fractions within classes" (Miles 1982: 157). Thus, an analysis of race relations situations involves the specification of both racial categorisation as well as class dynamics.

Lest the foregoing methodological discussion give the impression that we are engaged in a formalistic and mechanistic analysis of race relations and class in which the former is "reduced" to the latter as if in response to some iron laws, we argue for an historically specific analysis of each social formation. These formations did not follow a set course of evolution. Variations obtained depending on the pre-colonial social formation, type of colonial enterprises, extent of foreign investment, availability or importation of local/immigrant labour, and composition and role of the middle classes in the national independence movement. The race relations situations of overseas Indians were contingent upon these factors as they combined to constitute a specific colonial/post-colonial social formation and the attendant class structure.

NOTES

1. Besides Furnivall and Malinowski, Myrdal (1944) is also considered an important contributor to the theory of pluralism. According to Rex (1959), Myrdal's contribution lies in raising doubts about the possibility of achieving complete objectivity in any sociological investigation. For Myrdal the pluralness of American culture raised problems on a methodological level. So far as the race relations situations in the U.S. are concerned, "Myrdal looks at the conflict situation in American society as one between differing ideals as well as between interest" (Rex 1959: 122).
2. "Middleman minorities" were not necessarily the creation of colonial economies. In many cases they existed in pre-colonial and pre-capitalist societies (Blalock 1967). Chinese in Southeast Asia, Jains and Parsees in India, Jews in Europe provide some examples of such communities.
3. Operationally defined, colonialism refers to the social structure created within the colonised society characterised by economic exploitation and political subjugation of native people, structural inequalities, ethnic/racial pluralism and an ideology of native inferiority. In this work the terms "colonialism" and "colonial social formation" are used inter-changeably.
4. The concept of "peripheral capitalism" is in sharp contrast to the notion of "dual economy" in which the modern sector supposedly coexist with the traditional, apparently without affecting it.
5. Our conceptualisation of a colonial social formation is derived from a critique of the dependency/world system perspectives as developed in a number of recent works on the subject (e.g. Brett 1973; Howard 1978; Leys 1975: Penas 1978; Rodeny 1981; Stenson 1980). Besides putting more emphasis on class

analysis, these critiques also assume the articulation of the modes of production. Thus, although the dominant mode of production in the colonies was capitalism, subordinate pre-capitalist modes of production were also retained or even encouraged. The latter nevertheless showed a strong transitional tendency towards capitalism.

6. While discussing class formation in the colonial societies it must be stressed that in the early colonial period classes were not greatly differentiated entities. As Rodney (1981: 218) noted in the Guyanese context for the late nineteenth and the early twentieth centuries: "If classes are to be defined in their mutual opposition (as would seem logical), then the differentiation of the working class, peasantry and middle class was incomplete. The most sharply defined of the existing classes in British Guyana comprised the capitalists who owned most of the means of production, controlled the institutions of the colonial state, and secured most of the surplus alienated through wage labour or market mechanisms".
7. In the plantation economies the correlation between race and class was so strong that a number of important studies were done within this paradigm, though they mistakenly used the term "caste" in place of "race" (e.g. Dollard 1937; Myrdal 1944; Warner 1936). This caste school of race relations studies was later forcefully criticised by Cox (1948) and Dumont (1961), among others.
8. It should not be inferred that the various constituent elements in the plantocracy were always unanimous in their opinions. Occasionally, colonial officials and planters or planters and missionaries came in conflict with each other on certain issues, but their conflicts was usually resolved in favour of the planters' interests.
9. The split labour market situation was widespread in the colonial economies. Quoting Parliamentary Papers (India) Reports (1841, XVI (45), p. 6), Cumpston notes that in Guyana "the total annual receipts of a healthy coolie when fully paid in wages, food and clothes amounted to 8.10s 0d per annum and the wages of a free labourer, Negro or mulatto, at 1/2 dollar a day deducting the food and clothing, 32.8s 0d" (1969: 32).
10. The then Prime Minister Nehru (1947-64) had frequently exhorted the overseas Indians to identify themselves with the country of their adoption. In 1955 he declared that Indians in Africa could expect no help from India if they exploited Africans.
11. The term "post-colonial" simply refers to the post-independence period. In this connection the mid-1980s is the limit of our time-period in this study.
12. This becomes possible as in many less-developed countries "the ruling class is directly represented in the state, and in some cases the state-classes are combined features of society" (Petras 1978: 69).
13. Obviously not all of these ideologies or policies can be put on the same footing in terms of their content and real intent. In spite of some flexibility, apartheid essentially represents the continuity of colonialism, while other ideologies which emerged in reaction to imperialism have emancipatory content and reflect the neo-colonial reality.

3

Guyana: Indentured Labour and Race Relations

Unlike pluralist studies (Despres 1967; Glasgow 1970; Green 1974 and Newman 1962) which emphasise the institutionalised cultural and political differences between groups as the main cause of race relations tensions in Guyana,[1] in this chapter we argue for a class analysis of race relations. This argument is based on two major premises relevant to the post-emancipation Guyanese colonial society: *first*, it was predominantly a plantation economy, and *second*, all the Indian[2] immigrants arrived in Guyana as indentured labourers to work on the sugar plantations. It will be shown that given these circumstances, the first racial animosity experienced by Indian labourers emerged from their class exploitation by the European planters. The second form emerged from economic competition with African labourers. Indian immigration resulted in a "split labour market" situation within the working class. Further tension between the two groups arose outside the plantation when, following the availability of Crown land, an Indian peasantry began to emerge and entered into competition with Africans over the growth of agricultural produce for sale in local markets. In this connection the land settlement schemes designed for Indians in lieu of their return passage were additional complicating factors.

The post-war race relations situation in Guyana is sometimes explained in terms of cultural pluralism and racial politics. It is argued that since the mid-1950s Guyanese politics essentially represents the racial competition for political dominance between Indians and Africans, the two major racial groups in Guyana (Despres 1967; Glasgow 1970). As Raymond Smith (1971: 417) rightly pointed out, this simple model has many attractions, not least of which is the fact that it is used by many Guyanese themselves, and it does represent some important features of the real situation. However, the model leaves out a number of gaps in our understanding of Guyanese politics and race relations. For example, how do we explain the success of the nationalist Peoples Progressive Party in bringing together the Africans and Indians in 1950-53? Which racial group was dominant between 1953 and 1957, or were either? "Were the East Indians dominant in 1957-64, and if so how was it that strikes and riots fomented by the basically Portuguese United Force and basically African P.N.C. (Peoples National Congress) was able to cripple the Jagan Government?" (Post 1969: 91).

Any satisfactory answer to such questions lies not only in the plural nature of the Guyanese society but in the post-Second World War colonial history of Guyana and its relation to the United States of America and Britain. At every crucial point where the allocation of political power has been involved–the suspension of the constitution and the dismissal of the Peoples Progressive Party (P.P.P.) Government, the strikes and riots of the early 1960s, the adoption of proportional representation–it has been the U.S. and/or British policies that have decided the matter (Post 1969; Smith 1971). Thus, theoretically the most significant drawback of the plural model in the Guyanese case is its unaccountability for the external factors which shaped the course of political events.

It is our contention that some of these issues can better be addressed by taking into account a broader class perspective in conjunction with the plural reality of Guyana. With the analytical strength of a class perspective the major political events in Guyana which had repercussions on race relations can briefly be recounted as follows: the common oppression of Indian and African masses led to the formation of biracial P.P.P. and launching of the nationalist movement. The threat to British capital interests from the newly formed leftist P.P.P. government soon resulted in its dissolution along with the suspension of the constitution. Even after the split in the P.P.P. in 1955 when it continued to form the government, winning elections in 1957 and 1961, the American Government through the C.I.A. and the labour movement began to intensify its efforts to oust the P.P.P. government from office. It was during these efforts to topple the P.P.P. government in the early 1960s that the worst racial riots occurred in Guyana. Finally, with the imposition of proportional representation, the British and the U.S. governments were successful in installing the P.N.C.-U.F. coalition government in Guyana which was initially sympathetic to their economic and geo-political interests.

I. THE NINETEENTH CENTURY GUYANESE ECONOMY

Like other West Indian territories, from the very beginning Guyana has been a plantation economy.[3] In the early nineteenth century, coffee and cotton were the main crops in Guyana. With a slave population of about 101,000 in 1817, the plantation economy was a thriving industry. Soon, however, the price of cotton fell due to the increased production of cotton in the U.S., where the labour supply was abundant. Sugar, therefore, assumed an increasingly large proportion of production in Guyana. By the 1820s British Guyana had emerged as a major sugar producer in the world market.

The Aftermath of Slave Emancipation

The backbone of the Guyanese plantation economy until 1834 was Negro slavery. Although the Dutch and British tried to enslave the indigenous Amerindian tribes, they were unsuccessful. Instead, the Amerindians, with their knowledge of the terrain, were used as allies in catching the runaway Negro slaves (Menzes 1977: 51; Lutchman 1974: 2). As part of the Atlantic slave trade, Negro slaves were imported from West Africa. Their value as labourers was tied to the success of the plantation, since an estate without an adequate supply of them was useless. Indeed the value of an estate was largely the value of slaves upon it; so much so that this formed the most convenient criterion for taxation purposes" (Nath 1970: 1). It should not be surprising, therefore, that the economic consequences of emancipation in 1834 were disastrous for the economy.[4] Free Negroes were not willing to work on the plantations. They entertained the "idea that field labour is degrading and inconsistent with freedom" (Hancock 1840: 15). Instead some of them preferred to cultivate their own land which they had purchased in the best parts of the colony (Farley 1954). Others demanded high wages to continue to work on the plantations.

The most pressing need of the late 1830s was therefore for labour. The situation was further aggravated when the apprenticeship scheme, a modified form of slavery, came to an end in 1838. Some planters, however, were ready for this situation. In 1835, 429 Portuguese immigrants were introduced from Madeira. Efforts were also made to import 'surplus' Negro populations from the West Indies. Though these supplies, irregular and in small numbers, along with some Chinese and African indentured immigrants, continued throughout the nineteenth century, the experiment as a whole was not a success.

Indian Indentured Labour and the Revival of the Economy

In this situation of uncertainty John Gladstone, an estate owner, introduced 396 Indian indentured immigrants in 1838 on an experimental basis (Nath 1970: 11). Following the ill-treatment of these labourers by certain estate owners, an embargo on further emigration was placed between 1838 and 1844. The emigration was resumed in 1845 and in the next four years 11,841 Indian immigrants came to Guyana. This second experiment with Indian immigration during the 1845-48 period also failed on two counts:

(i) There was a high mortality rate on the estates as well as during the voyage, and
(ii) Many of the immigrants who were bound to a written contract, found the plantation work hard and instead preferred to become beggars. Indian emigration was again suspended for two years.

By 1854, migration from India, a short-term remedy for declining sugar crops, had become a permanent and regular traffic. As a result of this massive influx of an unskilled labour force throughout the rest of the nineteenth century, the Guyanese sugar industry revived.

According to Guyanese historian Dwarka Nath, about 240,000 men, women and children were brought to work on the plantations in British Guyana between 1838 and 1917, of whom about 65,000 returned to India between 1834 and 1955. In a demographic study of Indian immigrants who landed in British Guyana between 1865 and 1917, Raymond Smith (1959) found that the immigrant population was predominantly male and young.

Concentration of Capital

While the Guyanese economy was reviving following the influx of Indian immigrants in the middle of the nineteenth century, it was also facing stiff competition from other countries. The difficulty in getting cheap labour to work on the sugar estates and the British Government's policy towards equalisation of tariffs on colonial and foreign sugar put the colonial partners in a poor competitive situation with other sugar producing countries such as Cuba and Brazil where slavery was still a practice. This resulted in the bankruptcy of a large number of planters. Consequently, planters were forced either to abandon the estates or to transfer them to the creditors. Between 1838 and 1853, a total of 135 plantations were abandoned. Of these at least thirty-five had been in coffee and eighteen in cotton production (Adamson 1972: 161). Smaller plantations had higher mortality.

Of far greater significance than this, however, was the change in ownership of estates, mostly through forced sale at execution. According to Adamson (1972: 160), between 1838 and 1853 there were "no fewer than 201 such execution sales, in which 175 estates, or nearly 60 per cent of the plantations under cultivation in 1838, changed owners". Between 1834 and 1851 the resident estate population declined sharply from 84,915 to 39,375 (Mandle 1973: 20).

All these developments were having devastating effects on the level of sugar production, which dropped from an annual average of 57,197 tons during 1829-34 to annual average of 31,865 tons during 1838-46. Soon, however, because of a steady supply of indentured labour from India (see Table 3.1), a reduction in wage-costs, changes in production techniques, and the cheap initial cost of plantations on the part of new owners, production increased. But in the process, the highly differentiated plantation economy gave way to the growth and concentration of corporate capital and the dominance of big planters. This eventually resulted in absentee ownership, which was close to absolute domination in 1884. In 1872 such ownership and control amounted to 77.7 per cent of the total production and in 1884 it rose to 83.5 per cent (Adamson 1972: 205). At the same time, by the turn of the century, three major British multinational firms had gained control of most of the Guyanese sugar industry–a situation which lasted until a decade after independence. Of these firms, the Bookers' Sugar Estate Ltd., a subsidiary of the Manchester-based Booker Brothers, McConnell & Co. Ltd. was the most important. Besides owning more than two-thirds of the local cane industry, the firm was also engaged in shipping, retail distribution and a variety of other activities. It was not without reason that British Guyana came to be propularly known in the Caribbean as "Bookers' Guyana".

II. CLASS AND RACE RELATIONS IN THE LATE NINETEENTH CENTURY

Against this background of the plantation economy of Guyana it becomes possible of discuss the process of class formation and resultant race relations situations in the late nineteenth century. In the post-emancipation period, the three classes which found themselves in resource competition in the colonial economy, though by no means on equal terms, were: British planters, mainly African peasantry, and Indian and African plantation workers. Additionally, there existed a petty bourgeoisie consisting of Portuguese and Chinese traders, merchants and money-lenders.

TABLE 3.1: **Number of Contract Immigrants arriving in British Guiana, 1835-1918**

Country of origin	Years of immigration	Number of immigrants	Percentage of total
India	1838-1917	238,960	70.1
Madeira, Azores, Cape Verde	1835-1882	31,628	9.3
Malta	1839	208	0.1
West Indies	1835-1928	42,562	12.4
Africa	1838-1865	13,355	3.9
China	1853-1912	14,189	4.2
	Total	340,902	100.0

Source: Despres (1967: 56).

The planters' interest lay in importing cheap immigrant Indian labour and thereby maintaining the dominance of the plantation sector in the economy. In opposition to the planters' interests, the African peasantry was struggling for its survival. But at the same time a part of the peasantry was also dependent on plantations to supplement its income. Indentured Indians lacked power. Those who had moved off the estates were in the same predicament as African peasants. As the situation then existed, the planters constituted the ruling class in Guyana. Even the colonial administration was under the planters' thumb.[5] The latter's political dominance derived from the fact that under the existing constitution the planters effectively controlled the legislature, especially the Combined Court which was responsible for taxation, annual estimates, supplies and the salaries of the civil servants (Daly 1975: 258). For fear of criticism in the House of Commons, the imperial government could neither abolish the Combined Court nor withdraw its financial powers. Until the constitutional reforms of 1891, even merchants were not represented in the Combined Court, and it was in fact on their behalf that moderate reforms were introduced.

Representatives of the sugar oligarchy also dominated various statutory boards concerning drainage, health, transport and harbours, public works, lands and mines, and agricultural research and development (Despres 1967: 37-38). The overall economic policy as well as the various infrastructural facilities were designed and developed primarily to benefit the sugar industry rather than meet the needs of peasant production.

Class and Race Relations Between Europeans and Indians

Throughout the indenture period, the major goal of the planters was to maintain a long-term supply of cheap labour-power. Towards this end the planters in conjunction with colonial and imperial governments adopted a number of strategies which directly affected the class and race relations situations of Indians:

Legal Repression

Repression of indentured labourers was built into the Indian Immigration Ordinance through which immigrants were tied to the plantations and were rendered virtual slaves for the bonded period. Generally, the indenture system, as the Chief Justice Beaumont of Guyana put it in 1871 in his book *The New Slavery*, was

> a monstrous rotten system, rooted upon slavery, grown in its stale soil, emulating its worst abuses and only the more dangerous because it presents itself under false colours (quoted in Ruhomon 1947: 118).

More particularly, all legal measures of the slavery period were retained by the planters to the extent that "the immigrant charged for an offence under the labour laws was gradually reduced to the position of a criminal" (Nath 1970: 46). In the 1860s the maximum fine was raised substantially and the terms of imprisonment were established at two months hard labour. The defendants were not allowed to give evidence. The prosecution rate of labourers in Guyana was especially high. The 1871 the Des Voeux Commission had found that "over half the number of immigrants was at all times liable of prosecution" (Nath 1970: 44). In 1907, about 20 per cent indentured immigrants were convicted under labour law (Rodney 1981: 41). Similarly, the vagrancy law required the immigrants to reside on the plantations. Absence for seven consecutive days constituted desertion, an offence liable to prosecution and/or penalty or both. Thus the legal measures adopted by the planters guaranteed the year round accessibility of a regimented and cheap labour-force.

Land Settlement Schemes

The planters' second strategy towards maintaining a surplus labour-force involved Indian settlement in Guyana rather than their repatriation to India. Repatriation was not only expensive, it meant "the loss of accumulated wealth which the repatriates took with them", and which in the 1880s exceeded one million dollars (Mandle 1973: 35). Repatriation would also have pushed the wage rates upwards. In order to induce Indians to commute their rights to return passage, the government had launched several official land settlement schemes during 1880s and 1890s (Nath 1970: 93-101).

These schemes were only partially successful and they were indeed intended to be so. The availability of a cheap labour force in the vicinity of sugar estates was their major objective. The plots were small-sized and therefore not financially viable (Nath 1970: 103). In order to maintain their control on labourers, the planters had made the insecurity of tenure, both of tenements and of allotments, an invariable feature, which was intensified in times when a glut of labour rendered the management all-powerful (Kondapi 1951: 125). Nevertheless, partly because of land settlement schemes, and partly because of the availability of Crown land at cheaper prices, an Indian peasantry had begun to emerge in the 1890s.[6] Since then rice cultivation has been the mainstay of the Indian peasantry. In 1884, only 2,500 acres were under rice cultivation. This had increased to 61,200 acres in 1919. In addition to rice cultivation, Indians also established and were dominant in the cattle and dairy farming and coconut industries (Ramnarine 1977: 154-89).

Lack of Education and Occupational Mobility

In order to keep Indians attached to the plantation the third strategy of the planters was to check their intergenerational occupational mobility. This was done by not providing the necessary educational facilities for the immigrants' children. In the 1860s a certain Rev. E.B. Bhose of the Anglican East Indian Mission had found "the education of coolie children and even their attendance to be rather a thing desired than effected" (Quoted in Ruhomon 1947: 179).

This was partly attributed to the fact that these coolie children could earn as much as six pence a day for light work on the estate and therefore their parents were understandably indifferent about their school attendance. In spite of this argument, however, Rev. Bhose was convinced that the low attendance of the Indian children in schools was because the interests of the planters required that they should work on the estate.

The planters' vested interests formed one obstacle to the schooling of Indian children. Another was official apathy. In spite of the fact that primary education had been compulsory since 1876, the policy was not rigorously applied to the Indian population on the sugar estates. Thus in 1881, of the 102 estates then in the colony, forty-three were not provided with schools (Ruhomon 1947: 182). Officials were apprehensive that once educated, Indians would not settle down on the land as estate residents or part-time cultivators. Moreover, Indians, who were mostly Hindus and Muslims, were naturally apprehensive of the Christian denominational schools to the extent that "a number of parents would let their children grow up in ignorance rather than run the risk of their being converted as a result of attending Mission schools" (Phillai-Tivari Report 1922, p. 62 quoted by Kondapi 1951: 147).[7] Consequently, in the 1921 Census of Guyana there were 19,000 Indian children under the age of 10 years, of whom less than 50 per cent were attending schools.

Lack of education directly affected the degree of occupational mobility among Indians. As the Report of the Des Voeux Commission (1871: 123) noted:

For the great multitude there is nothing open but a re-indenture of

> the statutory footing. There is no provision for settling the people on the soil, and no trade or special calling can be said to be open to them. They are here to fill up one gap in the social system as agricultural labourers, and agricultural labourers they must remain.

Although some occupational differentiation among Indians occurred in the nineteenth century, especially after the end of the reindenture practice in 1873, such differentiation occurred more in terms of the growth of the part-time or independent peasantry rather than in terms of urbanisation. As late as 1931 Indians were heavily concentrated in agricultural occupations. Data in Table 3.2 also show that Indians were grossly underrepresented in the professional (including public service) and industrial occupations. In addition, unemployment among Indians was high, with close to 40 per cent unemployed in 1931.

These three factors–legal repression, land settlement policies and limited educational and occupational mobility of Indians–directly accounted for the super-exploitation of Indian labourers on the plantations. The cultural differences of Indians from Europeans also played a part. As Jayawardena (1963: 17) states:

> the culture of the coolies differed widely from the European culture of the Guianese society. Their language was outlandish, they knew no English; their clothes were strange and their religion was heathen. They lacked the cultural characteristics valued in the society, and in return the society withheld its rights and privileges from them. Indian culture or coolie culture as it was and is called, became a mark of low status in the eyes of the white upper status groups as well as of the coloured and black lower status groups.

The reaction of Indian labour to their class and racial exploitation ranged from seeking legal redress through the Agent-General to acts of violence on the estates. Mention has already been made of the high incidence of prosecution under the labour laws in Guyana that belies the docility and compliance of the Indian workers.

> Violent protests were occasioned by many specific and local grievances, such as overbearing behaviour by management, disagreement over tasks, sexual exploitation of women by overseers, the "stopping" of pay, and so on (Rodney 1981: 153).

TABLE 3.2: **Percentage of Indians to All Races in Each Class of Occupations, 1891-1931**

Occupations	Percentage			
	1891	1911	1921	1931
Class I				
Professional (including Public Service)	5.8	8.2	6.8	12.0
Class II				
Commercial	10.6	24.3	23.6	30.5
Class III				
Industrial	4.3	5.4	4.9	10.0
Class IV				
Agricultural	75.9	81.6	91.9	71.5
Class V				
Domestic	7.6	7.8	4.7	8.1
Class VI				
Unoccupied	19.8	31.1	38.8	39.9
Percentage of Indian population (Census figures)	37.9	42.7	42.0	42.0

Source: Nath (1970: 241).

The strikes on the estates tended to follow a general pattern. "Whenever workers gathered to seek for higher wages, or to give vent to a grievance, they were told to disperse, and when they did not do so the 'leaden argument' (police force) was used to bring them into submission" (Nath 1970: 133). Every strike was dubbed by management as a riot and the strikers were dealt with under the Criminal Penal Code of the colony.

In sum, in the nineteenth century the pattern of race relations involving the Indian immigrant labourers *vis-a-vis* the European planters fully coincided with the former's exploitation on the sugar estates. As such, the process of racial categorisation and class exploitation went hand-in-hand.

Race Relations Between Indians and Africans

Racial problems between Indians and Africans arose from the planters' attempt to suppress African peasantry on the one hand, and the continued immigration of Indian labourers on the other. Both these measures tended to create a surplus labour-force in the colony resulting in a split-labour market situation, strike-breaking and racial antagonisms between Africans and Indians. Two additional factors which further tended to exacerbate the tensions between Indians and Africans were related to the predominance of Africans in the police force and the occupational specialisation on the estates along social lines. These factors are discussed below.

Suppression of the Peasantry

Planters as a ruling class in the second half of the nineteenth century had placed many obstacles to the growth of an independent peasantry. The major one was the planters' monopoloy of a vast tract of cultivable land and thereby the unavailability of suitable land for peasant cultivation. A significant proportion of land was kept idle by the planters. Thus in 1884 it was estimated that about 43 per cent of land belonging to the sugar estates was kept idle (Adamson 1972: 202). By the 1930s this proportion rose to about 50 per cent. In 1949 the *Commission of Inquiry into the Sugar Industry of British Guiana* reported that 21 estates then in operation encompassed 155,000 acres, of which only about 60,000 acres were under cane cultivation. It was possible for the planters to maintain such a large amount of land in idleness because the rent charged by the government was very low. In 1950, for example, it averaged only five cents an acre for nearly 90,000 acres of idle land (Jagan 1954: 24). In 1951, a private member's bill which sought to withdraw the leases or to tax uncultivated land held by the sugar planters was defeated in the Assembly.

Planters and colonial officials presented many obstacles in the way of the acquisition of land by Africans. To deter settlement in the interior, the authorities stipulated that Crown land could only be purchased in minimum lots of 100 acres; later this was raised to 500 acres (Standing 1978: 54). The price of Crown land was deliberately set high by as much as five times that of other types of land being sold. Officials also discouraged cooperative farming by passing an ordinance which required the partition of a plot of land owned by a group of more than 10 persons. This resulted in inefficient land-holdings and fragmentation of land.

Perhaps even more important than these obstacles was the lack of large-scale government assistance, especially for sea-defence, drainage and irrigation which are vitally important for agriculture under Guyanese ecological conditions.[8] "This assistance was not forthcoming in the nineteenth century because the planters used their political power to prevent a development that would have undermined their control of the labour market" (Daly 1975: 218). Throughout the nineteenth century, the promotion of peasant crops in terms of credit, transportation, marketing and agricultural research was conspicuously lacking. In this regard the *West Indian Royal Commission Report* of 1897 strongly indicted the planters. The Commission noted:

> The settlement of the labouring populations on the land, and the encouragement of the products and forms of cultivation suitable for a class of peasant proprietors formed no part of their sugar policy; such measures were generally believed to be opposed to their interests which they regarded no doubt as indentical with the best interests of the community. What suited them best was a large supply of labourers, entirely dependent on being able to find work on the estates, and, consequently, subject to their control and willing to work at low rates of wages (*Report of the West Indian Royal Commission, 1897*, Appendix C, Vol. 2, Parts II-V, p. 17, quoted in Glasgow 1970: 81).

While the plantocracy attempted to suppress the African peasantry, at the same time it tended to encourage the creation of an Indian peasantry through various land settlement schemes. As already discussed, these schemes were meant to counter the repatriation exodus of time-expired indentured Indians. The preferential treatment given to the Indians was obviously not conducive to the unity of the two racial groups of the peasantry. The manner in which some of these land settlement schemes were executed engendered direct racial clashes between the Africans and Indians. Thus in the settlement called Huis t'Dieren in 1881, eighteen Africans with leases on the land had to be forcibly ejected, whereupon the driver of the operations was "set upon and beaten" (Minutes of the Court of Policy, March 1881, cited in Rodney 1981: 184).

There were a number of such incidents relating to the land-settlement schemes. Scarcity of fertile land (which was held by the planters) and land ownership remained a source of contention in the second half of the nineteenth century between the African and Indian fractions of the peasantry. On several occasions the land leased by Africans was sold to Indians for the former's non-payments of rents and taxes. Predominantly African villages were in this manner transformed into predominantly Indian villages. "When they owned land, African peasants sold fresh provisions to Indian sugar workers of the Corentyne district; but as the land changed hands, Indians entered into effective competition as food growers and hucksters–virtually reversing the roles of buyer and seller (Rodney 1981: 182).

Immigration

Africans naturally resented the suppression of the peasantry. They also disliked the continued importation of Indian indentured labour despite the local availability of labour. Continued immigration of Indian labour meant reduced opportunities in employment, lower wages, and increased costs of living for Africans, who, as earlier pointed out, were still struggling to establish themselves as independent peasants and many of whom were also dependent on plantations for seasonal or part-time work. Moreover, it was out of Creole tax-payers' money that one-third of immigration expenses were borne by the colonial government. Africans also protested the funding of estate medical staff from public finances for the benefit of immigrants alone (Rodney 1981: 175).

Although the Africans' objections to Indian immigration were in their own self-interest, it was also in the interest to ex-indentured Indians who were similarly facing the prospects of unemployment and underemployment as a result of continued immigration (Ramnarine 1977: 46). There is no evidence of any manifest tension between the ex-indentured Indians and the incoming immigrants. A number of ex-indentured Indians and pro-Indian intelligentsia consistently expounded the view that by the 1880s the indentureship had outlived whatever justification it had in terms of boosting scarce labour supplies, and that continued immigration was undermining the well-being of Creole as well as the Indian working class as a whole.

Prominent among those who held this view were the Rev. H.V. Bronkhurst and the Rev. H.J. Shirley; Joseph Ruhomon, a journalist of Indian origin; and an ex-indentured Indian Bechu who wrote to the press and appeared before the West Indian Royal Commission of 1897 (Rodney 1981: 177).

From the 1880s onwards, Africans strongly objected to Indian immigration and its dire consequences for them. The Indians were seen by Africans as a threat to their employment, as strike-breakers and as pampered planter proteges (Moore 1970: 132-82). In the 1880s and 1890s the protests were usually in the form of random petitions; between 1903 and 1906 these were structured through the People's Association, a Creole organisation which was founded in 1903. In 1903, in addressing the Colonial Office, the Association formulated a shrewd hypothetical situation regarding the impact of cheap immigrant labour on the British working class itself:

> An adequate conception of the injustice of state-aided immigration, as it obtains in British Guiana, might be gained by imagining the British workmen on a strike for higher and fair wages being taxed to pay for the introduction of *foreign* cheap labour, and the government justifying it on the ground that what would in such case be essentially a grant to capitalists was merely a grant to increase the population of the country (Colonial Office 111, 537, 14 July 1903, quoted in Rodney 1981: 176).

Deployment of the African Police Force

In the second half of the nineteenth century Africans, who predominated in the colonial police force, were often deployed by the government to suppress work-stoppage or strikes by Indians on the estates. In one such incident on the Plantation Devonshire in 1872, nine Indians were killed and several wounded (Kirke 1970: 101). In another incident on 16 June, 1948, five Indians were killed and 12 injured (Glasgow 1970: 93). This pattern of deploying the mainly African police force against Indian workers was to become common throughout the colonial periods. Indian representation in the police force was then disproportionately low, and continues to be so.

Occupational Specialisation

Occupational specialisation on the plantations occurred along racial lines. While Africans were mostly factory workers, the majority of Indians were field hands. In the hierarchical work of plantations, the racial tension between the two groups therefore was bound to arise due to wage differentials and the attendant status-consciousness. At times, the planters were successful in using this division of labour to prevent working class solidarity. This was evident in the 1905 Plantation Ruimveldt riots which occurred in Georgetown and in which mainly African stevedores, factory hands, cane-cutters and gold miners took part and the Indian sugar workers stayed away in their homes (Nath 1970: 136-37; Rodney 1981: 190-216). Indian porters were coerced to fill the places of Africans who had withdrawn their labour (Rodney 1981: 212).

As would be normal in such situations, intense economic competition between Africans and Indians led to the formation of mutual stereotypes which in due course took on their own relative autonomy and dynamics. In the nineteenth century Guyana while the Negroes were generally characterised by laziness, indolence, lack of thrift, unskilled in business, and lax in sexual ethics, the Indians were regarded as docile, thrifty, revengeful, excitable and "effeminate" (Moore 1970: 266-329). Most of these stereotypes reflected white planters' ambivalent attitudes towards each racial group. Stereotypes of Africans reflected the fact that the ruling class wanted the Africans "to learn the ethics of the working class; not of the Victorian English bourgeoisie or Africanism" (Moore 1970: 420). On the other hand, the emphasis on the "docility" of Indians not only served as propaganda of self-justification on the part of the plantocracy *vis-a-vis* indentured labourers, it also was helpful in justifying the continued importation of indentured immigrants from India.

In making a virtue out of the docility and thriftiness of Indian immigrants, the planters were indeed emphasising the centrality and importance of cheap indentured Indian labourers *vis-a-vis* Africans in the emerging division of labour in the sugar industry. The planters' propaganda led the Indians to believe that Guyana would have been ruined had not its sugar economy been saved by indentured immigration. According to Bronkhurst, a missionary who worked among Creoles and coolies in the second half of the nineteenth century, when Creole reproached coolie with having come to undercut established plantation labour, the answer was readily forthcoming: "Yes you rascal neegah man: me come from India dis forty-six year: supposing me and me matty no come dis side fo' work, you rascal neegah been a starve one time" (Bronkhurst 1888: 186, quoted in Rodney 1981: 180).

Whereas Indians in their perception of Africans succumbed more to the planters-generated stereotypes, the Africans viewed Indians as physically inferior, thrifty, violent, constant inmates of the estates, public hospital, or jail, and a financial liability to the society at large (Moore 1970: 319). The Africans regarded Indians' thrift as avarice. They alleged that the presence of Indians, far from contributing to the prosperity of Guyana, led to economic depression as Indians tend to be miserly in their diet and dress and only derive satisfaction in decorating their women with jewellery. Since the 1940s ambition appears to have been recognised as another major stereotype of Indians in Guyana (Landis 1973).

The planters derived great satisfaction from the fact that cultural differences and racial tension existed between Africans and Indians. They took every opportunity of playing off the two major racial groups against each other. In this connection, appearing before the West Indian Royal Commission of 1897, a planter named J.E. Tinne observed:

> The two peoples do not intermix. That is, of course, one of our great safeties in the colony when there has been any rioting. If the negroes were troublesome every coolie on the estate would stand by one. If the coolies attacked me, I could with confidence trust my negro friends from keeping me from injury (quoted in Rodney 1981: 188).

This kind of strategy of policing one segment of the working class by another prevented the emergence of working class unity on the one hand, and provided the necessary elements for the stability of the plantation society on the other. In spite of antipathy between the Africans and Indians, however, Guyanese historians unanimously agree that in the nineteenth century most of the Indian-African clashes were minor and were mostly confined to the plantations (Moore 1970: 263-64; Ramnarine 1977: 218; Rodney 1981: 188).

III. CLASS AND RACE RELATIONS IN THE INTER-WAR PERIOD

The position of Indians in the inter-war period did not change substantially from that of the late nineteenth century. Perhaps the major reason of this was the continuity of the same class and power structure in the colony. Although by the end of the nineteenth century, the plantocracy had begun to lose its control over the legislature in favour of the emergent middle-class Portuguese, coloured and African politicians, such changes were generally ineffectual in the overall governing of the colony (Lutchman 1974: 99-127). "The white planters and their attorneys were still represented on the new Executive Council to which they could be nominated by the Governor" (Smith 1962: 53). Moreover, the franchise was still very restricted as we see in Tables 3.3 and 3.4. In 1910, to be registered, a potential voter had to prove an annual income of 125 pounds. The literacy qualification required a voter to acquire an ability to read and write some language, either European or Asian. The inability to meet these qualifications disqualified a great majority of poor and illiterate Indian immigrants. The available data (Tables 3.3 and 3.4) highlight the extent of limited franchise and the colonial class character of franchise rights. As is evident from Table 3.4, while the Indians formed 51.8 per cent of the total adult male population of British Guiana, they formed a mere 6.4 per cent of the total electorate and only 0.6 per cent among them were registered as voters. In contrast, the whites with 1.7 per cent of the population and comprising 17.0 per cent of the total electorate had 46.1 per cent of the registered voters. Africans were also grossly under-registered. In other words, during the colonial period in British Guiana peasants as well as working classes were denied political rights. This situation more or less continued until the emergence of "mass politics" in the late 1940s.

A further constitutional amendment was enacted in 1928 resulting in greater solidarity between the government and commercial interests (including sugar) which clearly reflected in the composition of the government bodies. In a thirty-member Legislative Council of 1928 there were eleven ex-officio, five nominated and fourteen elected members. In the twelve-member Executive Council there were seven ex-officio members, including the governor as president, three nominated non-officials and two elected members of the Legislative Council. The racial composition was such that the whites were in a comfortable majority. Almost all the non-white members were upwardly mobile middle-class persons and essentially supporters of the colonial government (Lutchman 1974: 59-68; 197-201).

TABLE 3.3: **Registered Voters in Guyana, 1833-1929**

Year	Total adult male population	Total numbers of registered voters	Percentage
1833	39,560	621	1.2
1850	47,256	916	1.9
1915	93,377	4,312	4.6
1929	150,761	9,513	8.2

Source: Green (1974: 16).

TABLE 3.4: **Registered Voters by Race in Guyana, 1910**

Race	Percentage of each race in the adult male population	Percentage of each race in the total electorate	Percentage of adult males of each race registered voters
East Indians	51.8	6.4	0.6
Africans	42.3	62.7	6.8
Portuguese	2.9	11.4	17.7
British	1.7	17.0	46.1
Chinese	0.9	2.4	12.3

Source: Clementi (1937: 367); Green (1974: 16).

This power structure reflected the wider social structure in the inter-war period. In the existing Creole social hierarchy which was dominated by the Europeans and which consisted of Portuguese, coloured or mixed and African (in descending order of importance), Indians had virtually no place. Only a tiny minority of Indians had emerged as landlords, money-lenders, shopkeepers and rice millers. They also lacked positions of power and prestige in the legislature and civil service.[9] In the 1931 Census, only 12 per cent of the positions in professions including the civil service were held by Indians who as we saw in Table 3.2 comprised 42 per cent of the colony's population. In

1943, only 74 Indian civil servants were employed with a salary of 150 pounds and over, compared to 735 non-Indians (Nath 1970: 244). Lack of education was a major factor in this respect. Literacy among Indians was far below the national average in 1940s.

Nevertheless, when in the 1940s Indians began to become educated and socially mobile, the Creole hierarchy's reaction had both social and economic aspects; socially, Creoles continued to regard the Indian middle classes as 'coolies' and demanded 'creolisation' as the price of social integration. Economically, most middle class creoles regarded Indians as competitors.

As there were no political parties in Guyana until the end of the Second World War, much of this competition was organised and expressed through such ethnic and racial organisations as the British Guiana East Indian Association (BGEIA), Georgetown Branch of the Universal Negro Improvement Association, the League of Coloured People, the Negro People Convention, the Portuguese Benevolent Society, etc. All of these associations were based in Georgetown and their leadership was drawn from the urban middle classes. And although the African and Indian associations tried to associate themselves with the cause of plantation workers, they never gained the trust of the workers. The Plantation Ruimveldt incident of 1924 clearly illustrates this point when in a management-labour dispute BGEIA officials "associated themselves with the police in urging the coolies to disperse. They were manhandled by the crowd for being 'paid officers of the government' and were rescued by the police" (Jayawardena 1963: 61). The BGEIA never tried again to espouse the cause of the labourers. Although this incident was not likely an expression of developed class consciousness, it was certainly an expression of the fact that "the coolies saw themselves as participating in a social system distinct from that in which they participated as members of the Indian community" (Jayawardena 1963: 61).

More direct proof of emerging working class consciousness comes from the fact that Indian and African workers rallied together under the leadership of Hubert N. Critchlow in the industrial disputes in the first quarter of the present century for better wages and improved working conditions. Critchlow, who in 1922 had formed the first trade union in Guyana representing the interests of mainly Negro workers of Georgetown harbour, was usually known among Indian sugar workers as the "Black Crosby".[10] Indian workers frequently went to him with their work-related grievances. Thus a rudimentary form of working class consciousness transcending racial divisions was emerging among both Indians and Africans in the 1920s. In the 1950s an important axiom in the ideology of the plantation workers was "de punishment of de black and coolie people" (Jayawardena 1963: 60). This kind of consciousness among the workers reflects the then prevailing poor socio-economic conditions of the majority of the population in Guyana, both Indian and African, to which the *West Indian Royal Commission Report* (1939) also testifies.[11]

In summary, it can be said that the inter-war period does not provide any dramatic break from the past in terms of the changes in the economy, power-structure, and class and race relations situations. Although in this period bauxite had emerged as an important export item, its impact on the Guyanese society in terms of employment (only 4,139 people, mostly Africans, were employed in bauxite production in 1946) and industrial diversification away from sugar was extremely limited. There were no political parties until 1946. And although there had emerged a number of trade unions in this period, none of them was recognised by the authorities until 1939. The Middle class colonial politicians were without mass support and racially divided. On the whole, race relations in this period remained more or less the same as in the nineteenth century.

IV. CLASS AND RACE RELATIONS, 1950-1966

During the post-World War period, race relations between the Indians and Africans derived from a specific conjuncture of class, politics and race in an atmosphere which was charged with the ideologies of anti-colonialism and self-determination. These ideals were reflected in the formation of the mass-based Peoples Progressive Party (P.P.P.), and in the latter's policies and programmes. Its leftist orientation and the Marxist rhetoric of its leaders gave cause for concern among the Anglo-American capital interests who feared the spread of communism in the Caribbean. Consequently, the British imperial state was successful in its attempt to help split the party and subsequently force the P.P.P. government out of office. This led to the politicisation of racial differences between the Indians and Africans and racial riots in the early 1960s. It is in terms of this international context of class conflict that the race relations situation of Indians in this period is analysed.

The Peoples Progressive Party was formed in 1950 with L.F.S.

Burnham[12] as Chairman (a titular position), Janet Jagan as general secretary and Dr. Cheddi Jagan[13] as leader. The Peoples Progressive Party came to power in 1953 following its victory in the general elections. The Peoples Progressive Party government followed a popular mandate to introduce legislative measures such as bringing all schools under government supervision, universal adult suffrage without property limitations at the local government level, tax reforms, modernisation and diversification of agriculture, removal of colonial trade restrictions, encouragement of local industry, social security and workmen's compensation (Jagan 1972: 119).

Within four and half months, allegations of communist subversion led to the suspension of the Constitution by the British Government. The Peoples Progressive Party leaders including Dr. Jagan and his wife were imprisoned. The Chief Secretary to the British Government, John Gutch, issued the following statement:

> Her Majesty's Government has decided that the Constitution of British Guiana must be suspended to prevent Communist subversion of the Government and a dangerous crisis both in public order and in economic affairs. . . . The faction in power has shown by their acts and their speeches that they are prepared to go to any lengths, including violence, to turn British Guiana into a Communist state. The Governor has therefore been given emergency powers and has removed the portfolios of the Party Ministers.

These charges of an attempted communist takeover were repeated in a report of the British Guiana Constitution Commission (1954) in which the Jagans and several other P.P.P. leaders were described as the followers of "the 'classical' communist doctrines of Marx and Lenin", and Burnham and his two colleagues as "socialists" with the assertion that the latter "were as bitterly opposed as their communist colleagues to British colonial rule, but they were not communists" (quoted in Manley 1979: 6). Subsequent studies, however, have found that the charges lacked validity and can be properly understood in relation to cold-war circumstances (Despres 1969: 208-10; Smith 1962: 175-78) and in terms of the threat posed to British capital interests in Guyana by democratisation.

The P.P.P. government represented a broad popular national movement against imperialism. Peoples Progressive Party major-

support came from the workers, the peasantry and the middle classes. As pointed out earlier, its policies and programmes were anti-imperialist and were aimed at expatriate sugar planters and big local landlords.[14] The actual legislation passed by the P.P.P. government included the lifting of the ban on the West Indian leaders which the colonial government had imposed, the repeal of the Undesirable Publications Law, and the amendment of the Rice Farmers Security of Tenure Ordinance of 1945. The last measure particularly irked the landed class which held thousands of acres of Crown land in idle condition and sublet at very high rentals. Another law which affected the planters' interests was the Labour Relations Bill. The bill, passed only in the lower house and interrupted by suspension of the constitution, had a number of provisions: recognition by employers of the trade unions enjoying majority support, minimising inter-union rivalry, "seeking to prohibit victimisation of workers and . . . seeking the right of trade union officials to visit the place at which their members were employed" (Jagan 1972: 123). Thus, the P.P.P. government's policies were in direct conflict with the interests of the small but powerful national/expatriate bourgeoisie. The suspension of the constitution and the dismissal of the government was an attempt by the latter to reassert control.

The suspension of the constitution was obviously part of the wider political design of the imperial government. The report of the British Guiana Constitution Commission in 1954 (Robertson Commission) itself contains the basic outline of this design. The central message of this report was that in order for Guyana to restore "normal" constitutional government, it was necessary to get rid of the militant leadership in the P.P.P. and its anti-imperialist policies. The report concluded:

> We are therefore driven to the conclusion that so long as the P.P.P. retains its present leadership and policies there is no way in which any real measure of responsible government can be restored without the certainty that the country will again be subjected to constitutional crisis (quoted in Jagan 1972: 160-61).

The imperial government's strategy was to help split the P.P.P. and win the support of the "socialist" wing of the party. This eventually happened in 1955 and did not prove a difficult task as the P.P.P. was already riddled with factionalism along ideological (the Marxist Jagan *vs.* non-Marxist Burnham) as well as racial lines. These internal divisions within the P.P.P. were also compounded by rural-urban differentiation within the party: whereas Jagan's followers were mainly sugar workers and peasants, Burnham's electoral support was among urban middle classes and the industrial workers.[15]

The initial split in the P.P.P. did not follow racial lines; it was rather ideological. At the leadership level, the split took a Marxist *vs.* non-Marxist form. Thus, whereas Jagan retained the support of such prominent African leaders as Sidney King, Martin Carter and Rory Westmaas, Burnham got the support of Indian leaders, Dr. J.P. Lachmansingh and Jai Narine Singh. "Among the rank and file, the split by and large took on an urban-rural, rather than strictly racial, form" (Jagan 1972: 174). The 1957 and 1961 election results testify to this contention. In the 1961 elections, for example, the P.P.P. victories were in the sugar and rice areas. It also won four "marginal constituencies", where the two major racial groups were evenly distributed. The P.N.C. won seats in Georgetown and New Amsterdam and in the Bauxite area. The United Force got electoral support from the isolated Amerindian districts (2 seats) and the well-to-do districts in Georgetown (Bradley 1961).

Towards the late 1950s Guyanese politics was increasingly polarised along racial lines. Some African P.P.P. supporters (e.g. King, Carter and Westmaas) had defected to join the Peoples National Congress. Perhaps unwittingly, the Jagan government's economic developmental policies and programmes, which were designed to encourage the agricultural sector, especially the rice industry dominated by Indians, was also a contributing factor. Thus in the 1956-59 development program, of the total expenditure of $77.4 millions, 42.8 per cent was spent in the agricultural sector; the areas of development in which Africans were interested received only 22.3 per cent–19.2 per cent for urban housing, 1.7 per cent for education and 1.4 per cent for industrial development. Similarly, in the 1959-64 plan, agriculture was allocated about 55.0 per cent, housing, education and industry about 7.3 per cent, 3.8 per cent and 3.6 per cent respectively (Despres 1967: 245-46). Consequently, about 90,000 acres of land were made available to a large number of rice farmers, and rice production had doubled to 275,000 tons between 1957 and 1964 (Jagan 1972: 197-98). Although the government maintained that these developmental programmes were in line with rational economic planning and were not designed as an instrument of *apanjhat* politics (communal politics), the opposition leaders and intellgentsia were unwilling to see them in terms other than "Indian domination". This perception was not without foundation. In the late 1950s and 1960s, Jagan increasingly relied on the mobilisation of the Indian electorate. Not only did he receive the support of the Hindu Sanatan Dharam Mahasabha and Anjuman-e-Islam (Muslim association), but also the support of the Indian businessmen by forming the Junior Chamber of Commerce. It has been suggested that Jagan, who was otherwise a working class champion and non-racialist, justified these electoral strategies in order to counteract the openly racialist electoral mobilisation by Burnham and his party.[16]

If the Indians were rallying behind Jagan, Africans were doing likewise by following Burnham. In 1957 Burnham had lost the support of two major Indian leaders: Latchmansingh died, and Jainarine Singh resigned. Burnham received further African support when the United Democratic Party, which "contained militant anti-communist Catholics, equally militant African racist, and a number of Portuguese businessmen" (Despres 1967: 6), was dissolved and most of its African membership was taken into the P.N.C. Thus by 1960, both major political parties were organised on racial lines. In the same year this trend was further reinforced by the formation of the United Force Party (U.F.), which was founded by a prominent Portuguese businessman, Peter D'Aguiar. The party represented the interests of European, Portuguese and Amerindian populations. In its outlook the U.F. was pro-colonial as well as capitalistic, and therefore was immediately perceived as a "White man's" party aiming to maintain the *status quo*.

Although a party alliance between the P.N.C. and the U.F. was not formalised until the 1964 elections, during the 1962, 1963 and 1964 riots both shared a common goal: the removal of the P.P.P. government. Moreover, the two parties had more in common with each other in terms of class interest and cultural affinity, and the Creole value system, than with the P.P.P. Racially, the P.N.C.-U.F. alliance represented the Indian *vs.* non-Indian cleavage in the Guyanese society and politics, an important dimension of pluralism especially since the suspension of the constitution. Ideologically, it is difficult to understand the basis of the coalition of the "socialist" P.N.C. and the capitalist U.F., except in terms of their common opposition to the P.P.P. rule. The Portuguese, European and Coloured businessmen were opposed to the government because of the government's liberalised trade policies favourable to the emergent Indian and other businessmen at the expense of colonially established European, Portuguese and Chinese capital (Despres 1967: 233). The Africans were opposed to the government for two important economic reasons: (i) the Indian-dominated agricultural sector received developmental priority by the government over the African dominated industrial sector; (ii) Africans were experiencing competition in business and professions as a result of increased education among Indians. Additionally, the Africans feared that independence under Jagan would mean perpetual rule by Indians as the latter constituted about 50% of the total population and the growth rate among them was high. Thus the P.N.C.-U.F. alliance was to lose nothing and gain everything from destabilising the government. The local press (Portuguese owned),[17] trade unionists and the missionaries were also on their side.

Moreover, the P.N.C.-U.F. alliance had the blessings of the Anglo-American capital interests and their governments. As detailed earlier, most of the Guyanese colonial economy, especially its main prop, the sugar industry, was owned by the British companies. British involvement in the import-export sector was also substantial. In 1963, for example, the British Sugar Corporation "made a profit of between 3m. and 4m. . . . from sugar purchased from Guyana alone" (Nath 1970: 90). American and Canadian companies were involved in another important raw material of Guyana, bauxite (Girvan 1976). These companies were virtually exempt from corporate taxes. They bought Guyanese bauxite at substantially cheaper market rates than under the previous agreements (Reno 1964: 97-102). These imperial interests were at stake while the P.P.P. government was in office in 1953 and again during the 1957-1964 period. Some form of economic nationalisaion after the independence of Guyana was expected from the P.P.P. government. Additionally, the U.S. government was obsessed with Guyanese "communism".

Consequently, vertical integration was strengthened between the metropolitan and local bourgeoisie interests during the troubled years of the early 1960s. The major objective of this alliance was to oust the P.P.P. government from office. The participation of the multinationals in the 1963 strike clearly shows this. In that strike, bauxite and aluminum operations at Mackenzie were closed down. Bookers and Demerara sugar companies cooperated by locking out 18,000 to 20,000 sugar workers who did not support the strike. International airlines and shipping companies effected an air and sea blockade creating food and gasoline shortages (Reno 1964: 52-56).

The role of trade unionism, and particularly that of the British Guiana Trades Union Congress (T.U.C.)–a federation of a number of trade unions–was crucial in the 1963 strike. The T.U.C. was not only affiliated to the Inter-American Regional Organisation of Workers (O.R.I.T.) since 1956, it was also heavily dependent upon O.R.I.T. for financial and other assistance. In 1960, T.U.C. had a total income of $15,911.84, of which O.R.I.T. (American) grants and other financial assistance from overseas amounted to $12,500.00. The corresponding figures for the year 1961 were $16,970.25 and $13,000.00 approximately (Chase 1964: 216). So far as the financial assistance to the 1963 strike was concerned, the American Federation of Labour

> had put up the money for the strike, reportedly $30,000 to $50,000 a week (U.S. $) to begin with, and as the strike dragged on, $130,000 a week. . . . When the cost had mounted over an estimated $1.2 million the T.U.C. at last signed an agreement with the government to end the strike on July 7, 1963 (Reno 1964: 56-57; also Manley 1979: 7).

Additionally, from the same overseas sources the T.U.C. received a variety of office equipments including loud-speakers, projectors, typewriters and duplicators; "and special funds for paid organisers" (Chase 1964: 216). At the same time, at least a dozen trade unionists from Guyana, including the M.P.C.A. president, received training at the Washington-based American Institute of Free Labour Development in the techniques of anti-communist campaigning. "Six of these were still drawing salaries from the institute in June of 1963" (Reno 1964: 52; see also Chase 1964: 290-95). The P.N.C. opposition leader himself acknowledged that the "assistance was received from the American trade union movement . . . and from many sections and quarters not normally friendly to the workers." He, however, contends that "the workers kept full control of the struggle" (Burnham 1970: 100).

It was against this backdrop of the changing class alliance as well as racial polarisation that racial violence occurred in the early 1960s. The P.P.P.'s third successive victory in 1961, in spite of "gerrymandering" in favour of the opposition parties, was seen by the latter as the victory of Indians over other ethnic groups who were therefore determined to 'contain and repel' the P.P.P. The first occasion to attempt to do so arose in February 1962 when, in order to meet developmental needs and raise the salaries of civil servants, teachers and policemen, the government introduced a budget. The budget was introduced following the recommendations of Nicholas Kaldor, a Cambridge University economist and was aimed at reforming the existing tax structure which favoured the propertied classes. Additionally, the government also proposed some indirect taxes, such as customs and excise on a variety of items, including luxury and semi-luxury goods, alcoholic drinks, beverages and tobacco. As Dr. Jagan (1972: 214) himself puts it, the budgetary measures "were likely to hit hardest the expatriate companies and the wealthy Portuguese and Indians".

However, both opposition parties vigorously opposed the budget dubbing it simultaneously "anti-working class" and "communistic".[18] In their opposition they were also joined by the Chamber of Commerce, the local press, the Trades Union Council and the Civil Service Association. *The Daily Chronicle* owned by the U.F. party president D'Aguiar began to publish reports, articles and letters calling for the overthrow of the government. "Georgetown merchants did their part by raising prices and ascribing the price increases to the proposed taxes" (Reno 1964: 39). The Chamber of Commerce welcomed the proposed strike, and employers agreed to pay their workers while they were out against the government. Although in the end the government had decided to withdraw the budgetary measures regarding indirect taxes and was in negotiation with the Trades Union Council and Civil Service Association, the opposition leaders and trade unionists were intent upon a showdown. Week-long tension finally resulted in widespread arson, looting and violence, causing the death of five people, injury to eighty and destruction of property estimated at about \$30.0 million in the business centre of the city of Georgetown (Lutchman 1974: 228; also Daly 1975; 304-05; Despres 1967: 264-65). Race relations were strained. Looting was directed particularly at stores owned by Indians. African mobs roamed the Georgetown streets beating Indians. When word of this spread, Indians fought Africans in the villages.

In 1963 there was a "general strike" in British Guiana which lasted eighty days and paralysed the country's economy. Partly at issue was a P.P.P. proposed labour relations bill which sought to give the government the power to certify unions for purposes of representation of workers. The legislation was intended to get legal recognition for the Guianese Agricultural Workers Union (GAWU), which had support of the majority of the sugar workers and was backed by the P.P.P. The existing union, Man-Power Citizens Association, which was recognised by the Sugar Producers Association but did not have majority support, was obviously opposed to the legislation. The whole issue became politicised as in 1962, and this time too the opposition politicians and trade unionists found an opportunity to discredit the government.

The year 1964 also proved violent following a call for a strike by the Guiana Agricultural Workers Union (a P.P.P. supported sugar workers union). The major issue was the same as in 1963, i.e., the recognition of the GAWU. Also at issue was the imposition of proportional representation, a form of electoral system the P.P.P. opposed. The strikers were mainly Indians. The sugar planters attempted to break the strike by employing scabs, mostly Africans from Georgetown. Thus an industrial dispute soon turned into a racial conflict. Disturbances were country-wide. The most tragic incident occurred at Wismar, a village near the mining town of Mackenzie where arson, killing and rape affected about 1,000 people, mostly Indians. On the whole, in the 1964 incidents "176 persons were killed, 920 injured, 1,400 homes destroyed by fire, and about 15,000 persons forced to move their houses from one district to another in order to settle in communities where people of their own ethnic group predominated" (Daly 1975: 306-07). The large majority of displaced people were Indians.

The Jagan government was finally ousted not by racial violence but by the introduction of proportional representation which was imposed by the British government with pressure exerted by the U.S. government (Schlesinger 1965: 774-79; Smith 1971: 417-18).[19] In the 1964 election held under the proportional representation system[20] the P.P.P. with 45.8 per cent of the votes were allocated twenty-four seats, the P.N.C. with 40.5 per cent of the votes, twenty seats, and the U.F. with 12.4 per cent of the votes, seven seats. The P.N.C. and the U.F. formed a coalition government. Guyana achieved its independence on 26 May, 1966.

To sum up, the emergence of the P.P.P. in the early 1950s represented the emergence of a working class coalition as well as a comprehensive nationalist movement. For a very short period of time in Guyana class forces appeared to win over racial cleavages in politics. However, a combination of internal and external forces led to the split in the P.P.P. and subsequently to the polarisation of politics along racial lines. Race relations between the Indians and Africans deteriorated and resulted in widespread racial violence in the early 1960s. During this period of racial politics and violence, the old stereotypes were revived and used against one another.

V. CLASS AND RACE RELATIONS IN THE POST-INDEPENDENCE PERIOD

Class and race relation in the post-colonial period in Guyana are essentially the derivatives of those that obtained on the eve of independence. The P.N.C.-U.F. coalition which achieved independence for the country from the British represented the absentee British bourgeoisie; Portuguese, Chinese and Coloured petty bourgeoisie; urban middle classes (mainly coloured and African) and industrial workers (African). The opposition P.P.P. was supported mainly by Indian peasantry and sugar workers and a minority of middle classes. Following the 1968 elections the ruling party had further strengthened its position, despite the break-down of the P.N.C.-U.F. coalition. In the 1968 elections, the P.N.C. won 30 out of the total of 53 seats in the National Assembly. An analysis of the 1968 election shows that "between the 1964 and 1968 elections there was a net shift of party support to the P.N.C. from the P.P.P. and U.F. respectively" (Green 1974: 135). Better party organisation and political patronage appeared to be the factors responsible for this shift towards the P.N.C. support.

Thus by 1968 the ruling party had gained not only an independent base among the African electorate, but also some support among the Indians, particularly the urban petty bourgeoisie. Until then the ruling party's economic orientation was only covertly socialistic. The economy was still dominated by the British and North American capital interests. However, the opposition party's continued adherence to Marxism-Leninism and its criticism of the government policies in conjunction with the worsening economic situation forced the government to seek the needed revenues to stay in power by nationalising first the Canadian-owned Demerara Bauxite Company in 1971 and subsequently other industries (Premdas 1977: 70-71). Simultaneously, Guyana was declared a Co-operative Socialist Republic. The Guyanese Government's economic policies and programmes, however, did not bring about the desired results of reducing poverty among the masses. On the contrary, the economic situation worsened. To stem the tide of popular discontent as well to stay in power, the ruling class has increasingly adopted authoritarian state policies which represent a complex balance of forces of class and racial conflict. In the following pages we attempt to show that race relations situations of Indians in Guyana emerge not merely from racial party politics, but also from the imperatives of economic transformations, emerging class conflict and state policies and practices. We elaborate upon this argument by first highlighting some of the salient features of the post-colonial Guyanese economy.

The most significant feature of the Guyanese economy after independence was its emphasis on the radical decolonisation policy. As part of this process, the two major industries–sugar and bauxite–were nationalised in the first half of the 1970s. By 1978, official estimates suggest that eighty per cent of the productive sector was public. Thus, significant change occurred in the ownership of the plantation and mining sectors and the corresponding class formation in these sectors. As the management of the nationalised industries was placed in the hands of state corporations, the state bureaucracy replaced the absentee metropolitan bourgeoisie. This meant that the state petty bourgeoisie has gained control of the public sector of the economy. The major implication of this change has been the augmentation of the bureaucratic petty bourgeoisie which was already dominated by Africans (Enloe 1973: 88). In spite of the rapid increase in government services, a large number of Indians experience difficulties in finding employment. Consequently, an increasing number of Indians have been emigrating abroad reversing the ethnic pattern of migration from Guyana. "By the 1970s, with the P.N.C. in power, the majority of all categories of migrants together–permanent, temporary and students–were East Indian" (Bacchus 1980: 52).

In spite of the nationalisation of the plantation and mining industries, the Guyanese economy was not diversified. It remained dependent on the export of raw materials. The two major products, sugar and bauxite, continued to dominate the economy. Between them these two items accounted for 26.86 per cent of output in 1977 as opposed to 31.33 per cent in 1965 (Sackey 1979: 33). The nationalisation of sugar and bauxite industries has not resulted in the transformation of production relations. On the contrary, class conflict between the new ruling class (the state petty bourgeoisie) and the labourers has intensified. This is clearly evident in the increased number of industrial disputes involving both sugar and bauxite workers (Table 3.5).

TABLE 3.5: **Industrial Disputes Involving Stoppage of Work in Guyana, 1960-77**

Year	No. of work stoppages	No. of workers involved	No. of man-days lost[1]	Wages lost (G$)
1960	43	6,300	17,000	-
1961	55	10,700	29,000	-
1962	48	13,400	45,000	220,000
1963	54	62,900	1,360,000	4,300,000
1964	45	15,300	1,168,000	5,740,000
1965	146	48,300	133,000	701,000
1966	172	37,600	109,000	696,000
1967	170	30,300	152,000	841,000
1968	136	56,489	306,009	1,652,858
1969	126	17,878	38,660	250,030
1970	159	84,056	453,928	2,821,754
1971	199	41,447	141,816	623,529
1972	175	44,597	135,599	717,425
1973	172	34,695	75,955	666,676
1974	136	61,932	150,991	1,300,991
1975	129	82,484	339,218	2,738,544
1976	284	110,158	352,317	1,973,161
1977[2]	247	120,191	361,499	3,809,023

Notes: 1. The above figures reflect only minimum losses.
2. Excludes the figures for the 135-day strike in the sugar industry in 1977.

Source: Sackey (1979: 43).

In a situation of post-colonial economic crisis and mass discontent, the plight of mainly Indian sugar workers has worsened considerably. The general conditions of labour exploitation continue to persist in the face of low wages, increasing inflation and unemployment. In Guyana, unemployment is particularly high in rural areas. In a 1965 manpower survey, unemployment rate was 15.2 per cent in the agriculture sector, where Indian population is concentrated (Bacchus 1980: 48). Since then this trend does not appear to have reversed as government nationalisation and militarisation policies have resulted only in strengthening of the service sector (where Indians are under-represented).

In addition to these problems, a major grievance of sugar workers involved the government's denial until 1976 to recognise the Guyanese Agricultural Workers' Union, which the majority of workers supported and which was the cause of the 1964 strike and violence. The government increasingly appeared to be unsympathetic to the workers' demands and grievances. In 1977, the sugar workers went on a four-month strike demanding higher wages and better working conditions. The government "countered the strike by ordering the defence force and party loyalists into the sugar plantations. Hurriedly passed prohibition bills limited the ability to sustain the strike much longer" (Sackey 1979: 42).

The progressive decline of the rice industry, which is dominated by the Indians, is another setback to the post-colonial economy of Guyana. This decline is attributed to a reversal of the economic policy by the new government. Thus, in the 1966-70 development plan, the Indian-dominated agriculture sector was accorded the lowest priority. Compared to 50-55 per cent expenditure on agriculture in the P.P.P. government plan during the 1956-64 period, only 16 per cent of the total expenditure was allocated to this plan (Green 1974: 53). This reduced expenditure meant less input into infrastructural facilities in agriculture. The government's interference in administrative and marketing agencies further led to the deterioration of the industry. Thus, the Rice Marketing Board which is responsible for purchasing rice from farmers has been reorganised by the P.N.C. government in the manner that from an elected body by the farmers the Board has been reduced to a government-appointed body. With an expanded bureaucracy in rice marketing, the cost of handling rice increased from $2.1 to over $4.0 per bag (Tennassee 1982: 12). In 1966, the Board had reduced the purchasing prices of rice and paddy to those prevailing in 1955 thus affecting the margin of profits to the farmers. Subsequently, "although the industry made profits of $13.1 m. between 1967 and 1973 there was no significant increase in the net income earnings of the rice farmers" (Sukdeo 1976: 218). The farmers therefore have less incentive with the result that not only rice acreage but rice production also declined from 171,500 tons in 1963 to 144,800 tons in 1972 (Sukdeo 1976: 214). The contribution of rice to the Gross Domestic Product fell from 5.7 per cent in 1966 to 2.9 per cent in 1971 to 2.1 per cent in 1973 (Premdas 1977: 69). Consequently, food imports in Guyana increased from $25.0 m. in 1960 to $38.0 m. in 1970 (Jagan 1972: 383). These figures highlight the perception among Indians that the governments' policies are detrimental to the interests of the Indian peasantry.

Another major feature of the post-colonial Guyanese economy is the adoption of co-operative socialism as the desired socio-economic order. The country was declared a Co-opertaive Socialist Republic in

1970. According to Burnham, co-operative socialism should be "the principal institution for giving the masses the control of our economy" (quoted in Sackey 1979: 38). It was also supposed to be the instrument for "minimising" the private and state sectors and this followed from the "declared objective of making the co-operative sector the dominant sector eventually" ("Declaration of Sophia", address by Prime Minister Forbes Burnham, 14th December, 1974, quoted in Sackey 1979: 38). Unfortunately, this has not happened; co-operativism plays only a marginal role in the overall economy of Guyana. The total investment (shares and savings) in 1,327 co-operative societies in 1975 amounted to less than G$ 1·3 million with about G$416,000 in reserve funds (Sackey 1979: 39).

Most of the co-operative societies are controlled by ruling party members, who "tend to use the co-operative as an instrument of personal gain" (Sackey 1979: 41). Moreover, Guyanese co-operativism is antithetical to the values of socialism as (a) the majority of farmers are "barred from using credit facilities" (Singh 1972), and (b) working class repression and class disparities continue to increase. In spite of its marginal role in the functioning of the peripheral state capitalist economy, co-operative socialism in Guyana has a number of ideological functions externally and internally. Externally, it is palatable to the West because it is opposed to the Marxism-Leninism of Jagan. Internally, besides providing employment and patronage through the likes of board memberships to Africans,[21] it has also co-opted a small section of the Indian bourgeoisie and petty bourgeoisie, which is least attracted to Jagan's "communism".

The response of the ruling class to the faltering economy and its inherent contradictions has been both political and ideological. The ideological functions of co-operative socialism have already been noted. Politically, since independence Guyana has increasingly adopted authoritarian measures to suppress popular discontent. The security and police forces have been expanded beyond any reasonable assessment of the country's requirements and economic capacity. In the mid-1970s, the period which marks the beginning of economic decline and intensified class conflict in Guyana, the government embarked on militarisation as a developmental strategy. In 1975 and 1976, the existing Guyana Defence Force was strengthened by the inauguaration of two new paramilitary institutions, the Guyana National Service, and the Guyana People's Militia. The expressed object of the first was stated as "moulding the new Guyana man" and of the second as making "every citizen a soldier" (Danns 1978).

In 1964, the total number of armed forces in Guyana was 2,135 (including the Police numbering 1,635). In 1977 this number increased to 21,751. "In 1964, there was about one military personnel for every 284 citizens; in 1976, there was one for every 37 citizens, hence presenting a conspicuous feature of everyday life in Guyana" (Sackey 1979: 46; Danns 1978). In the 1970s, the government expenditure on economic development generally tended to be the half of that for defence.

Nationalisation and militarisation appear to be complementary processes in independent Guyana. Just as nationalisation resulted in the emergence of a privileged class of state petty bourgeoisie, militarisation has also created a privileged group of military personnel. The interests of both class fractions at present are mutually complementary, and evidently in contradiction to those of the majority of workers and peasants. As a cadre of disciplined loyalists of the ruling regime, the members of the security forces enjoy all the benefits and privileges of their political and administrative counterparts in the emergent state enterprises. On the other hand, the police forces have been frequently used in the suppression of labour demands. In this connection the suppression of the 1977 sugar workers' strike has already been mentioned. In 1979, a general strike involving about 20,000 members of the Guyana Mine Workers' Union, Commercial and Clerical Workers' Union and Guyana Agricultural Workers' Union was similarly suppressed by using the riot police to break demonstrations and by arresting the trade unionists (*Keesing's Contemporary Archives* 1981: 31059-60).[22]

The constitution and expansion of these forces have distinct racial overtones in that they do not reflect the broad cross-section of the population. The participation of Indians in these forces is weak. Thus in 1965, of the total security forces of 3,671 only 733 (about 20%) were Indians. In 1970, the racial distribution of Guyanese defence and police forces was as follow: total 4,145–African 2,840 (69%), Indian 995 (24%), and other 310 (7%) (Green 1974: 75, fn 15). The Indians had first raised this question of imbalance in the public service (Table 3.6) as well as in the police forces in the early 1960s when during racial upheaval the predominantly African police force was used against the Indians. For the Indians, who constituted over half of Guyana's population as early as 1960, such an imbalance in various public services as well as police forces amounts to racial discrimination.

TABLE 3.6: **Racial Distribution (%) in the Security Forces, the Civil Service and Other Government Agencies, 1965**

Body	Indians	Africans	Others	Total
The Security Forces	19.9	73.5	6.6	100
The Civil Service	33.1	53.0	13.9	100
Government Agencies and Undertakings	27.2	62.5	10.3	100
Percentage of Total Population	47.8	32.8	19.2	100

Source: Adapted from Robert and Byrne (1965: 33).

Another area in which state repression has virtually become institutionalised in Guyana is national and local elections. This includes faulty electoral lists, use of overseas voters,[23] abuse of proxy voting[24] and miscounting of ballots. On all these counts, the results of the 1968 and subsequent elections have been vehemently criticized by the opposition parties and international observers (Green 1974: 29-32; Manley 1979: 11-16; Spinner, 1980, 1982). It was on account of these electoral frauds that the P.N.C.-U.F. coalition was ended in 1968.

From the above discussion it is obvious that the post-colonial economy of Guyana suffers from a number of contradictions. Notwithstanding the radical nationalisation policies boldly followed by the government, the economy continued to be dependent and underdeveloped. The agricultural and manufacturing sectors generally stagnated, and the service sector over-expanded. Contrary to the government's claim of building a co-operative socialistic society, its economic policies only tended to perpetuate the elitist bias in society with the result that the pattern of development has tended to reinforce the class differences and racial cleavages in Guyana.

In Guyana, racial boundaries generally coincide with both rural-urban as well as class divisions. The majority of Indians who constitute the peasantry and a segment of working class are also rural residents. Party politics in Guyana since the mid-1950s has also followed these divisions. The post-colonial economic development, emergence of state capitalism and militarisation have intensified class conflict in Guyana between the ruling class consisting of state petty bourgeoisie and the masses (peasantry and the working class). To the growing mass discontent, the ruling class has responded by increased state repression and curtailment of civil liberties.

Since the late 1970s, the economic crisis in Guyana has generalised into a society-wide crisis.[25] The ruling class response to this crisis has been to escalate state repression. Not only the right to work and right to strike have been undermined by the state, the repression has also extended to all opposition as well as independent social/political groups (Thomas 1982: 57-58).[26] The state has been constitutionally restructured (1978 and 1980) and the security apparatus of the state further enhanced. However, one important outcome of the increased state repression has been the blurring of the traditional racial boundaries within the work force as revealed in several major industrial strikes in the late 1970s (Spinner 1980, 1982; Thomas 1982). The organised force behind these attempts to unite working classes has been the country's third major political party, the Working People's Alliance (W.P.A.) founded in 1975 by the late Dr. Walter Rodney and Eusi Kwayana (the former Sidney King). The party has been engaged in campaigning for "free and fair elections and elections free from fear". The W.P.A. also advocates a kind of "politics that rejects all forms of racism and exploitation" (*Caribbean Contact*, Sept. 1984: 6). It remains to be seen whether the W.P.A. will be able to change the racial nature of Guyanese politics, if and when free and fair elections are held.

In sum, although there has not been any overt racial conflict in the post-independence period in Guyana, perhaps mainly due to the authoritarian stance adopted by the government, racial discrimination and antagonism directed against Indians have nevertheless been present. For Indians, their presence is felt in the form of continued exploitation of a segment of the Indian working class and alienation of the peasantry under the P.N.C. regime, which ruthlessly adheres to the principle of "paramountcy of the ruling party" over other institutions in Guyana.

VI. SUMMARY AND CONCLUSIONS

Historically, race relations involving Indians and Africans in Guyana primarily emerged not from their cultural or phenotypical differences, but from the dynamics of the plantation economy and society. In the post-slavery period, instead of paying higher wages to ex-slaves, the dominant planter class preferred to import and employ Indian indentured labour on the sugar plantations. Subsidised by the colonial state, indentured labour was much cheaper than ex-slave labour. The planters continued to import indentured labour resulting in a surplus labour force in the colony. As a result of this move, employment opportunities for Africans were severely restricted and wages depressed. Consequently, by the 1880s the Africans had begun to protest against the indenture system and continued to do so until its abolition in 1917 (Moore 1970: 132-82; Rodney 1981: 174-78). Thus, late in the nineteenth century the two racial groups had developed competing economic interests.

Relations between the Indians and Africans in Guyana were further complicated by racial stratification on the estates in which the majority of Africans worked in the factory and the Indians in the field. The wage differentials and the attendant status-consciousness not only prevented the emergence of working class consciousness and unity but at times led to strike breaking (Nath 1970: 136-37; Rodney 1981: 190-216). Additionally, the deployment of the predominantly African police force by the colonial government to suppress work stoppages or strikes by the Indians on the estates often led to racial tensions throughout the colonial period.

Further tensions between the two groups arose in off-the-estate situations when, following the availability of Crown land, Indians began to buy land and entered into competition with Africans in growing food–virtually reversing the roles of buyers and sellers. During and after the 1880s various land settlement schemes were designed to check the growing repatriation of ex-indentured labourers. This was in sharp constrast to the earlier practice of the colonial government whereby attempts were made to suppress the African peasantry by not providing it with infrastructural facilities and by not allowing it to own the cultivable land which the planters held idle (Adamson 1972: 202, Standing 1978).

In spite of this conjuncture of antipathy and racial separation between Africans and Indians since the late nineteenth century, it is remarkable that there were few serious violent inter-racial conflicts. The most intense racial conflict occurred in the early 1960s when in the midst of the decolonisation process, Anglo-American capital interests were eventually successful in creating a rift between the two racial fractions of the united working class in 1955 and, subsequently in 1964, in toppling a duly elected democratic socialist government in favour of the one which was deemed to be less hostile to capitalistic interests.

There is no doubt that the pre-independence years of the early 1960s in Guyana represent a period of bitter political rivalry between Africans and Indians which led to the politicisation of ethno-cultural differences and communal violence. However, as Rodney (1981: 189) rightly pointed out, the specificity of the early 1960s can scarcely be used "as a springboard for historical enquiry" as many pluralists have argued (e.g. Despres 1967; Glasgow 1970).

We have argued that the nature of race relations involving Indians in the post-colonial period is derived from the conjuncture of class, race and politics during the late colonial period. The Peoples National Congress-dominated government that was put in power by the imperial government through the imposition of the electoral system of proportional representation initially represented the interests of the absentee British bourgeoisie; and following nationalisation of sugar and bauxite industries, of the emergent state petty bourgeoisie. The main opposition party was supported by the Indian peasantry and Indian sugar workers, and a fraction of Indian middle classes. This class and political polarisation has further been reinforced by the emergent state capitalism and its crisis. Consequently, the majority of Indians, who constitute over half of the total population, have been effectively denied any participation in the government. This has been accomplished by the government through increasing state repression and electoral malpractices (Green 1974: 29-30).

Within the above configuration of class, race and politics, Indian peasantry and sugar workers find themselves in a distinctly disadvantaged position. Under the Burnham regime, agriculture has not only received lowest priority, the farmers are also not getting a fair price for their main produce (rice) as it is bought by a state marketing board which also fixes the price. The Indians in rural areas are facing unemployment in the wake of a growing population and increasing mechanisation of agriculture. Similar problems are faced by the Indian sugar workers on the plantations. Additionally, until 1976 they had little bargaining power as the trade union of their choice was not recognised by the government. This racial antagonism directed against Indians in Guyana has been economically and politically advantageous to the African-dominated ruling class.

NOTES

1. During the British period Guyana was known as British Guiana. However, except in the quotations throughout this study we shall refer to Guyana, the name of the independent nation.
2. Although it is customary to refer to Indians as East Indians in the Western hemisphere including the Caribbean, for the sake of uniformity we have retained the term Indian in the Guyanese context. Exception is made regarding the quotations.
3. Guyana has a territory of about 83,500 square miles, and is approximately the size of Britain. With a population of about 900,000 in 1981, it is both underpopulated and overpopulated. It is underpopulated in the sense that Guyana has a very low density of population (about 11 per square mile), and overpopulated in the sense that more than 90 per cent of the population lives on five per cent of the land–a 10 to 20 miles wide strip that runs along the 270 miles of coast line.
4. There were about 100,000 slaves in British Guiana in the early 1830s. The actual number for which compensation was claimed was 82,824.
5. Planters exercised a great influence at that time. "They dominated the colony and wielded a power strong enough to coerce the Government in any matter affecting their interest. . . . (In 1835, 1840 and 1848-50) they threatened to bring the machinery of government to a standstill by refusing to vote supplies" (Nath 1970: 48-9). "Des Voeux, the stipendiary magistrate who tried to protect indentured workers against abuses of the labor laws, found his life made unbearable by the combined hostility of planter and administration. Chief Justice Beaumont was suspended and ultimately removed from office after a judicial committee of the Privy Council found that he had been 'indiscreet' and wanting in 'judicial temper'" (Adamson 1972: 264). Plantocracy in Guyana lasted until the 1891 constitutional reform which, according to the Report of the Constitutional Commission, 1950-51, broke its power.
6. In 1890 the statutory price per acre of Crown land was reduced from ten dollars to one dollar, which was further reduced to fifteen cents in 1898. In the same year the stipulated minimum size of a lot for purchase was reduced from 100 acres to 24 acres (Mandle 1973: 37).
7. The so-called "dual control" was another feature of the colonical education system which prevented the growth of education among Indians in Guyana. Under this system, while the schools were owned and managed by Christian Churches, the financial burden of running the schools was borne by the government. Informed by utilitarianism this policy of combining education with evangelisation was earlier implemented with a view to transforming a rebellious slave population into a peaceful and obedient working class (Smith 1962: 145).
8. In Guyana most of the land is either savannas or equitorial rain forest; only four per cent of the coastal land which contains a narrow strip of rich alluvium is suitable for agriculture. The coastal lands comprise a low-lying area of five to eight feet below sea level at high tide. A dual need stems from this

ecological condition: that of preventing flooding by sea water and that of draining off the water that flows from the hinterland and accumulates in the coastal belt. The solution to this problem necessitates an elaborate system of drainage ditches, dams and sea walls, which the impoverished African peasantry in the nineteenth century found extremely difficult to build and operate on their own.

9. One early exception to this situation was the election in 1916 of an Indian lawyer, J.A. Lackhoo, who was elected to the Combined Court defeating a white candidate. Obviously, Lackhoo was supported by predominantly African voters and their organisation called the Peoples Association (Ramnarine 1977: 252).

10. Mr. James Crosby was the Immigration Agent-General in Guyana between 1858 and 1880. Crosby had so endeared himself to the immigrants that whenever they had a grievance they went to the Immigrant Department with full confidence that a speedy redress would be obtained by him on their behalf (Nath 1970: 48).

11. The West Indian Royal Commission (Moyne Commission) Report which was completed in 1939 was so critical of the colonial government and administration that only its recommendations were made available at the time, the detailed survey of conditions not being made public until 1945.

12. The Prime Minister of Guyana during 1964-80 and the President during 1981-85, Mr. Linden Forbes Sampson Burnham was born in 1923 and educated in England as a barrister. He was the leader of the Peoples National Congress since its inception in 1957. He was president of the Guyana Labour Union from 1952 to 1956 and from 1963 to 1965. He was leader of the Opposition in the 1957-61 and 1961-64 legislatures.

13. Dr. Jagan, who subsequently became the Prime Minister of Guyana, was the son of an Indian estate 'driver'. He was born at Port Mourant on 20 March, 1918. After his secondary education in Georgetown, he went to the U.S. where he studied for seven years in Washington and Chicago to become a dentist. It was during this period that he was influenced by Marxism. He married an American Jewish woman, Janet Rosenberg, who was a trained nurse and shared Jagan's interest in Marxism. After his return to Guyana in 1943, he became treasurer of the M.P.C.A. In 1946 he formed a quasi-political party named the Political Affairs Committee, which became a stepping-stone for his political career (see Jagan 1954, 1972).

14. The anti-P.P.P. and pro-imperial interests in the 1953 election were organised in the form of the National Democratic Party (NDP) which was closely associated with the League of Coloured People (L.C.P). "The N.D.P.-L.C.P. nucleus of the middle class African and creole elements of the society received the backing of the commercial community and the established churches, mainly Roman Catholic and Anglican" (Green 1974: 36). Among the N.D.P.'s Indian leaders were Sheik Mohammed Shakoor, a wealthy businessman and the then general secretary of the powerful sugar workers' trade union, the Manpower Citizens Association (MPCA), and Lionel Lackhoo, a barrister who was later to become Guyana's High Commissioner to London and the Acting Chief Justice of the Supreme Court of Guyana.

15. There were a number of other reasons behind this split. Besides the personality differences between Dr. Jagan and Burnham, it has been suggested that the two leaders were also "under foreign and local pressures to pursue different policies after the breakdown of the 1953 government" (Glasgow 1970: 107). One major issue around which these opposing policies crystallised was whether Guyana should join the West Indian Federation. Jagan was opposed to the idea of joining the federation. It has been claimed that this stance of Jagan was influenced by Trinidad Indian leaders as well as two successive Indian High Commissioners whom Pandit Nehru allegedly directed to give Jagan needed advice and help. It should be pointed out here that Jagan, consistent with his anti-imperialist beliefs, repeatedly declared that the issue should be decided by the Guyanese people only after being granted dominion status. In the case of Burnham, who was initially reluctant to denounce communism and was also not in favour of the federation, pressure was applied by the West Indian leaders, as well as Pan-Africanist African leaders, particularly Nkrumah. In 1957, on the occasion of the first independence celebrations of Ghana, Burnham along with Jamaica's Norman Manley, Barbados' Grantley Adams and West Indian British Labour Party official Dr. B. Pitt conferred with Nkrumah. This was arranged by the Trinidad-born writer, the late George Padmore, and Jagan was excluded from it. "At the conference, Jagan's activities were all condemned. There was a suspicion that if he did not turn British Guiana into a Russian satellite, he would turn in into an Indian state. . . . The assembled leaders told Burnham that they were prepared to help British Guiana regain her constitution, provided that he came out on an anti-communist platform before it was too late" (Glasgow 1970: 110). Burnham well heeded the advice and denounced Jagan as "a communist inspired stooge".

16. I am grateful to Dr. Robert J. Moore of the Canadian International Development Agency for clarifying, in personal communication, this and many other aspects of Guyanese politics.

17. During the period under discussion, four major daily newspapers were published in Guyana. These included the *Daily Argosy*, the *Daily Chronicle*, the *Guiana Grapic*, and the *Evening Post*. All four were predominantly owned and controlled by a combination of big business and sugar interests. "Needless to say, editorial policies have been mostly conservative with respect to economic and political issues. Reflecting both the general and specific interests of their owners, these papers have emphasized the economic, social and cultural values attached to British colonial ties. . . . At one time or another, all of these papers have been critical of most of Guiana's nationalist parties and their leaders" (Despres 1967: 132-33). Similarly, in the late colonial period, the radio broadcasting services were also owned and operated by the same business interests that owned and controlled the major newspapers.

18. In contrast to the allegations of the opposition parties about the budget, the Commonwealth Commission of Enquiry into the Disturbances in February 1962 had found the budget economically sound and courageous in the sense that it was geared towards self-help. The Commission had strongly criticised

the attitude and behaviour of the opposition leaders, trade unionists and the Chamber of Commerce officials. It described the attitude of the P.N.C. leadership as "callous and remorseless" and drew attention to the strangely unfeeling attitude of the political leaders when passions aroused by them had been let loose on the town" (quoted in Jagan 1972: 218). Regarding the role of the trade union leaders the Commission noted: "There is very little doubt that despite the loud protestations of the trade union leaders to the contrary, political affinities and aspirations played a large part in shaping their policy and formulating their programme of offering resistance to the budget and making a determined effort to change the government in office" (quoted in Jagan 1972: 211).

19. President Kennedy's advisor Prof. Arthur M. Schlesinger, Jr. (1965: 774-79) had described how Jagan and Burnham visited Washington one after the other in 1961 and 1962 respectively and made different impressions on the President. According to him, while Jagan seemed to be "endowed . . . with unconquerable romanticism or naivete", whose "party lived by the cliches of an impassioned, quasi-Marxist, anti-colonialist socialism, Burnham's visit left the feeling, as I reported to the President, that 'an independent British Guiana under Burnham (if Burnham will commit himself to a multi-racial policy) would cause us many fewer problems than an independent British Guiana under Jagan'. And the way was open to bring this about, because Jagan's parliamentary strength was larger than his popular strength: he had won 57 per cent of the seats on the basis of 42.7 per cent of the vote. An obvious solution would be to establish a system of proportional representation. This, after prolonged discussion, the British Government finally did in October 1963; and elections held finally at the end of 1964 produced a coalition government under Burnham. With much unhappiness and turbulence British Guyana seemed to have passed safely out of the communist orbit."

20. Under the proportional representation system the votes are cast in favour of lists of candidates, each list representing a political party. Depending on the number of votes cast for each list, 53 Assembly seats are allocated to each party in proportionate manner.

21. For instance, political patronage to the ruling party members and other Africans was extended through the organisation called the African Society for Cultural Relations with Independent Africa (ASCRIA), which was formed in the late 1960s to promote ethnic consciousness among Africans.

22. In this strike, the leaders of ASCRIA along with the newly formed multi-racial leftist political party, the Working Peoples' Alliance, played a militant role (Norton 1984: 431; Spinner 1982).

23. In the 1968 elections the P.N.C. government introduced a bill enabling overseas Guyanese to vote. In this election about 66,000 overseas voters were registered. "Independent television program 'World in Action' alleged that (Guyanese diplomats) fabricated most of these names: only 4,700 of the 11,750 voters registered in America were found to be genuine, and of the 44,000 registered in Britain less than a quarter could actually be located. The survey was conducted by Opinion Research Centre, a skilled, professional body" (Tinker 1977: 83, fn 1).

24. In Guyana proxy voting allows one person to be appointed to vote for up to five electors. In 1968 elections as many as 7 per cent of the total votes were cast by proxies. As early as 1964 a team of Commonwealth observers reported that the proxy system was liable to abuse (see, Green 1974: 29-30).
25. During the summer of 1979 several government buildings were fire-bombed and mass demonstrations occurred on an almost daily basis against the Burnham regime. In October 1979 a government Minister of Education was fatally shot. In June 1980 Dr. Walter Rodney, the leader of the neophyte opposition group called the Working People's Alliance (WPA) was killed in a mysterious car explosion which many people think was an assassination orchestrated by the PNC. See, for example, Spinner (1980).
26. The U.S. State Department's report on human rights in Guyana in 1980 pointed out the "significant curtailment" of civic and political liberties in Guyana and referred *inter alia* to: (i) evidence that the government was implicated in the death of Dr. Walter Rodney; (ii) the use of 'repressive measures' in response to discontent caused by worsening economic conditions; (iii) 'excessive use of force by police officers' (19 people having been killed by armed police in the year to February 1981, with no inquests on the victims); (iv) a lack of guarantees of judicial independence and integrity in cases 'perceived to be political in nature'; (v) the breaking up of demonstrations by police and 'unidentified *thugs*', many of whom were presumed to be connected with the House of Israel, sect, 'which has apparently received official protection and has strong connections to the PNC' and (vi) 'official meddling' in the internal affairs of trade unions (the validity of the election of a pro-government candidate as president of the Trades Union Congress in September 1980 having been challenged by several member unions). (*Keesing's Contemporary Archives*, 1981: 31064).

4

Malaysia: Kangani Labour and Race Relations

Ever since the publication of Furnivall's work on the neighbouring countries of Burma and Indonesia, pluralism has been the dominant paradigm in the study of ethnic and race relations in Malaysia (Arasaratnam 1970; Freedman 1960; Lent 1977; Mahajani 1960; Mohammed 1970; Nagata 1975; Ratnam 1965; Silcock 1965; Tinker 1977; Wiebe and Mariappen 1978). As we observed in Chapter 2, it is typical of this paradigm that racial, cultural, religious or linguistic diversities have been given prominence. Economic disparities are sometimes considered, but seldom systematically or as a central variable. It is our contention that even though the plural society approach might seem most appropriate in accounting for race relations in Malaysia, a focus on economic variables and class is required to explain these relations.

In regard to the Indians in Malaysia, two major forms of race relations can be identified. The first emerges from the exploitation of labour on the rubber estates and the second in relation to the Malays. It is argued that the latter form of race relations was shaped by two interrelated aspects of class relations. The first of these involved the class conflict between the Indian money-lenders and the Malay peasantry and the second was based on the intra-class conflict between the Indian and Malay middle class segments. The competing Indian and Malay communal nationalisms tended to confound and exacerbate these two forms of class and race relations. The type of race relations experienced by Indians cannot be analysed fully without due consideration to that of Chinese, who along with the Indians are known in Malaysia as "non-Malays"

I. COLONIAL ECONOMY AND INDIAN IMMIGRATION IN MALAYSIA

Indians' contact with the Malay Peninsula, which was largely confined to trade and cultural exchange, dates back at least to the second century B.C. Indian influence in the area continued until the fall of the Malacca Sultanate in 1511 to the Portuguese, the first Europeans to arrive in Malaysia, followed by the Dutch and the British. Racial and cultural tolerance appears to have existed in the Malacca Sultanate (Arasaratnam 1970: 6-8). Perhaps the most important reason for this was the nature of trade, which was complementary and barter-like rather than competitive and coercive.

An even more important aspect of this pre-colonial contact was the fact that it did not lead to large-scale immigration and settlement of Indians in Malaysia. When the Straits Settlements were established between 1786 and 1824 there were few Indians, and these were mainly traders, in Penang and Malacca (Jackson 1961: 8). However, as soon as the European and Chinese began commercial agriculture in the Straits Settlement, which included production of pepper, betelnut, sugar and spices (cinnamon, nutmeg, cloves, etc.) in Penang and Province Wellesley, and gambier and coconut in Singapore (Turnbull 1972: 142-54), Indian and Chinese indentured labourers were brought to work on these plantations. The indigenous Malays engaged in fishing and subsistence farming rarely sought work as hired labourers.

There are no reliable statistics about Indian labour immigration in Malaysia for this period, but it is probable that on the average 1,800 Indian labourers arrived each year in the Straits Settlements in the 1840s, 2,360 in the 1850s and 5,117 in the 1860s (Sandhu 1969: 304, App. I). Consequently, by 1871 there were an estimated 33,385 Indians in the Straits Settlements (Table 4.1). The latter figures also included a tiny minority of Tamil Muslim Chulia traders, South Indian Chettiar money-lenders and north Indian petty traders (Arasaratnam 1970: 8; Turnbull 1972: 8).

The success of plantation agriculture and the possibility of the exploitation of economic resources, especially in the Malay States for which the Singapore-based European and Chinese entrepreneurs were clamouring for quite some time, led the British in 1874 to formally "intervene" in the Malay Peninsula (Caldwell 1977a: 14-22). By 1914 all Malay states were incorporated into the British empire. The four states of Perak, Selangor, Negri Sembilan and Pahang, collectively known as the Federated Malay States (FMS) after 1896, with Kuala Lumpur as the federal capital, were directly ruled and the remaining states (Kedah, Perlis, Kelantan, Trengganu and Johore) were under "indirect rule". The introduction of the British Residential system replaced the traditional Malay administrative system by a western-type bureaucratic system which provided the basic foundation for the development of a capitalist economy in Malaysia (Khoo 1972: 226). In spite of resistance from the Malay peasantry (Amin 1977: 64-71), the British were able to consolidate their rule with the help of traditional Malay elites and the Malayan Civil Service (Heussler 1981).

TABLE 4.1: **Indian Population of Penang, Malacca and Singapore, 1794-1871**

Penang		Malacca		Singapore	
Year	Population	Year	Population	Year	Population
1794	1,000	1817	2,986	1821	132
1812	7,113	1834	2,403	1833	2,324
1833	10,346	1860	1,026	1850	6,284
1871	18,611	1871	3,277	1871	11,501

Source: Sandhu (1965: 175).

"The basic principle underlying the British policy in the Peninsula in the latter part of the nineteenth and early twentieth centuries was:

> to protect and encourage economic enterprise and to keep out other foreign powers [especially Russia, France, and the Netherlands] whose intrusion would endanger the security of India and the sea route to the Far East passing through the Straits of Malacca.[2]

The British were generally successful regarding this policy in the region. By the end of the First World War, not only was the whole Malay Peninsula under their political control, there was also remarkable growth in production and trade. Tin production rose from 4,200 tons in 1874 to 51,335 tons in 1913. Rubber exports soared from 104 tons in 1905 to 56,782 in 1915, in value terms an increase from $529,000 to $93,660,000, or from 0.7 per cent of total export value to 57.7 per cent" (Caldwell 1977a: 32). According to Sir Frank Swettenham, then High Commissioner of the F.M.S. (1948: 348), the value of trade had increased from 3.0 million pounds in 1885 to 15.0 million pounds in 1905 to 64.0 million pounds in 1925.

British colonial policies, especially regarding land, labour and social welfare, were obviously directed toward these economic ends.

Thus the major objective of the land policy was to reserve suitable land for European planters. In 1897 special land regulations were introduced in the F.M.S. which were favourable to European planters' interests. In 1905 in Selangor, alienation of land to natives was prohibited without the previous permission of the Resident. In so doing, the Resident was "attempting to concentrate native gardeners in specified areas, and to discourage the occupation by them of land which may be usefully reserved for scientific planting" (quoted in Caldwell 1977a: 23). In addition to land, generous official loans were made available to European planters. Cheap and docile Indian labour was readily available to work on these plantations and was further organised through the Indian Immigration Committee and Fund in 1907.

Social policy, too, was geared to the needs of Western enterprise. In order of decreasing priority, government expenditure was made on (a) construction of roads, railways and docks, (b) internal security and the defence of the Straits of Malacca, and (c) public administration. The last measure involved the education and training of a small group of Malay elites drawn from the traditional ruling families. In this connection the following statement of the Inspector of Malay Schools of the F.M.S. from 1903 to 1906 is worth mentioning, clearly showing that the British were fully aware of the implications of their English education policy:

> We are, at best, creating an Asiatic governing class rather than Asiatic races capable of self-government (quoted in Roff 1967: 28, fn. 82).

Thus, by the first decade of the present century the political and administrative foundation was laid for further exploitation of the Malay peninsula. By then Malaysia had emerged as the foremost producer and exporter of tin and rubber. It was in connection with these primary commodities of the colonial economy that Chinese and Indian labour immigration took place on a massive scale in Malaysia. These immigration patterns are briefly described below:

Tin Mining and Chinese Immigration

From the middle of the nineteenth century, substantial expansion of tin mining in Malaysia was made possible by Chinese enterprise. The

Chinese merchants, who were often interested in tin as a trading commodity, supplied not only capital but also the Chinese immigrant labour to work in the mines. In order to increase their income from rents, royalties and river-tolls, Malay chiefs themselves encouraged the Chinese enterprises. Sometimes they "went into active partnership with the Chinese *towkay* (businessman); sometimes Chinese miners worked in small groups subject to the Malay chief" (Kennedy 1970: 192). The Chinese remained dominant in the industry until the late 1920s when their dominance was broken by Europeans, who had begun to obtain mining concessions in the Malay States in the 1880s and 1890s.[3] In 1929, European-owned mines produced 61 per cent of the total tin produced in Malaysia, and the Chinese-owned only 39 per cent. However, the labour-force in the mining sector remained predominantly Chinese and continues to be so.

As a result of massive Chinese immigration encouraged by the British *laissez faire* policy regarding labour and capital, the Chinese population in Malaysia grew substantially during the last quarter of the nineteenth century and the first quarter of the twentieth century. In 1860 there were over 96,000 Chinese in the Straits Settlements (Purcell 1948: X-XI). Their population increased to 693,000 in 1911 and 1,285,000 in 1931 constituting about one-third of the total Malaysian population (Table 4.2). By 1931 the Chinese had also diversified themselves considerably with a large majority of them employed in urban petty bourgeois occupations rather than in mining and agriculture.

Rubber Plantations and Indian Immigration

If the expansion of tin mining in Malaysia encouraged Chinese immigration, the growth of rubber[4] plantations accelerated the volume of Indian labour immigration around the turn of the present century. As mentioned earier, indentured Indian labourers had already been immigrating to Malaysia to work on sugar and spice plantations at least since 1840s. But the system of indentured "recruitment through agents and sub-agents in Southern India was costly", and the labourers were "an unselected lot, poor in physique and unable to do outdoor work", with no experience in agriculture (Jain 1970: 198-99). Therefore, coffee and rubber planters were in favour of *kangani*–recruited "free" immigrants who were found satisfactory by the planters in Ceylon. Thus as early as 1890s, when the indentured system was still in effect, the *kangani* system was started for the planters of the F.M.S.

TABLE 4.2: **Ethnic Composition of West Malaysia, 1911-1980**

	Population in Thousands					
	1911	1921	1931	1957	1970	1980
Malays	1370	1559	1864	3126	468	6050
Chinese	693	856	1285	2334	3122	3876
Indians	239	439	571	707	932	1158
Others	37	43	68	112	70	83
Total	2339	2907	3788	6279	8810	11167

	Percentage Distribution					
	1911	1921	1931	1957	1970	1980
Malays	58.6	54.0	49.2	49.8	53.2	54.2
Chinese	29.6	29.4	33.9	37.2	35.4	34.7
Indians	10.2	15.1	15.1	11.3	10.6	10.4
Others	1.6	1.5	1.8	1.8	0.8	0.7
Total	100.0	100.0	100.0	100.0	100.0	100.0

Source: Wiebe & Matriappen (1978: 8), *Europa Year Book* 1985: 2111.

The *kangani* labour system proved immensely profitable to the planters, and the demand for such labour was tremendous in Malaysia. It was in response to this demand that Indian labourers immigrated at the rate of 20,000 per annum between 1890 and 1904. Following the boom in the rubber industry after 1905, this volume increased to an average of 90,000 labourers per annum between 1911 and 1930 (Courtenay 1972: 102; Sandhu 1969: 158). The immigrants were largely Hindus (over 80%) dominated by the Tamils from South India. Besides *kangani* labour, other forms of labour immigration also took place in Malaysia. According to Sandhu (1969: 97), the proportion of each labour immigration type between 1844 and 1941 was as follows: indentured 9.1 per cent, *kangani* 43.7 per cent, assisted voluntary 10.7 per cent, non-assisted voluntary 29.9 per cent, others 6.6 per cent.

Non-Labouring Indian Immigrants

In addition to the labourers, who constituted about 72.5 per cent of Indian immigrants until 1941 (Table 4.3), there were groups of immigrants who were often recruited for the specific needs of the colonial economy. These included Chettiar (Tamil Hindu) bankers, money-lenders, and owners of real estate, land and housing property; Marakkayar (Tamil Muslim) shopkeepers; Gujarati merchants; Punjabi policemen and watchmen; Ceylonese Tamil, Tamil and Malayalee administrators and clerks, teachers, doctors and lawyers. These various groups, which constituted the Indian petty bourgeoisie in Malaysia, were an extremely heterogeneous community fragmented along linguistic, regional, caste, religious and occupational lines (Sandhu 1969: 225). Until at least the mid-1930s they were not only divided among themselves, they also remained aloof from the more numerous Indian labouring class. Additionally, their subordination to the European employers and their impermanence in Malaysia inhibited the growth of leadership among Indians.

TABLE 4.3: **Composition of Total Indian Immigration into Malaya, 1786-1957**

Period	Total number of arrivals	Percentage			
		Labourers	Non-Labourers	Total	
				South Indians	North Indians
up to 1941	3823812	72.5	27.5	92.3	7.7
up to 1957	4245990	65.3	34.7	91.3	8.7

Source: Sandhu (1969: 159).

II. CLASS AND RACE RELATIONS IN THE COLONIAL PERIOD IN MALAYSIA

The compartmentalised colonial economy, consisting of plantation, mining and peasant agriculture, had been decisive in the formation of the class and racial structure in Malaysia. As a result of the colonial land and labour policies, occupational specialisation largely followed racial lines. The plantation sector was owned by the Europeans and the labour was predominantly Indian. Until the late 1920s the mining sector was owned by the Chinese and thereafter by the Europeans. The Chinese labourers worked on the mines. Malay capital or labour was conspicuously absent from these two sectors of the colonial economy. Instead peasant agriculture was the stronghold of the Malays (Table 4.4). Through legislation, the government had prevented the alienation of land to non-Malays, especially to the Indian money-lenders.

TABLE 4.4: **Ethnic Composition of Labour Forces in the Federated Malay States in 1931 in the Estate, Mining and Paddy Sectors**

	Estates		Mines		Paddy	
	No.	%	No.	%	No.	%
Malays	4,821	3	813	1	89,122	97
Chinese	32,916	23	70,704	92	1,038	1
Indians	104,767	74	4,168	7	1,892	2
Total	142,504	100	76,685	100	92,052	100

Source: Lim Mah Hui (1980: 137).

In addition to their relations with Europeans, two other types of class relations were significant for the type of race relations experienced by Indians. They were those existing (a) between the Indian business and commercial groups and the Malay peasantry, and (b) between the Indian middle classes and their Malay counterparts. These three forms of class and race relations during the colonial period in Malaysia are discussed below.

Class and Race Relations Between Europeans and Indians

The exploitation of Indian labourers was made possible by the fact that after the First World War the labour supply normally exceeded demand. For the reasons mentioned earlier, South India became a source of unlimited labour supply to the Malaysian plantation industry. Not only was such labour supply abundant, much of it was also of a migratory nature, the average stay of South Indian labourers in Malaysia being about three to four years. Thus, carefully manipulated immigration meant that there was always a pool of unemployed labour (Caldwell 1977b: 59). Whenever supply exceeded demand, thousands of Indians were shipped back to India. During the depression of

1930-33, nearly 250,000 Indian labourers were deported (Sandhu 1969: 106). The migrant status of Indian labourers also meant that there was no provision for old age pensions and/or other benefits for the retired workers: repatriation awaited them as soon as they were past productive work. A common metaphor in this connection was that of "sucked oranges".[5] Thus, South Indian villages largely shared the social cost of reproduction of the Malaysian estate labour force not only in caring for these repatriated elderly Indians but also in rearing and supporting future migrants in their childhood and youth.

Colonial Malaysia was a low wage economy. At least until the Second World War, the wages of Indian labourers were close to a subsistence level. The Indian Immigration Committee which since its inception in 1907 effectively controlled labour immigration to the planters' advantage, was also responsible for recommending wages. The Committee went to great lengths in calculating the monthly cost of individual subsistence and then setting the wage rates (Parmer 1960: 278). In doing so the labourers were left with a very small margin of savings, which either could be used to pay for the workers' return passage or else remitted to India, or as was more likely the case, spent on the purchase of "toddy", an alcoholic drink to which many of the labourers became addicted (Stenson 1980: 21). According to one historian, small savings, and remittances which Indian labourers made were often done "at the cost of a parsimonious and stingy existence at bare subsistence level, injurious in the long-term to the labourers general health" (Arasaratnam 1970: 63). In this connection, the following observation made by a planter in 1911 gives a good idea of the conditions of Indian labourers in Malaysia:

> The Tamil struck me as being a poor specimen, both in physique and morale, and of being abject, cowardly and generally lacking in vitality. . . . The Tamils, one and all, had a half-starved look about them, and seemed to be thoroughly dissatisfied with their lot in life. . . . The blind admiration for the white man by these Tamils is really rather pathetic (quoted in Stenson 1980: 17).

There was also widespread indebtedness to the *kanganies* among the Indian labourers in Malaysia. An inquiry conducted in 1934 by the Malacca Planters' Association had revealed that

> in only one district the indebtedness was as high as $60,000

> through pawn-shops alone. . . . This figure was so staggering that the other planters' associations gave up their inquiry (Kondapi 1951: 78).

In addition to subsistence wages and indebtedness, the following demands which were made in 1941 and which occasioned a bloody strike in the Klang district of Selangor State in the same year further highlight the class and race relations situation of the Indian plantation labourers in Malaysia:

1. Parity of pay for Indian and Chinese labourers.
2. The removal of estate staff who were brutal and their replacement with Tamil-speaking staff.
3. The provision of 'proper' education for children.
4. An end to the molesting of labourers' womenfolk by Europeans and 'black' Europeans.
5. The provision of proper medical facilities.
6 The closing of toddy shops.
7. The granting of freedom of speech and assembly.
8. Free access to estates for relations and friends.
9. Permission for labourers to mount bicycles in front of European managers and Asian staff.
10. The abolition of working days of 10 to 12 hours.
11. No victimization of those presenting grievances.
12. Permission for the labourers to have an association to look after their interests and put forward their grievances.[6]

While most of these demands are self-explanatory, some need elaboration. The story behind the demand for "the closing of toddy shops on the estate" was that initially the government and the planters themselves had encouraged the habit of toddy drinking among the workers by allowing toddy shops to be opened on the estates. For the government it was an easy source of revenue and for the planters a means to attract labour.[7] However, when the Planters' Association of Malaya realised the injurious effects of toddy to the health of the labourers and pressed for the government action in the matter, the government tried to whitewash the problem by declaring that pure unadulterated toddy was not injurious to health (Arasaratnam 1970: 71). Throughout the colonial period, the government never opted for total prohibition. On the contrary, the number of toddy shops on the estates had increased from 107 in 1951 to 286 in 1955 (Mahajani 1960: 212).

The foregoing list of demands, reflects a regimented life on the estates organised along military/industrial lines and its abuses by the estate bureaucracy. The estate labourers lived in employer-provided 'lines', which were often situated in isolated areas. Until the 1930s when buses and bicycles began to open up communication, estate workers generally had no contact with the outside world. The trespass laws, which were designed to insulate workers from communist and socialist ideological influences, made it difficult for workers' friends and relatives to even visit the estates. The rigid, hierarchical social structure of the plantation was headed by the European *Periya Durai* (lord or master). "Below the *Periya Durai* and *Sinna Durai* (assistant manager) were the Asian supervisory and clerical staff, usually Ceylon Tamils or Malayalees; heading the Tamil labourers were the *kanganies*, who were the main recruiting agents until the 1930s and who acted as field foremen" (Stenson 1980: 25).

In the actual functioning of this social structure, the *kanganies* "were for long the recognised leaders of Indian labour, and also its recognised exploiters" (Arasaratnam 1970: 79). As recruiters in India and foremen on the estates, *kanganies* had an effective hold on labourers. Many *kanganies* were shopkeepers on the estates and a majority of labourers were indebted to them. Labourers' indebtedness also obtained from the fact that "the passage and other expenses incurred in bringing the labourer were treated as a loan which he had to settle within two years" (Arasaratnam 1970: 17). Thus, as V.S. Srinivas Sastri pointed out in 1937, the labourer had a concealed obligation to the *kangani*, which acted to his disadvantage.[8]

Aspects of regimented plantation life are further reflected in the above-mentioned demands number 2, 4, and 9. Asian staff members (*kiranis*) on many estates were South Indian Malayalees and/or Ceylon Tamils, and tended to be insensitive towards Tamil labourers. The labourers often resented "being bossed by these Indian officers" (Arasaratnam 1970: 79). In order to exercise their full authority over the workers the *kiranis* had devised and insisted on an elaborate code of conduct for the workers. The *kiranis*, for example, would insist "that a labourer must get down from his bicycle when passing a staff bungalow or that a Tamil coolie must not put on shoes or must groom his hair only in the traditional style, with a tuft" (Jain 1970: 390). The *kiranis* as well the European managers and assistants also had sexual liaisons with labourers' womenfolk, which the estate authorities tended to view as part of a welfare paternalism strategy on the part of the officials involved.[9]

Besides maintaining a surplus supply of the labour-force through carefully manipulating the immigration process, two major strategies which planters in Malaysia adopted in order to fully exploit the labourers were: (a) denying educational facilities on the estates, and (b) the legal repression of workers. These are briefly discussed below.

Lack of Educational Facilities

Until the 1923 Labour Code, which stipulated the provision of a school on every estate containing ten or more children of school-going age, the planters opposed any move for educational facilities on the estates. They were against the schools on the estates mainly on the ground of cost. Perhaps the planters' attitude is best reflected in the following remark which one of their representatives made during the debate on the subject in the Federal Council in 1923:

> So long as they let the Controller of Labour pass my smoke factory with the word "school" written up in large letters I shall be quite happy (Proceedings of the Federal Council, 1923, B 107-8, cited in Arasaratnam 1970: 179).

The same attitude of indifference and neglect was very much in evidence in the actual operation of these schools. "The school was often a dilapidated shed, set apart to concur nominally with the provisions of the Code" (Arasaratnam 1970: 179). Until after the Second World War, very few of them had qualified teachers; *kanganies*, clerks and even literate labourers would function as teachers. Most of the schools were one-teacher, multi-class schools (Sandhu 1969: 260). Attendance was seldom compulsory. Moreover, in the 1920s estates provided employment for children above the age of ten. "This incentive, coupled with the general ignorance and illiteracy of the parents and the need for the children to work in order to supplement the family income, meant that most children left school after a few years" (Sandhu 1969: 260). Consequently, the drop-out rate was excessively high. In any case, with the medium of instruction in these primary schools being Tamil, Telugu or Malayalam, this education was neither useful for further schooling, nor for job opportunities, as in either case the knowledge of English was necessary. Thus for lack of education, the generational mobility of domiciled Indian estate labourers was effectively blocked in the colonial period.

Legal Repression

The repression of workers occurred at both the individual and collective level. Until the enactment of the 1923 Labour Code, purely industrial offences were treated as criminal offences" (Arasaratnam 1970: 55). At the collective level, the colonial policies regarding land and labour made it difficult for a non-communal labour movement to grow.

> The hostility of employers, the continuation of the contract system of employment, the geographical and social isolation of most tin mines and plantations and the general availability of labour, combined with the difficulties of class organization in a multi-racial society, militated against the development of trade unionism (Morgan 1977: 152).

Nevertheless, when trade unionism among Indian workers emerged in the late 1930s subsequently resulting in a major strike in the Klang district of Johore state in 1941, it was quickly suppressed through the declaration of a state of emergency. The labourers were forced back to work after the death of four strikers and the arrest of over three hundred. For a majority of Indians, the violent suppression of the strike was a traumatic experience. According to an Indian leader, the events of 1941 "tended to create a feeling of suppressed anger among Indians" (quoted in Stenson 1980: 70). This partly explains why a section of Indian leaders so enthusiastically welcomed Japanese occupation of Malaya. The 1941 incident taught the Indians the lesson that they could not rely solely on the strength of communalism. They had failed to seek support from the Chinese workers and the Malayan Communist Party.

The organised labour movement remained suppressed during the Japanese occupation (1942-1945).[10] Following the Japanese surrender, the colonial government promoted only non-communist trade unions. In 1947, trade unions among Indian workers were formed in a number of states in Malaysia. In 1953, these unions were merged into a newly formed Plantation Workers' Union of Malaya. In 1954, it was expanded and renamed the National Union of Plantation Workers. This union had 80,000 members, the majority of them being Indians. Its leadership was also predominantly Indian, and continued to be so even after Malaysia's independence. In 1963, of its total membership of 241,505, about 52 per cent were Indians, 28 per cent Malays and 19 per cent Chinese (Arasaratnam 1970: 143). The relatively low participation of Chinese labourers can be explained by the fact that they were organised through a separate union called the Pan Malayan Rubber Workers' Union, which was formed in the mid-1950s. The Chinese rubber workers also drew higher wages than their Indian or Malay counterparts.

During the national emergency of 1948-1960 which was declared in the wake of the communist insurrection, the National Union of Plantation Workers operated under state surveillance and therefore generally tended to be "accommodative" of the colonial interests (Jain 1970: 353, 373; Morgan 1977). Thus, it is contended that legal repression, coupled with lack of educational facilities, were the major determinants of class and race relations of Indian workers in colonial Malaysia.

One would expect that because of its free legal status *kangani* labour in Malaysia was less exploited than its indentured counterpart in Guyana. However, this does not appear to be the case. There were at least three important reasons responsible for this situation:

(i) The proximity of Malaysia to India and the private organisation of *kangani* labour tended to create a situation of surplus labour in Malaysia that was severe compared to the one in Guyana. The bargaining position of *kangani* labour was therefore weaker in Malaysia.

(ii) Unlike in Guyana, in Malaysia there was no provision for land settlement schemes. This not only prevented Indian labourers from engaging in peasant production and thus escaping the consequences of plantation life, but also forced a large number of them in their old age to migrate back to India. Lack of English schooling on the estates also tended to block the intergenerational mobility of those who stayed in Malaysia.

(iii) The repression of trade unionism in Malaysia was more thorough than in Guyana. In Guyana the emergency period was relatively short and the emergency measures initiated by the colonial

> authority were directed against the Jagan government. In Malaysia, on the other hand, the emergency lasted for 12 years and was imposed due to threat from the outlawed Malayan Communist Party which had considerable support among Indian as well as Chinese workers. During the emergency Malaysia was virtually turned into a police state. In 1948, "no fewer than 185 leading trade unionists had been imprisoned" (Morgan 1977: 190). A year later, more than 10,000 people, both Chinese and Indians, were deported under the Banishment Act (Morgan 1977: 190). Such a widespread suppression of the labour movement led to a massive reduction in the number of man-days lost due to strikes: from 370,464 in 1948 to 5,390 in 1949 (Morgan 1977: 198, fn 176). The inevitability and severity of this suppression becomes clearer in the light of the fact that in the post-war years Malaysia was the most important 'dollar-earner arsenal' in the British empire (Hua 1983: 91).

Thus, the *kangani* labour in Malaysia, in spite of its free legal status, was more exploited than indentured labour in Guyana.

Class and Race Relations Between Indians and the Malays

Patterns of race relations between Indians and Malays were shaped by two interrelated aspects of class relations. The first of these involved antagonistic class relations between the Indian money-lenders and the Malay peasantry and the second involved the intraclass competition between the Indian and Malay fractions of the middle class. The two aspects tended to overlap giving the impression of communal rather than class relations between the two communities.

Class Relations Between the Indian Money-lenders and the Malay Peasantry

Because of the compartmentalised nature of the colonial economy, class and race relations between the Malays and Indians did not develop in the sphere of production; however, they did develop in the sphere of exchange. A section of the Chinese as well as Indian petty bourgeoisie had been involved in trade and commerce in Malaysia since pre-colonial times. As colonial economic development began to effect the Malay agricultural sector, the Malay peasantry inevitably came into contact with non-Malay traders or money-lenders either as producers or consumers. Such "middlemen"-peasant exchange relations are always exploitative, though they are tolerated and rationalised in various ways by the exploited party. As early as the late 1920s in the wake of Malay nationalism, Malays had begun to resent non-Malay, especially Chinese dominance in retail and wholesale trade and the Chettiar Indians' role as money-lenders and rural creditors.

The Chettiars who were primarily money-lenders and bankers "provided credit to a variety of groups–European entrepreneurs, Chinese speculators, Indian hawkers and peddlers, and Malay royalty and peasants" (Arasaratnam 1970: 92). Although the government generally supported their commercial activities, their practice of money-lending to Malay peasants in return for the mortgage of land and housing property became increasingly questionable as more and more Malay land was passing into the hands of Chettiars. Before we analyse the extent of exploitation and its effect on relations between the Malays and Indians, it will be useful to briefly discuss the conditions of the Malay peasantry in the colonial economy.

Malay Peasantry in the Colonial Economy: At the time of British intervention, Malays were largely confined to subsistence agriculture. Organised into *kampongs* (villages of varying sizes), they lived on the banks of rivers and cultivated dry or wet paddy depending on the suitability of land. "Land had no value in the Malay States of 1874 and it was the custom for anyone to settle where he pleased on unoccupied and unclaimed land" (Swettenham 1948: 136). The Malay peasants therefore were not particularly inclined to take to wage labour. Even after 15 years of British intervention, the Perak Annual Report for 1889 noted that a Malay "absolutely refused to hire himself out as a labourer on any term that a planter could accept" (quoted in Jackson 1961: 94). Obviously, the limited wants of the Malays as well as the harsh working conditions in the plantations and the mines discouraged them from moving into these sectors of the colonial economy. Consequently, the Malays remained confined to the subsistence sector of the colonial economy, cultivating paddy, coconut, fruits and vegetables and, later on, rubber. In 1931, of the total working Malays numbering 241,754 in the F.M.S., 204,644 or 84.6 per cent were engaged in "agricultural pursuits", the majority directly or indirectly associated with wet-rice cultivation (Roff 1967: 121). Of the remainder, a large proportion was involved in rubber planting on small-holdings. Although rubber cultivation was most profitable to the

Malay peasants, statutory restrictions, existing more or less uninterrupted since 1922, had inhibited the growth of small and medium rubber holders. Therefore, paddy cultivation had a virtual monopoly of the Malay work-force. In 1931, of the total paddy cultivators, about 97 per cent were Malays, while the Indian and Chinese share was 2 per cent and 1 per cent respectively (Table 4.4). Since then the situation has remained more or less unchanged.

The F.M.S. government encouraged the Malays to remain on the land and cultivate the traditional staple. Malay ownership of land was achieved by passing the Malay Reservation Enactment of 1913 which limited the ability of Malay to mortgage or lease land held in reservations to non-Malays. Four years later, due to food shortage and the growing popularity of rubber among the Malay peasants, another piece of legislation know as the Rich Lands Enactment was passed laying down the condition that no state land suitable for paddy cultivation might be alienated for any other purpose. Besides this legislation, the general discouragement of English education among the Malay peasants further confined them to the village (Caldwell 1977a: 25; Roff 1967: 201).[11] Consequently, throughout the Colonial period the rate of urbanisation and proletarianisation among the Malays *vis-a-vis* non-Malays was extremely low. From a political point of view, it was in the British interest to keep the Malays as peasants rather than to proletarianise them, for the Malay peasantry was better "integrated" into colonial society than ununionised plantation labourers (Lim 1980: 137; Lee 1973). The protection of Malay land and the preservation of Malay peasant life indeed was the declared British policy in Malaya.[12]

The Malay peasantry generally did not fare well in the colonial economy. Among their many problems were the uneconomic farming units (Lim 1973: 57),[13] "indebtedness of a variety of kinds to non-Malay rice millers, rubber marketing agents, village shopkeepers, and money-lenders" (Roff 1967: 124), and general poverty. In 1957, the average rural Malay family income was only 49 per cent and 60 per cent of those of the rural Chinese and the rural Indians, respectively (Lim 1973: 55).

Agricultural indebtedness among the Malays was principally of two forms: (1) amongst the rice cultivators who were indebted to "Chinese shopkeepers, rice millers, and others for advances in cash and kind to help satisfy consumption needs during the maturation of crops" (Roff 1967: 204) and (2) amongst the rubber producers with small land holdings who were indebted to Chettiars in the form of mortgages and other liens on land. The latter form of indebtedness with which we are concerned here first surfaced in the early 1920s when rubber prices fell. At that time the government thought it "neither possible nor desirable to intervene in the private contract between parties" (Federal Council Proceedings, quoted in Roff 1967: 206). Consequently, by 1928 Indians held 176,719 acres of land of which 101,681 acres was in ownership and 75,038 acres in mortgage (Table 4.5). With the onset of the depression of 1929-33 the problem became acute and many Malay farmers were rendered landless. In the course of debates in the Federal Council it was revealed that Chettiars had loaned $125 million to small-holders in the F.M.S. on security (Arasaratnam 1970: 94). The Perak state was most affected, and therefore in 1930 the Sultan of Perak pressed the British Resident for suitable legal measures. The British themselves were concerned with the political implications of Malay poverty and indebtedness. Consequently, in 1931 The Small Holdings (Restriction of Sale) Bill was passed by the Federal Council. This was followed by the Malay Reservation Act of 1933 which was more stringent than the similar one of 1913. These acts were aimed at forbidding the transfer of land from the Malays to non-Malays and at curtailing the mortgage practice. The 1933 Act appears to have had some desirable effects, for in the F.M.S., land held by Indians under mortgage had declined from 75,038 acres in 1928 to 65,970 acres by 1938 (Table 4.5). A similar law known as the Money-lenders' Ordinance was passed in the Straits settlements in 1935. The Chettiars, protested vigorously against these legislative measures, but to no avail.[14]

Although no evidence is available of any untoward incident between the Malays and Indians resulting from the Malays peasants' indebtedness to the Chettiars, it has been pointed out that "these events brought a lot of unwelcome attention on the Chettiar community, who were held up before the public eye as extortionate and heartless exploiters of the poor" (Arasaratnam 1970: 95). Following the Second World War, however, the Chettiars' clientele had changed from rural Malays to clerks and shopkeepers. The Money-lending Licensing Act of 1951 further diverted the capital of many Chettiars into industries and real estate (Mahajani 1960: 99-100).

TABLE 4.5: **Land Owned and Held in Mortgage by Indians in the F.M.S. (in acres)**

	1919		1928		1938	
	Owned	Mortgage	Owned	Mortgage	Owned	Mortgage
Perak	18,506	23,641	48,680	30,816	69,632	28,872
Selangor	N.A.	11,872	27,081	12,523	40,100	10,271
Negri Sembilan	7,835	23,724	17,154	11,243	28,000	10,483
Pahang	N.A.	10,033	8,766	20,456	15,111	16,334
Total	26,341	69,270	101,681	75,038	152,843	65,970

Source: Arasaratnam (1970: 96).

Class and Race Relations Between the Indian and Malay Middle Class Factions

For at least two important reasons the intra-class competition between the Indian and Malay middle class fractions had greater implications than the class conflict that obtained between the Indian money-lenders and the Malay peasantry: (i) the former directly or indirectly involved almost all the Indians in Malaysia while the latter's scope was much narrower; (ii) given the urban context of the former, it was easier for the contending parties to articulate it in terms of antagonistic ideologies, i.e. communal nationalisms. The Indians in Malaysia were influenced by nationalism in India where movements for "Home Rule", and even full independence were gaining momentum in the late 1920s and the 1930s. The source and inspiration of Malay nationalism on the other hand was Indonesia. The two competing nationalist ideologies tended to intensify class competition between the Indian and Malay middle classes. A brief discussion of the development of the Indian and Malay nationalist ideologies will be followed by an analysis of class and race relations between the two communities.

Indian and Malay Communal Nationalisms: Indian non-labouring immigrants since the late nineteenth century came in trickles and were dispersed in various towns. Their ethnic differences kept them apart from each other. Therefore it took some time to get them organised. In the first and the second decades of the present century, a number of Indian associations were formed.[15] Still there was no coordination among them (Arasaratnam 1970: 83-84). In the 1930s, two sets of forces tended to unite the Indians in Malaysia: (i) the impact of Indian nationalism, and (ii) the British pro-Malay policies that were generally contradictory to non-Malay interests. One expression of this tentative unity among Indians in Malaysia was the creation of the Central Indian Association of Malaya (C.I.A.M.) in 1936. The C.I.A.M. was a federation of a number of existing Indian Associations and Chambers of Commerce. Mainly supported by English-educated Indian intelligentsia, the C.I.A.M. soon became a vehicle of Indian communal nationalism, and liberal radical politics in Malaysia. It highlighted the plight of Indian estate labourers, including the problem of *toddy* drinking. It successfully appealed to the Indian Government to ban assisted labour migration to Malaysia in 1938 with a view to preventing the imminent wage-cuts of Indian labour (Arasaratnam 1970: 99-100; Stenson 1980: 48-49). The C.I.A.M.'s secretary K.A. Neelakantha Aiyer wrote a brilliant polemic in 1937 on the situation of Indians in Malaysia entitled *Indian Problems in Malaya* which provided the common core of demands of Indians just before and after the Japanese occupation in 1942. The following were the main demands: full rights of citizenship and equal political status, establishment of minimum wage rates not affected by fluctuations in the rubber market, land settlement schemes, government schools and other amenities for estate labourers (Stenson 1980: 50). In its efforts towards realisation of these demands, the C.I.A.M. received encouragement and support from a number of Indian leaders. Prominent among them were Pandit Jawaharlal Nehru and H.N. Kunzru who visited Malaysia in 1937 and 1938 respectively. In fact, the C.I.A.M. tended to become an overseas arm of the Congress movement in India.

Obviously, the British were not happy with the activities of the C.I.A.M., especially its importation of nationalist ideas from India. Therefore, it was not recognised by the government as a mouthpiece of Indian opinion in Malaysia. Instead, the government encouraged the Dravidian movement which was embraced by a section of Tamil intelligentsia. This form of Tamil nationalism was generally concerned with the issues of social reform and was therefore parochial in scope; it showed "little appreciation of the need for unity in face of the repressive force of the colonial regime" (Stenson 1980: 79). In spite of fostering divisive tendencies in the Indian nationalist movement in Malaysia, the British could not prevent it from increasingly taking an anti-imperialist stance, especially after the Japanese occupation (Arasaratnam 1970: 107-08). The formation of the Indian National Army and the Indian Independence League in 1942 and a provisional government of *Azad Hind* (Free India) in 1943 under the leadership of Subhash Chandra Bose and the involvement of these organisations in mobilising the Indian population throughout Southeast Asia clearly shows that the Indian middle class in Malaysia was prepared not only to work for the liberation of Indian, but also that of Malaysia (Arasaratnam 1970: 105-06; Mahajani 1960: 146-49; Stenson 1980: 94-97).[16]

In contrast to Indian nationalism, Malay nationalism,[17] especially that stream of it which was to succeed and gain widespread support after the Second World War, "arose in response to Malay fears, especially among the English-educated in government employment, that specifically Malay interests were about to be lost by default to locally domiciled aliens, particularly the Chinese" (Roff 1967: 256). Malay nationalism was loyal to both the traditional Malay aristocracy and the British colonial rule. Protagonists of the movement at that time considered the British rule "as the bulwark of the time being of Malay interests against the rapacious demands of Malayan domiciled aliens" (Roff 1967: 256).

Class Conflict: The Main Issues

Centred around the question of the Malay *vs.* non-Malay rights and privileges, the communal nationalisms in Malaysia served as a catalyst in the intra-class competition between different factions of the middle class. The following were the main issues on which this form of class competition obtained:

The Political Status of the Domiciled Indians

The first major issue which divided Malays and Indians was the political status of the domiciled Indians in Malaysia. Since the late nineteenth century, a considerable number of Indians had immigrated with the intention of permanent settlement. A major reason behind this desire was better economic opportunities in Malaysia. Besides the long domiciled Indians, there were those Indians who were locally born. In the 1931 Census, about 21.4 per cent of the total Indian population in Malaysia was enumerated in the latter category. The comparable figure for the Chinese, who were in a similar situation, was 29.9 per cent. The leaders of these non-Malay communities therefore aspired and demanded citizenship rights and equality of status in the Malay states. They urged the government "that the British law of *Jus Soli* should be applied to the Malay states and that all persons born in Malaya should be considered as subjects of the (Malay) Rulers" (Mahajani 1960: 133).[18] After the Second World War, Indian demand for citizenship rights became more vocal. In 1950, the Malayan Indian Congress rejected the idea of dual nationality, and urged the Indians to "pronounce unequivocally for single nationality".[19]

The Malays, who regarded themselves the "sons of the soil",[20] were generally opposed to the continued non-Malay immigration, especially of non-labouring Indians.[21] On the question of citizenship rights of non-Malays, the British Government described non-Malays as "aliens" (in the 1931 Census). The government also maintained the myth of the sovereignty of the Malay Sultans and their right to deny non-Malays citizenship rights. The Malay reaction, however, was sharp following the Second World War when amidst the British proposal of forming a unitary Malayan Union (comprised of nine Malay states and the two Settlements of Penang and Malacca), and of granting citizenship rights to non-Malays, the Malays protested by organising themselves into the United Malay Nationalist Organisation (UMNO). Consequently, the short-lived Malayan Union was replaced by the Federation of Malaya, in which the special Malay rights were safeguarded. Non-Malay protests followed and there emerged an alliance of non-Malay moderate and leftist parties. Thus in the late 1940s, colonial politics in Malaysia was polarised along left-right ideological lines. On the left were the Malayan Communist Party (formed in 1930 and largely supported by the Chinese), the Malayan Indian Congress formed in 1946, and the Malayan Nationalist Party (a multi-racial party for the advancement of democracy and independence with the concept of greater Malaysia/Indonesia).

On the right was the United Malay Nationalist Organisation. While the former demanded immediate advancement towards democratic politics and independence, the latter were apprehensive of Chinese domination; nevertheless they were content with British colonialism and its policies of paternalism. The consequence of this political polarisation included the suppression of trade unionism in

1948 (Morgan 1977), imposition of a state of emergency during 1948-60, and prolonged guerrilla warfare by the outlawed M.C.P. (Short 1975).

Employment Opportunities in Government Services

The second issue on which the Indian and Malay middle class fractions had developed competitive interests pertained to job opportunities in the government. In spite of the government's pro-Malay policy after the early 1920s, non-Malays and especially Indians dominated in government service. The reason for Indian dominance in government was twofold: (i) the colonial education policy for the Malays–English education for the elites and vernacular education for the masses–turned out insufficient numbers of qualified Malays (Hua 1983: 62), and (ii) there was availability of many English-educated Indians due to unrestricted immigration policy. Thus, as late as 1938, 3,181 Indians and 1,169 Chinese were employed in seven key government departments of the F.M.S. as compared to only 1,742 Malays (Table 4.6). Moreover, the Malays were largely employed in subordinate services. In 1934, a Malay Federal Councilor, Dato Abdullah of Rembau remarked:

TABLE 4.6: **Government Employment by Ethnicity in the F.M.S. in 1938**

	Tamils	Chinese	Malays	Others
Clerks in General State Services	537	465	336	97
Public Works Overseers and Sub-Overseers	175	3	55	7
Teachers, Government English Schools	102	64	24	35
Technical Assistants	419	73	329	78
Asiatic Employees, Railways*	1,277	302	485	263
Asiatic Employees, Posts and Telegraphs*	414	175	408	81
Dressers and Hospital Assistants	257	87	105	27
Total:	3,181	1,169	1,742	588

*"Excluding menials".
Source: Roff (1967: 120, fn. 82).

> It is, no doubt, pleasing to see so many Malay peons, Malay messengers, Malay punkah-pullers, Malay sailors, Malay police

> constables and Malay gateman in the employ of the railway but, Sir, the Malays also desire to have a fair share of the higher appointments (Federal Council Proceedings, 1934, p. B 58, quoted in Roff 1967: 120, fn. 81).

At the same time, during the depression of the early 1930s the government's retrenchment programme to reduce public expenditure was also causing concern among the Malays. Although, the programme affected a far lesser number of Malays compared to non-Malays,[22] the Malay concern arose from the fact that government employment was the only avenue open to the educated Malays and with the retrenchment programme in operation this avenue was closed. At that time as a result of low urbanisation among Malays, presumably due to government's "preservation of the Malay peasantry" policy, the Malay commercial class was virtually non-existent and its Chinese and Indian counterparts employed their own people. Therefore, as Roff (1967: 203) stated, with "an increasing recognition of the competitive claims of Chinese and Indians, retrenchment seemed to urban Malays to constitute a serious threat to their attempts to enter more fully into public life".

Although Indians enjoyed a superior position regarding government services, they were denied admission to the Malayan Civil Service,[23] particularly in the F.M.S. After much pressure from the Chinese and Indian communities, in 1932 the Malayan Civil Service in the Straits Settlement was partially opened to non-Malays, "who were admitted as district officers, magistrates and in legal services" (Mahajani 1960: 133). In 1934, the Indians demanded a similar scheme of reservation for them, a certain proportion of appointments in the F.M.S., to which the government response was as follows:

> There is already in existence a Malay Administrative Service which is considered adequate for the needs of the country and there would not appear to be any justification on purely administrative grounds for the creation of a parallel service open to non-Malays (Federal Council Proceedings, 1935, p. B55, quoted in Mahajani 1960: 133).

On another occasion in 1936 the F.M.S. High Commissioner stated:

> I could not support the proposal for the appointment of

> non-Malays to posts in the Federation. I know of no country . . . that appoints a foreigner, i.e. a native not of the race of the country or a non-Englishman, to an administrative post (Proceedings of the Federal Council, 1936, B18, quoted in Arasaratnam 1970: 91).

Demand for Equitable Political Representation

This demand arose from the Indians' desire in the late 1920s to share in the decision-making process of the colony. In 1923, one Indian was appointed to the S.S. Legislative Council. But there was no political representation in the F.M.S. Federal Council until 1928 when an Indian member was included in the Council. The Chinese as well as Indians strove for more equitable political representation in these bodies. "The All-Malaya Indian Conference in its annual session from 1928 to 1931 passed unanimous resolutions" to this effect (Mahajani 1960: 131, fn. 84). Consequently, one Indian member was included in each of the State Councils of Perak, Negri Sembilan and Selangor. Beyond this, however, the government was opposed to any move towards further democratisation of the colonial policy-making on the following grounds:

> The adoption of any kind of government by majority would forthwith entail the complete submersion of the indigenous population, who would find themselves hopelessly outnumbered by the folk of other races (Sir Hugh Clifford's statement, 1927, cited in Emerson 1964: 174).

Opposition to the "Decentralization Policy"

Another major issue between the Malay and non-Malay middle classes was the policy of decentralisation which the British pursued in the 1920s. Although the express objective of this policy was to enhance the position, authority and prestige of the Malay Sultans and the Malay people, the following were the real motives behind the policy:

(a) by delegating some power to the Rulers and State Councils in the F.M.S., the British wanted to pursuade the Unfederated Malay States to opt for a similar political structure. Eventually some sort of a federal political structure of all nine states was contemplated. "Decentralisation was therefore a preliminary to recentralisation"

(Allen 1967: 5);

(b) Decentralisation of administration to the individual Malay States and the reassertion of their Malay character was designed to effectively contain the Chinese and Indians, who as non-Muslims were ineligible to be subjects of the Malay Rulers (Stenson 1980: 37).[24]

Under the scheme it was proposed that certain federal departments be transferred to the State Councils. Chinese as well as Indian commercial interests opposed this measure because they found it more convenient to deal with a strong central government than with several different local authorities. Additionally, Indians feared "that the transfer of greater powers to the States would lead to the erosion of their prosperity and the little influence they enjoyed in governmental matters" (Arasaratnam 1970: 89). The policy eventually failed, not so much due to the non-Malay opposition, but because of the fact that there were other interest groups that opposed it. These included some Colonial Office officials, European business interests in the F.M.S. and the S.S., retired Malayan Civil Service officials and last but not least, the Malay Rulers and the Malay establishments themselves (Allen 1967: 5-6). Thereafter, until, the Japanese occupation, the British attempted to defuse the issue by doing nothing about it, or following the policy of "drift" (Stenson 1980: 52 fn. 7).

In sum, the differences in interests between the Malay and non-Malay middle class segments were central to the race relations situations between the Malays and Indians. Economic and demographic dominance of non-Malays, especially of the Chinese after the First World War, had aroused Malay fears of subordination in their own homeland. In fact Malay nationalism before the Second World War was largely shaped by these fears. The exploitation of Malay peasantry by the non-Malay petty bourgeoisie (the Indian moneylenders, Chinese rice millers, shopkeepers, etc.) further contributed in shaping Malay resentment towards non-Malays.

Much of the Malay resentment against non-Malays, however, was directed against the Chinese who were far more numerous and prosperous than the Indians. The impact of the Japanese occupation was an additional complicating factor in Malay and Chinese relations.[25] Communal rioting pitting Malays against Chinese in the rural areas immediately after the Japanese surrender provides evidence of the deteriorated Malay-Chinese relations. During the month-long period between the Japanese surrender and the British reoccupation, the predominantly Malay police force was withdrawn for retraining and the Malayan People's Anti-Japanese Army, which consisted mainly of 5,000 Chinese guerrillas "roamed the countryside paying off old scores against those people (mainly Malays) who had been suspected informers" (Gullick 1969: 100). Malays reprisals resulted in several violent incidents of which the massacre of forty Chinese villagers, mainly women and children, in Negri Sembilan was the most gruesome.

By the mid-1950s relations between the Malays and the Chinese had deteriorated even further. This occurred in at least three ways: first, unlike the Malays who volunteered in large numbers for service in the enlarged security forces, the Chinese not only did not do so, but in addition some 6,000 of them fled to China to avoid conscription in 1951; second, it was believed by many Malays that wealthy Chinese contributed to M.C.P. funds under the threat of terrorism; and finally, following the installation of the Alliance government in 1955, the M.C.P.-supported subversive activities were in direct conflict with Malayan nationalism (Gullick 1969: 119-20). Throughout the emergency period, distrust between the Alliance Government and the M.C.P. was so deep that in 1955 and 1957 the government was not willing to allow the outlawed M.C.P. to resume normal political life without restraint. In view of the Anglo-Malayan Defence Treaty, the M.C.P. leaders considered Malaysian independence under the Alliance Party as nothing more than another form of "neo-colonialism".

Thus for most of the colonial period in Malaysia the Chinese remained the target of Malay hostility. For this reason, middle class Indians did not experience any overt racial hostility or violence *vis-a-vis* Malays. Nevertheless, the oppression and exploitation of Indian estate labourers, whom the colonial authorities often referred to as a "peaceable and easily-governed race", continued throughout the colonial period and continued even after independence.

III. CLASS AND RACE RELATIONS IN THE POST-COLONIAL PERIOD

Since the first general elections in 1955, Malaysia has been governed by the Alliance of the United Malay National Organisation (UMNO); the Malay Chinese Association (MCA, formed in 1922); and the Malayan Indian Congress (MIC). All these three are moderate communal parties. "In the inter-communal negotiations of 1956 the Malays had made concessions to the other communities over citizenship and the franchise in exchange for an entrenchment in the constitution of Malay 'Special rights'" (Gullick 1981: 114). This coalition was based on behind-the-scenes communal bargaining and was confined to elite accommodation. As an observer wrote in 1968: "there is no 'Alliance' except at the top. The separate parties go their own way, perpetuate their own jealousies, indiscretions, communal demands . . ." with "little contact at the local branch level" (Grossholtz 1968: 338).[26] Political power among the Malays is exercised by a small section of the upper class, and "is certainly not in the hands of the Malays as a race" (Cham 1975: 458). Similar arguments can be made about the Chinese and the Indian partners of the Alliance. The MCA basically represented Chinese capitalists. The MIC was supported by the Indian petty bourgeoisie consisting of entrepreneurs, merchants and upward-aspiring administrators and professional men" (Stenson 1980: 194). It lacked the support of workers and the trade unions (Ratnam 1965: 155).

The Alliance served the interests of the ruling elites and foreign powers and prevented the decisive transformation of the economy prior to 1969. In spite of structural changes towards diversification in the West Malaysian economy it was still dominated by the rubber and tin industries. These two export items amounted to 69 per cent of total exports in the 1966-69 period (Lim 1973: 122). During the 1960s the *laissez faire* industrial policy continued to promote "the patterns and imbalances in industrial ownership and employment that the nation had inherited–and accepted–at the time of independence" (*Area Handbook for Malaysia* 1977: 321). In the same period, Malay's economic position did not "show any marked improvement" *vis-a-vis* other communities (Lim 1973: 142). Even after 10 years of independence the majority of Malays remained employed in low-paying occupations. Among the youth the unemployment problem was pressing, especially in the urban areas. In spite of rural development programmes initiated by the Alliance Party, poverty among the Malays remained more or less unchanged. At the same time over 50,000 Tamil estate workers were rendered unemployed as a result of the on-going subdivision of estates in the 1950s, which the European and Chinese planters encouraged (Stenson 1980: 196). "Subdivision of estates was creating not a class of peasant proprietors but rather of absentee landlords and urban investors in land" (Arasaratnam 1970: 156). This situation continued into the 1960s.

In the face of this uneven economic development, and economic dissatisfaction among various sections of the Malaysian population in the late 1960s, non-Alliance political parties worked for reducing the strength of the Alliance government from an absolute to a simple majority in the 1969 general elections. The opposition parties agreed not to split their votes, and the Malay-dominated Pan Malayan Islamic Party (PMIP) was also brought into non-Alliance agreement. The Federal election results were predictable. In the elections not only Malay but the Chinese votes were also split, and the M.C.A.'s strength was reduced from 27 seats in 1964 to 13 in 1969. In the Selangor State elections, the M.C.A.'s performance was worse; it could win only one seat out of 12. The 1969 elections thus "signalled the demise of M.C.A., and perhaps, the death of the Alliance formula" (Gagliano 1971: 15). All this gave rise to anxiety among U.M.N.O. activists that the political power was slipping out of their hands.

In the post-election atmosphere of crisis and uncertainty, especially regarding the formation of government in the Selangor state whose capital is Kuala Lumpur (also the national capital and the headquarters base of every political party), "the victory celebrations by supporters of the opposition parties set off counter demonstrations by U.M.N.O. youth, which quickly escalated into race riots" (Stenson 1980: 197). These riots which began on 13 May, 1969, claimed by 30th June, 1969, 196 dead, 439 injured, and 9,143 people arrested and charged in court. By 31st July, 40 Malays and 5 Chinese were awaiting trials for murder and arson. At the same time 39 people were still listed as missing (see the N.O.C.'s report: *The May 13 Tragedy*, 1969: 88-96). There was also widespread damage to property.[27] On 15 May, a nation-wide State of Emergency was proclaimed. This lasted for the next 18 months and was supervised by an eight-member National Operations Council.

The riots prompted the ruling Alliance to seek grass-roots support from the Malays. Consequently, a two-pronged strategy was adopted: (1) The Alliance entered into a pact according to which the entrenched constitutional provisions protecting special rights for the Malays were exchanged for the liberalisation of non-Malay citizenship rights. A Constitutional Amendment Act of 1971 made it illegal to question, whether inside or outside parliament, certain ethnically sensitive issues such as Islam (religion of the majority of Malays), Malay language and certain other Malay privileges in the fields of education and industry.

Thus the pact effectively instituted *bhumiputerisation* as the state ideology according to which the *bhumiputeras* (meaning "the sons of the soil"), that is, the Malays, were accorded special status.[28] Taken in conjunction with the New Economic Policy (to be discussed shortly) the pact meant that the state actively encouraged and supported the creation of the Malay bourgeoisie, petty bourgeoisie and proletariat at the expense of their non-Malay counterparts. (2) The government launched a New Economic Policy aimed at the removal of Malay poverty and the restructuring of society, i.e. the creation of a Malay industrial and commercial class as well as urban proletariat. The major operational goal of the Policy was to achieve 30 per cent Malay ownership and management of industries by 1990 by reducing the foreign ownership, which in 1970 was over 60 per cent (*Area Handbook for Malaysia* 1977: 323). In 1970 the Malay ownership and share capital of limited companies accounted for less than 2 per cent of the total (Table 4.7).

TABLE 4.7: **Percentage Ownership of Share Capital in Limited Companies by Ethnicity and Sector, West Malaysia, 1970**

Sector	Malay	Chinese	Indian	Foreign
Agriculture, Forestry, Fisheries	0.9	22.4	0.1	75.3
Mining, Quarrying	0.7	16.8	0.4	72.4
Manufacturing	2.5	22.0	0.7	59.6
Construction	2.2	52.8	0.8	24.1
Transport and Communication	13.3	43.4	2.3	12.0
Commerce	0.8	30.4	0.7	63.5
Banking and Insurance	3.3	24.3	0.6	52.2
Others	2.3	37.8	2.3	31.4
Total in per cent	1.9	22.5	1.0	60.7

Source: Wiebe and Mariappen (1978: 110).

By the end of the Plan, the New Economic Policy was considered successful in terms of the growth of new industrial ventures, capital formation (especially in the Malay and state sectors), and the creation of new jobs (Lim Mah Hui and Canak 1981: 217-18).[29] However, due to "the inadequacy of the domestic market and the difficulties of penetrating overseas market" the same rate of economic growth could not be sustained in the Third Malaysian Plan (1976-80) and subsequently (Gullick 1981: 185). Moreover, the increasing state intervention in the economy brought about new contradictions in Malaysian capitalism. Fundamental to these contradictions is the fact that state capital, which essentially represents Malay bureaucratic interests, is in competition with private capital of different fractions–Chinese and Malay. While state capital has been generally accommodative to foreign capital,[30] "Chinese capital both large and small, but especially the latter, is most negatively affected by the emergence of state capital" (Lim Mah Hui and Canak 1981: 219). Thus a potential for racial conflict continues to exist in Malaysia between the Malays and Chinese. This is more so in view of the fact that in the rural areas the rural transformation schemes have not done much in tackling land reforms to attack the structural cause of poverty. Instead, in the process only the landowning class from which the Malay bourgeois class draws its main support has been strengthened (Purcal 1975).

In the post-independence period, the Chinese community generally advanced and differentiated into a variety of strata consisting of artisans, technicians, industialists, financiers, and professionals. However, the Indian community continues to show its pre-independence composition. As before, the Indian community is divided into two classes: mainly urban dwelling middle classes and the estate workers. The earlier class division based on immigration patterns has been reinforced by the New Educational Policy as it affects the Indians. The crux of this policy is that while the children of Indian middle classes receive their education in English medium schools, the children of estate labourers continue to be taught through Tamil schools which have been in existence since at least the turn of the century. In 1968 there were about 680 Tamil primary schools, mainly on the estates. As there are no secondary Tamil schools, the mobility of estate children is completely blocked, unless they happen to be perceived as exceptional and allowed to devote the extra required year to be admitted to English schools. Moreover, the Tamil schools are staffed by inadequately-trained teachers. Due to the general neglect on the part of the government as well as the Indian community, Tamil schools remain cut off from mainstream education (Colletta 1975).[31] Consequently, there has been a low level of upward and out-of-estate mobility coupled with a high degree of unemployment among the younger generation of estate workers.[32] This situation is further exacerbated by the fact that as a result of the on-going technological innovation on the estate, employment opportunities are decreasing.

Thus the rubber-estate labour force fell from 285,300 in 1960 to 198,000 in 1971, and Indian employment on the estate from 148,500 in 1950 to 79,800 in 1971 (Stenson 1980: 204). Besides modernisation, competition from Malay and Chinese workers is an additional cause of dwindling employment opportunities for Indians on the estates. In 1971, for example, the estate labour-force consisted of 79,800 Indians, 63,800 Malays and 54,400 Chinese. The estate population in general and its Indian constituent in particular continue to be economically vulnerable. According to the Third Malaysian Plan, about 40 per cent of the estate workers of all races were estimated to be in poverty.

While the Indian estate population has thus been isolated and socially immobile, the Indian middle classes took the fullest advantage of English education immediately after the Second World War. "The English educated Indians attained their maximum influence and prosperity in the 1950s and early 1960s" (Arasaratnam 1970: 195). In that period they predominated in the technical, clerical and professional services. This position, however, could not be sustained for the rest of the 1960s and 1970s, mainly for two reasons: one, lack of mobility among the Indian estate labourers and two, increasing competition from the government-sponsored Malay *bhumiputera* participation in the public services. In 1970, over 49 per cent of the Indian working population was engaged in the agricultural sector, 24 per cent in services, 13.3 per cent in manufacturing and construction, and 10.6 per cent in commerce. Although representation of Indians in commercial activities is commensurate with their proportion in the total Malaysian population, their ownership of share capital in corporate companies is only one per cent of the total (Table 4.7). In other words, Indian capital remained tied to traditional specialities, and with a few exceptions, most of the Indian petty traders remained in petty trading, rather than becoming entrepreneurs and industrialists (Stenson 1980: 198; Tinker 1977: 110).

The New Economic Policy has also adversely affected the other segments of the Indian middle class, particularly professional, technical, managerial, clerical, and sales personnels. Between 1970 and 1980, the Indians in all these occupational categories have lost their share, mainly to the Malays. The irony of this situation and its further impact on the Indian middle classes in terms of possible unemployment can fully be appreciated from the fact that during the same period the number of Indian students enrolled in post-secondary institutions has jumped eleven-fold, that is from only 600 in 1970 to

6,771 in 1980 (Hua 1983: 178-79). In addition to decreasing employment opportunities, the Indian middle classes have also experienced the curtailment of chances for promotion, business opportunities, scholarships, and their children's educational opportunities (Hua 1983: 117).

To sum up, the 1969 riots in Malaysia involving the economically dominant Chinese and the politically dominant Malays occurred in an atomosphere of persistent poverty among the Malay peasants and proletariat within the context of neo-colonialism. In spite of its failure, communal politics in Malaysia continues with constitutionally-protected special Malay rights regarding religion, language and certain other privileges. At the same time, in a largely foreign owned capitalist economy, state capital is being invested with a view to increase the Malay participation and wealth in the economy. Thus the potential for racial tension has increased as the Malay bourgeoisie and petty bourgeoisie is being created at the expense of its Chinese and Indian counterparts.

In the tripartite racial situation in Malaysia, the Malays and Chinese are more likely to be in conflict with each other than any other combination of races. so far the Indian community, or at least a segment of it, has "benefited" from this situation in that it has not been the specific target of racial violence. The major reasons for this situation are:

(i) Race relations in Malaysia continue to be perceived in terms of "nativism", that is, in terms of Malay *versus* non-Malay. As the Chinese are both numerically and economically the dominant group, Malay hostility is usually directed towards them. On the other hand, Indians constitute a small proportion of the petty bourgeoisie and are not perceived as strong competitors *vis-a-vis* the Chinese.

(ii) The continuation of the underground communist insurrectionary movement, manned mainly by the Chinese guerillas, tends to discredit the Chinese in the eyes of the Malays. Additionally, Communist China is perceived as a threat, particularly by Malays with strong religious convictions and with a stake in capitalism. India is not perceived as so much of a threat.

(iii) In various middle class occupations to which the Malay masses aspire, the Indians have lost more ground than the Chinese. In fact, the proportionate share of Indians in both agriculture and manufacturing has increased, whereas that of the Chinese has decreased (Hua 1983: 178). Thus, for the Malays the Chinese appear more as competitors than do the Indians.

Thus in the post-independence period in Malaysia, both Indian estate workers as well as middle classes continue to experience increasing racial antagonism resulting from their specific class situation.

IV. SUMMARY AND CONCLUSIONS

Unlike Guyana where Indian immigrants belonged exclusively to labouring classes, the Malaysian case represents a situation where the Indian community from the very beginning has been divided into two classes: (a) the working class which mainly consisted of rubber estate workers, and (b) segments of the petty bourgeoisie (traders and money-lenders, government servants, teachers, lawyers, doctors, etc.). Except during a brief period of subcommunal nationalism in the 1930s when, in order to raise its status in the eyes of other communities, the Indian petty bourgeoisie showed some concern about the oppressed condition of Indian workers and provided them with organisational leadership, the two classes have been isolated from each other.

Taking first the race relations situation of Indian rubber estate workers, it must be said that they constituted one of the most exploited working class segments in the post-emancipation period in the British empire. Although unlike indentured labourers the *kangani* labourers were legally free, their initial indebtedness, low wages, illiteracy, isolation on the remotely located rubber plantations and legal repression made it possible for the planter class to exploit them even more thoroughly than indentured labourers (Stenson 1980). There were no land settlement schemes or social welfare measures for the retired and that compelled a great majority of them to return to their homeland in South India. Welcomed as belonging to "a peaceable and easily-governed race", the Indian labourers past productive age were thrown out of Malaysia like "sucked oranges".

In the plural society of Malaysia it is remarkable that there did not develop any structured tensions between the Indians and Chinese. The main reason lay in the compartmentalised colonial economy in which the mining sector was predominantly served by Chinese labour, the plantation sector by Indian labour and the peasant agricultural sector was the stronghold of the Malays. This occupational specialisation prevented any significant degree of contact between different groups and undoubtedly bred ignorance about each other. Apparently, the Chinese and Indian petty bourgeois class segments also did not develop any contradictory economic interests. Instead the dominance of both groups, known as non-Malays, was resented by the upcoming Malay middle class.

The conflict between Malay and non-Malay obtained in terms of several economic and political issues. One major issue in the 1920s and 1930s was the non-Malay demand for citizenship rights and equality of political status in the Malay states. Apprehensive of non-Malay economic and demographic dominance, the Malays were obviously opposed to this demand. Another issue was the non-Malay dominance in the government service, which the Malays resented. But on the other hand, the colonial administrative service was the exclusive preserve of the Malays and the non-Malays demanded it be accessible to all. Other issues involved the demand by non-Malays for proportionate political representation in various legislatures, the opposition to the "decentralisation policy", discrimination regarding educational funding, etc. (Arasaratnam 1970: 91; Mahajani 1960: 133; Roff 1967: 120, 203). These contradictions were not resolved until after independence, and all through the colonial period the colonial state generally tended to protect the Malay interests. The government portrayed non-Malays as "aliens" and "transient" and demanded them to behave accordingly.

Much of the Malay resentment against non-Malays was directed against the Chinese who were far more numerous and prosperous than the Indians. Nevertheless, a fraction of the Indian petty bourgeoisie to which the Malays were not favourably disposed consisted of the Chettiar money-lenders who held some of the Malay peasant land as mortgage. They had also advanced loans worth $125 million to the Malay small holders in the Federated Malay States alone during the great depression of 1930s. Although in the wake of growing landlessness among the generally improverished Malay peasantry, political expediency required the government to enact suitable legislation and thereby to help ease the situation, communal relations for the time being were strained. The Chettiars were "held up before the public eyes as extortionate and heartless exploiters of the poor" (Arasaratnam 1970: 75).

In sum, the Indian-Malay race relations situation in the colonial period emerged from two interrelated aspects of class relations. The first of these involved antagonistic class relations between the Indian money-lenders and the Malay peasantry and the second involved the intra-class conflict between the Indian and Malay middle class fractions. The two aspects tended to overlap giving the impression of communal rather than class relations between the two communities.

The post-colonial race relations situation in Malaysia is the political and ideological expression of the continuing uneven economic development and the attendant class structure characteristic of neo-colonialism. The 1969 riots adequately highlighted the economic and political contradictions inherent in the Malaysian society. The New Economic Policy followed by the ruling elites further deepened these contradictions by promoting only the Malay interests. Within these parameters, the racial discrimination against the Indians finds expression in (a) the continuing exploitation of the rubber plantation workers, and (b) the increasing competition between the Indian petty bourgeoisie and its Malay and Chinese counterparts. In order to maintain the Malay supremacy at any cost the state in Malaysia is increasingly assuming the authoritarian stance.

NOTES

1. In this chapter we are mainly concerned with Peninsular or West Malaysia which until 1963 was known as Malaya or British Malaya. Politically Malaysia evolved slowly. First were established the Straits Settlements of Penang, Malacca and Singapore between 1786 and 1824 and united into a single political unit as such in 1826. Following the British intervention in Perak in 1874, the Federated Malay States (F.M.S.) were created in 1896 with three other states (Selangor, Negri Sembilan and Pahang). The Unfederated Malay States consisted of Johore, Kedah, Kelantan and Trengganu which along with the F.M.S. became a British Protectorate at various dates between 1896 and 1914. Following the Second World War the short-lived Malayan Union (1946-48) was replaced by the Federation of Malaya. The Federation of Malaya achieved independence in 1957. Singapore, which was outside the Federation since 1946, was merged in the Federation in 1963 and left it in 1965. Since 1963 the Federation of Malaysia also consisted of the States of Sarawak and Sabah (in northern Borneo).

   The word 'Malay' refers to the indigenous people of Malaysia and 'non-Malay' to others, in this case mainly Chinese and Indians.

   The name of the independent nation, that is, Malaysia is used in this chapter for the entire period of its history.
2. Eunice Thio, "The British Forward Movement in the Malay Peninsula,

1880-1889", in *Papers on Malayan History*, edited by K.G. Tregonning, Singapore, 1962, quoted in *Malaysia: Selected Historical Readings*, compiled by John Bastin and R.W. Winks, Oxford University Press, Kuala Lumpur, 1966, p. 228.

3. The reasons for European business failures lay partly in expensive over-staffing at top levels, and partly in the insufficient attention given to trial-boring. The European firms were also inclined to place too much faith in the economies of expensive apparatus before it had been carefully tried and tested in local conditions (Kennedy 1970: 195).
4. The rubber plant was originally native to South America. In 1770 its use as an eraser of pencil marks was discovered. In 1873, with the object of obtaining seeds or plants for growing in India, an expedition was sent to Brazil. A few of the plants thus procured were raised at Kew, but six of these sent to Calcutta died. In the next expedition 70,000 seeds were brought. Only 4 per cent of these germinated at Kew, but from these a few plants reached Singapore via Ceylon. Of the twenty-two plants that were successfully grown in Ceylon the progeny is to be seen today in the millions of acres now under crop throughout Southeast Asia (Purcell 1946: 111).
5. According to Mahajani (1960: 115), the term was first used by Neelkantha Aiyer (1938) and has been widely used by Indians.
6. *The Hindu* (Madras), 2 June, 1941, cited in Stenson (1980: 64).
7. According to a Central Indian Association of Malay's memorandum submitted in 1937 to the Agent of the Government of India, in the year 1935, the government revenue from *toddy*, at 40 per cent of the sale price, was \$2,081,718, which meant that the total amount spent by the labourers on *toddy* for that year was \$5,204,295 (Arasaratnam 1970: 70). There were 107 *toddy* shops in the rubber estates in 1951 and 286 in 1955 (Mahajani 1960: 212).

   Just as the Indians drank *toddy*, the Chinese smoked opium. The S.S. Government earned huge sums of revenue from this source amounting to as much as 53.3 per cent of the total in 1906. In the S.S. during 1898-1906 period, the actual amount of revenue varied from over \$2.3 m. to \$6.3 m. a year (Purcell 1948: 188).
8. Mr. V.S. Srinivasa Sastri, an important nationalist leader was deputed to Malaya by the Government of India in 1937 to report on the conditions of Indian labour there. His Report on the 'Conditions of Indian Labour in Malaya' was published from Madras and later reprinted in Kuala Lumpur in 1937. The Sastri Report "regarded as a vindication of the contention that Indian labourers were well-treated in Malaya" was received badly in India. . . . "His reluctance to comment at length on the political and social status of Indians in Malaya was what angered Indians the most" (Parmer 1960: 68).
9. "The pre-war European planter often rationalized his sexual liaison with native women as an efficient means of learning the language–the so-called 'sleeping dictionary' method–and maintaining informal contacts with the labourers. On Pal Melayu [the name of the plantation which the author studied] this method seems to have been popular with European managers and assistants in the past, and knowledge of such liaisons was fairly widespread in the labour lines" (Jain 1970: 414).

10. Indian estate workers had suffered considerably during the Japanese occupation. Production and management on the estates was disrupted. Local rice production fell by one-third (Gullick 1969: 96). Consequently, malnutrition and undernourishment took a heavy toll of Indian labourers. The social provisions of public health, housing and education all had declined. Moreover, the labourers were recruited forcibly to build the Siam-Burma Railway. It is believed that between 50,000 and 70,000 labourers had perished on this Japanese project, later known as the "Death Railway" (Mahajani 1960: 192).
11. The colonial administration deliberately held back English education from the rural Malays, because as the Raja of Perak said, English-educated Malays ". . . would not take kindly to the pursuit of their forefathers (i.e. paddy growing)" (Roff, 1967: 203).
12. Time and again the British emphasised their "trusteeship" policy regarding the Malays. For example, in A.D. 1934 Haynes, the then Secretary of Agriculture, said that the British colonial administration should be consistent with Malay peoples' "welfare and happiness, not only for today but for the future ages. That aim will be obtained rather by building up a sturdy and thrifty peasantry living on the lands they own and living by the food they grow, than by causing them to foresake the life of their fathers for the glamour of the new ways . . . (and) . . . to abandon their rice fields for new crops which they cannot themselves utilise and the market for which depends on outside world conditions beyond their orbit" (cited in Latiff 1977: 80-81). It must be pointed out that "building up a sturdy and thrifty" peasantry was merely rhetoric. Throughout the colonial period, Malaysia remained dependent on imports for her rice supply. In the last decade of her colonial rule, for example, the country annually imported nearly half of its rice requirements.
13. As late as 1960, 67 per cent of all farms were under 4.75 acres. According to the Federal Land Development Authority of Malaysia, the minimum economic holding–that is one which can give the farmer a fair to good standard of living –is between 8 to 10 acres (Ooi Jin Bee 1963: 187). Obviously a large number of Malay farmers had uneconomic holdings. At the same time 80 per cent of the rice farms were not owned by the cultivators (Lim 1973: 57).
14. So far as the Indians were concerned, "the aggravating factor in this policy was that the most recent immigrant Malays from the Dutch Indies were accorded equal recognition with the native Malays, and were made eligible to hold land in reservations, while Indians, though settled for generations, were rigorously excluded" (Kondapi 1951: 123).
15. According to Arasaratnam (1970: 83), the first Indian association in Malaya, formed in 1906, was the Indian Association of Taiping. In 1909 the Selangor Indian Association was formed with backing from Indian businessmen, professionals and clerical workers. Soon similar associations were formed in Lower Perak, Penang, Malacca, Negri Sembilan and in 1923 in Singapore. In 1925 the Singapore Indian Association began to publish a monthly journal called *The Indian.* In 1932 the Selangor Indian Association published *The Selangor Indian.* Similarly, Indian Chambers of Commerce were formed at

various places in Malaya.

16. A great orator and a charismatic personality with martial bearing, Subbash Chandra Bose was a militant Indian nationalist. He was the president of the Indian National Congress in 1939. Dissatisified with the liberal Congress politics regarding the question of Indian independence, he fled to Germany in 1941 from where he went to Japan to launch an armed struggle for the liberation of India. He was "the innovator of the idea that India could use the struggle between the Axis powers and the West to secure her freedom" (Arasaratnam 1970: 104). He had arrived in Singapore in July 1943. In 1945 he died in an aeroplane crash on his way to Japan.

    Indians in Southeast Asia showed great enthusiasm towards Bose's efforts for the liberation of India. Thousands of them volunteered for the Army and donations were made of cash and jewellery. The Indians' enthusiasm about their new legal status as "free Indians", however, had soon lapsed into disillusionment following the defeat of the Indian National Army on the Imphal front in Burma in 1944.

17. Malay nationalism expressed itself through at least three major contending movements and elite groups: the Arabic-educated religious reform movement, the largely Malay-educated autochthonous intelligentsia, and the English-educated bureaucracy, "itself drawn mainly from the traditional elite in metamorphoses" (Roff 1967: 254). However, in the end, the movement led by the English-educated professionals and the Malay aristocracy dominated and it was also this movement from which stronger expressions of anti-immigrant sentiments came. "On the whole, the politicisation of the Malays occurred less along class lines and more in terms of ethnic consciousness" (Lim Mah Hui 1980: 145).

18. In 1932 Permanent Under Secretary of State for Colonies Sir Samuel Wilson visited Malaya and took note of the fears of the Chinese and Indians resulting from (i) the cry of "Malaya for the Malays" in the previous years, (ii) preferential treatment to Malays in services, and (iii) greater use of the Malay Land Reservation Enactments. Although Sir Wilson recommended provision for the same professional and business opportunities for non-Malay immigrants as for the European British subjects, he did not clarify the British policy on political representation of non-Malays. The report was criticised for this in India and by the Indian Agent and other leaders in Malaya (See Mahajani 1960: 132).

19. *The Indian Daily Mail*, Singapore, 8 August, 1950, cited in Mahanjani (1960: 240).

20. According to Mahajani (1960: 118, fn 52), this expression was first used in 1927 by Raja di Hilir in the Federal Council.

21. In 1938 the Selangor Malay Association had proposed that all non-Malay immigration should be stopped and that Indonesian immigration be increased "because the Indonesians come from the same stock as the Malays" (Roff 1967: 203).

    The immigration of non-Malays was tightened after the passage of the Immigration Ordinance of 1952 which came into force on 1 August, 1953. "While the Indians and the Chinese viewed the new ordinance as fairly stringent and prohibitive, the Malay nationalists considered it inadequate and full of loopholes" (Mahajani 1960: 250).

22. The data on retrenchment are not available strictly in racial/ethnic terms, especially for the non-Malays. However, it can be said that the number of Malays so affected was not very large in absolute terms. According to the Federal Council Proceedings of 1933, only 541 Malays were retrenched between July 1930 and February 1933. In about the same period (July 1930 to December 1932) 4,100 foreign-born officers were retrenched as against 1,198 locally born. Apparently, the foreign-born officers largely consisted of Indians and Chinese.

23. On the distinction between government service and civil service, in the Malaysian context, the civil services refer to the higher categories of administrative services for which candidates are selected through a country-wide competitive examination and the successful candidates are given specialised training. Government services, on the contrary, included a wide variety of occupations such as teaching in schools and colleges, and supervisory, technical and clerical services in government offices, public works departments, police and army, ports and railways, post offices, etc. Also included in the government service category were the lowly paid office servants (peons), a conspicuous feature in many colonial/post-colonial Third World countries.

24. The pro-Malay policy was based on the conventional definition of a Malay, as one who habitually speaks the Malay language, habitually practices Malay customs and follows the religion of Islam. Since the post-World War II constitutional developments this definition has now become legal.

25. During the Japanese Occupation the Chinese suffered the worst hardships. At least 40,000 Chinese suspected of being communist were massacred and the whole community was compelled to donate $50 million to the Japanese (Purcell 1948: 251-53). Their businesses were taken over by the Japanese. It was to resist these hardships that the Malayan People's Anti-Japanese Army was organised through the Malayan Communist Party. Ironically, this Army was supported by the British who had fled Malaysia at the first sign of Japanese invasion.

26. The nature of the coalition of the Alliance Party and its class interest is dramatically illustrated by an incident in which during 1961 the Minister of Agriculture, Aziz-bin-Ishak, who "had promised the (largely Malay) rice growers in Perak and Wellesley province that he would transform private rice mills, largely owned by Chinese, into cooperatives", was sacked from the cabinet (Nesh 1967: 225). For the M.C.A. the issue was so contentious that it was ready to leave the Party unless the move was revoked. In the end the M.C.A. won its case and the Prime Minister had to resort to the drastic action of removing the Minister.

27. "Almost all fighting in May was between Malays and Chinese, the Indians kept behind closed doors. However, as the Malays paraded triumphantly in the wake of the riots, the cry was heard: 'We have finished off the pigs: now for the goats!' (just as the Chinese are fond of pork, so Indians are supposed to favour curried goat.) On 28 June there was an attack upon a group of Indians

in the Malay Lampong suburb of Sentul; fifteen were slashed to death, and others wounded. In the evening several Indian huts were burned, and about seventy Indians moved into a refugee centre" (Tinker 1977: 108). About 60,000 Indians had returned to India in the aftermath of the 1969 riots.

28. On the eve of the 1974 general elections two opposition parties were forced to join the new coalition by the then Prime Minister Tun Razak. The coalition was renamed the *Barisan National* or the National Front. In the 1974 general elections the National Front had achieved almost total hegemony by winning all but seven seats. This coalition is still in power under the leadership of Dr. Mahathir Mohamad.

29. In order to implement the New Economic Policy a number of state enterprises were established which had increased from 10 in 1957 to 82 in 1974, of which 65 were wholly-owned subsidiaries. Additionally, there were 185 joint ventures with the private sector (Lim Mah Hui and Canak 1981: 217). The figures for capital growth rate of limited companies during the Second Malaysian Plan were as follows: state capital 68 per cent, Malay 34 per cent, foreign 18 per cent, and local non-Malay 27 per cent (Malaysia 1979: 49). During the Second Malaysian Plan new jobs were created at the rate of 20,000 per annum as compared with 2,000 per annum in the 1960s (Gullick 1981: 196, fn 46).

30. In the 1970s, besides the traditional sources of foreign capital, i.e., Western countries, the major source of foreign capital appears to be not the Western countries but a few Asian countries like Japan, Hong Kong and Singapore. However, in the cases of Singapore and Hong Kong, "it appears not unlikely that the supplying companies residing in these countries are themselves affiliates of multinational corporations who have their head offices in London or New York" (Hoffmann and Tan Siew E.E. 1980: 219).

31. In this connection Stenson (1980: 207) writes: "One cannot help suspecting that the decision to maintain the separate estate Tamil school system with the Tamil medium of instruction, even after 1970 when the former English medium schools were obliged to teach in Malay, was motivated as much by the desire to maintain divisions amongst the working class as by the desire to appease the Tamil cultural nationalist".

32. According to the Mid-term Review of the Second Malaysian Plan (1973), the unemployment rate among the Malays, Chinese and Indians was 8 per cent, 7.4 per cent and 11 per cent respectively (Wiebe and Mariappen 1978: 113, fn 1).

5

Kenya: The "Middleman Minority" and Race Relations

The situation of Indians in Kenya[1] differed from their situation both in Guyana and Malaysia. Whereas the Indians in Guyana consisted exclusively of labourers and in Malaysia of both labouring and middle classes, in Kenya it was exclusively the middle classes that constituted the core of the Indian community. The Indian community in Kenya consisted mainly of merchants and traders, middle-level government servants and artisans and occupied a middleman minority position in the overall social structure of Kenya. As shown in Chapter 2, the major burden of the "middleman minority" theory is placed on certain attributes of the group such as its sojourning orientation, preference for liquidable occupations (trading, truck farming, laundry business, etc.), self-segregation, maintenance of distinctive cultural traits, and resistance to out-marriage and assimilation. These supposed attributes are then used to explain (a) why such minorities remain "strangers" in the host society, and (b) why they do not have a strong commitment regarding their long-term stay in their country of adoption. These features, it is argued in turn, promote hatred for the minority from among the members of the host society. In a critique of this theory it has been argued that in its present form it is not rooted in sufficient ethnographic and historical details of the various middleman minorities whose situations it purports to explain, and that its key concepts such as "liquidable occupation", sojourning attitude, etc. are of questionable value (Zenner 1980).

Thus, the middleman minority theory is not in itself sufficient to explain all aspects of the position of overseas Indians, whether in colonial and post-colonial East Africa, or in the other overseas territories dealt with in this study. The alternative approach adopted in our analysis is to treat the middleman minority status as a dependent variable (or emergent property) to be taken into account, and we thus propose to incorporate political power (or dominance) as well as economic power into the analysis. These two variables in turn are linked to the racial dimension, all of which give rise to particular forms of race relations and class conflict in the interaction among the component groups. In the case of Kenya, it will be shown how racial cleavage and class interests among the three principal groups led to racial antagonism and class conflict in both epochs.

From the perspective of political dominance, it can be seen that the European settlers manipulated both the racial factor and the economic factor to create a three-tier social structure based on ethnic/social stratification, a familiar characteristic feature of colonial race relations situations. The middleman minority position of the Indians was thus a socially and economically imposed status not necessarily deriving from the group's cultural characteristics as the proponents of the middleman minority theory claim.

The presence of the Indians in Kenya provided the colonial governing elite with a practical social and economic barrier between the European settlers and the indigenous Africans. It was from this ascribed position that there developed among Indians a petty bourgeoisie based on commercial interests centered around trading rather than large-scale industrial and agricultural enterprises. Hence, their middleman position was a direct consequence of the juxtaposition of the three major racial groups in Kenya. The tripartite race relations conflict consequently involved European/Indian, European/African, and Indian/African dimensions, and through economic forces also resulted in ethnically-segmented class positions and class conflict.

An adequate appraisal of race relations in Kenya must consider that the colonial enterprise in East Africa (as elsewhere) was primarily economic and dependent on the efficient exploitation of the subordinate population and the maintenance of intergroup cleavage as a safeguard for European dominance. Economic opportunities were thus allocated to the component communities according to the functional interests of the dominant British colonial settler population. It will be shown in this study how the monopolisation of land and large-scale economic enterprises by the British settlers and the controlled distribution of small-scale enterprises according to racial lines to the subordinate groups resulted in fractionalised class interests which vitiated against class solidarity between Indians and Africans. Competitive economic activities were at the base of the social fragmentation and discordant race relations throughout the colonial period, and subsequently became manifest in the independence era in the guise of African nationalism and economic disenfranchisement of the Indians.

Kenya, unlike any other British colony, was the only colonial territory whose social and economic fabric was somewhat modelled not on the "mother country" but largely on that from which the subordinate Indian minority originated. The British transplanted to Kenya a number of legal precepts and administrative institutions from India as well as military and police personnel. The (Indian) rupee became the standard currency of Kenya until 1921. By these actions the British intended to re-create in Kenya an African counterpart of British India but the policy met with fierce opposition from the European settlers and was finally abandoned. It is from these special conditions that the examination of the position of the Indian minority in Kenya makes such an interesting case study particularly in view of the long history of pre-British settlement in East Africa. The next section details the background to the evolution of the Indian community in East Africa leading to their "middleman" position during the British colonial and post-colonial era.

I. THE COLONIAL ECONOMY OF KENYA

Indian Immigration and Merchant Capital

In spite of the ancient connection between India and coastal East Africa, Indian settlement before A.D. 1500 was very small. In the sixteenth century, the Portuguese, the first European coloniers of East Africa, had noted the presence of a small number of Gujarati merchants trading on a substantial scale. In the Portuguese East African colonies, Indians, especially Goans, played an active role in trade and administration.[2] Indian labour was used to construct forts along the Coast. "By the nineteenth century Asians were an informal advance guard of Portuguese influence in Central Africa" (Singh 1965: 2).

A somewhat similar role for Indians can be observed with respect to the beginnings of German and British colonial rule in East Africa. In the first half of the nineteenth century, Indians were extensively involved in the Zanzibar-based Arab-Swahili caravan trade of ivory and slaves. The Indians also financed the Arab-owned, slave-run clove plantations on the islands of Zanzibar and Pemba (Mangat 1969: 2-26; van Zwanenberg 1975: 169; Wolff 1974: 31). According to one historian, around the middle of the nineteenth century, the Indians in Zanzibar "owned or financed almost all the business. They possessed by purchase or by mortgage more than half the landed property" (Copland 1939: 391). Additionally, Indian firms collected customs duties.[3] In 1840 there were over 1,000 Indians in East Africa; by 1860 there were some 6,000 (Mangat 1969: 7; Singh 1965: 3).

These Zanzibar-based Indians, who were British subjects, played an important role in British expansion on the mainland. Before the Imperial British East Africa Company was granted the royal charter in 1888, Indians had already monopolised trade on the East African coast. Sir Bartle Frere who led a special mission to investigate slavery in the Zanzibar Sultan's dominion in 1873 noted "the preponderating influence" of the Indian trader. He reported: "Along some 6,000 miles of sea-coast in Africa and its islands, and nearly the same extent in Asia, the Indian trader is, if not the monopolist, the most influential, permanent, and all-pervading element of the commercial community". Encouragement of Indian settlement and enterprise in East Africa therefore was one of the reasons for official backing of the Company whose preamble of the charter stated:

> The possession by a British Company of the Coastline would be advantageous to the commercial and other interests of our subjects in the Indian Ocean who may otherwise become compelled to reside and trade under the government or protection of alien powers (quoted in Mangat 1969: 28).

British East Africa Company officials continued to emphasise the desirability of Indian colonisation until 1895 when the East African administration was taken over by the Foreign Office.[4] Among these Fredrick Lugard was perhaps the most vocal advocate of the scheme. He wrote that the police and military personnel as well as the labourers, both artisans and coolies, would be recruited from India and that their presence in the midst of Africans would have encouraging and civilising effects on the latter. He continued:

> Moreover, the methods of agriculture, the simple implements of the Indian *ryot*, the use of the bullock, the sinking of wells, the system of irrigation and manuring the soil, etc., would soon be imitated by Africans and the produce of this land would thus be vastly multiplied. . . . It is not as imported coolie labour that I

> advocate the introduction of the Indian, but as a colonist and settler (Lugard 1968, I: 486-89).

Similar sentiments were echoed by many other officials and travellers to East Africa such as Sir Harry Johnston, Special Commissioner in Uganda (1899-1901), Winston Churchill (1908), then Under-Secretary of the State for the Colonies, and W.W.A. Fitzgerald (1970: 549-50), a traveller, who published his accounts in 1898. Sir Henry Johnston's oft-quoted pronouncement was as follows:

> On account of our Indian Empire we are compelled to reserve to British control a large portion of East Africa. Indian trade, enterprise and emigration require a suitable outlet. East Africa is, and should be, from every point of view, the America of the Hindu (quoted in Mangat 1969: 63-64, fn 2).

In 1901 and in 1902, Commissioner Eliot approved the immigration of Indian agricultural settlers. In addition to land grants in the Highland, he supported a scheme of free seed distribution and agricultural loans to prospective Indian settlers. Unfortunately, the scheme did not materialise, as in 1906 the Pubjabi agriculturists were willing to emigrate only in village communities and not individually, an undertaking the imperial government deemed too expensive.

Meanwhile, in the last decade of the nineteenth century, the volume of voluntary Indian immigration into East Africa had increased considerably. The "opening up" of the interior provided a variety of economic opportunities to the "passage" or "free" immigrants, including trade and commerce, government services, employment on the railways and public works, and a variety of artisan jobs. The construction of the Uganda railway appears to have been a major factor in stimulating the Indian voluntary immigration. The 572 mile-long railway was mainly constructed with the help of Indian indentured labour. In all, 31,983 "coolies" were imported for this purpose between 1896 and 1903 when the railway was completed (Table 5.1). Of these, while 16,312 Indians returned home, 6,454 were injured, and 2,493 had died (Gregory 1971: 52; Mangat 1969: 39), the remaining Indians had settled as artisans, market-gardeners, cultivators and traders (Kuczynski 1949: 159).[5]

TABLE 5.1: **Importation of Indentured Indians in the East African Protectorate, 1895-1904**

Year	From Bombay	From Karachi	Total
1895-96	0	1,123	1,123
1896-97	3,900	0	3,900
1897-98	1,383	330	1,713
1898-99	0	9,479	9,479
1899-1900	28	9,903	9,931
1900-01	0	8,032	8,032
1901-02	4	0	4
1902-03	0	172	172
1903-04	0	25	25
Total	5,315	29,064	34,379
1904-22	1,926	3,466	5,392
Grand Total	7,241	32,530	39,771

Source: Adapted from Gregory (1971: 53).

The construction of the Uganda railway with the help of Indian immigrants was accompanied by the transplantation of the institutions of British India: British Indian laws, Indian police, Indian postal and currency systems and Indian administrative practices. The impact of the construction of the Uganda railway on the process of voluntary emigration from India was explained by the Protector of Emigrants at Bombay, who in 1896 reported:

> The people are flocking to Africa of their own free will, at their own expense, and on the chance of doing better there . . . many classes and professions are represented in the exodus . . . numbers of Indians are going to East African ports, not as Emigrants, but as adventurers, if I may venture to call them so . . . many have embarked for Mombasa . . . in the hope of finding work on the Uganda Railway, or in connection with the trade and wants that will spring up with the Railway Construction (quoted in Mangat 1969: 48).

No systematic data are available regarding the volume of Indian immigration into East Africa. Figures vary from over 600 in 1898 to about 2,000 in 1901 to 6,218 in 1906-07 and 5,995 in 1907-08 (Mangat 1969: 48; Ramchandani 1976: 52). By 1911 there were 11,787 Indians living in Kenya (Table 5.2). This figure had more than doubled in the next census of 1921. About 43,623 Indians were enumerated in the 1931 Census and 87,687 in the 1948 Census. In 1962, the year of Kenya's independence, the Indian population was 176,613 representing 2.2 per cent of the total Kenyan population (Table 5.2). These figures pertaining to the total number of Indians in Kenya and their proportion to the total population of Kenya remain unsurpassed in Kenya's history.

The majority of Indian immigrants in East Africa have been Gujaratis–both Hindus and Muslims. An important characteristic of the Indian population is its high degree of urbanisation–"a factor which has been responsible for the 'Indian look' of almost all the major towns and cities in East Africa" (Ghai 1965: 93). At least since 1911, the Indians have been the most urbanised community in East Africa. In Kenya in 1962 about 85 per cent of the Indian population was living in the five largest towns. According to the 1969 Census, of the total population of 139,037 Indians, Nairobi had 67,189 (i.e. 48.3%) and Mombasa 39,049 (i.e. 28%).

With the opening up of East Africa, the foundation was laid for the colonial economy in which Indian immigrants emerged as a petty bourgeois class. Since the early twentieth century, the Indian traders–the major component of the Indian petty bourgeoisie–had established themselves all over East Africa: along the railway and old caravan routes, at the administrative posts and in the interior. The Indian *dukawalas* (shopkeepers) traded Indian and European goods (cotton cloths, beads, earthenware, glass and other household items) for a variety of native produce such as cotton, hides, wax, rubber, ivory, copper, grain and foodstuffs. Thus the Indian became an indispensable link in the exchange economy of East Africa. With the advancement of the colonial economy, the Indian traders' role as middlemen was only to grow and be further strengthened.

The other major component of the indian petty bourgeoisie in East Africa was made up of lower-level government employees who worked in an extensive variety of capacities: as artisans, clerks, policemen, customs collectors, cashiers, mechanics, suveyors, draughtsmen, posts and telegraphs assistants, and hospital assistants, etc. In Kenya such Indian employees numbered 866 in 1912 and 1,447 in 1921 (Mangat 1969: 76). In addition, about 1,254 Indians were

TABLE 5.2 **Population in Kenya in Different Census Years, 1911-1979**

	Census Year					
	1911	1921	1948	1962	1969	1979
African			5,251,120	8,365,942	10,733,202	15,101,540
Non-African						
Asian	11,787	25,253	87,687	176,613	139,037	78,600
European	3,175	9,651	29,660	55,759	40,593	39,901
Arab	9,100	10,102	24,174	34,048	27,886	29,146
Other	99	627	3,325	3,901	1,987	67,874
Total Non-African	24,161	45,633	154,8[illegible]6	270,321	209,503	225,521
Total (African & non-African			5,405,966	8,636,263	10,942,705	15,327,061

Source: Kenya, *Statistical Abstract, 1981*, p. 12.

employed on the railways in 1905. This number had increased to 2,000 in 1914 and remained at approximately the same level until 1921 (Mangat 1969: 74). A majority of these employees were Goans.

European Settlement and Plantation Production

The growth of the Indian petty bourgeoisie in Kenya represented only the merchant capital sector of the colonial economy. It was instrumental in creating capitalist social relations at the level of exchange. The other branch of imported capital that created capitalist social relations at the level of production was white settler agriculture. It was the introduction of this second form of capital that was to have far reaching implications on the socio-political evolution of the colony and for whose survival and growth the colonial state vigorously pursued interventionist policies (Lonsdale and Berman 1979). In order to locate the specifically Indian situation in the context of the larger race relations scene in Kenya, it is necessary to provide some detail on settler agriculture and its impact, especially on Africans.

Only a few Europeans entered the East Africa Protectorate before 1900. However, following the passage of the Crown Land Ordinance of 1902 which allowed a maximum of 640 acres of cultivable land and up to 1,000 acres of free-hold land, many Europeans and South Africans were attracted to the colonisation scheme. In the early years of colonisation the European population was as follows: 1902: 506; 1905: 954; 1906: 1,184 (Wolff 1974: 53). The 1911 Census enumerated 3,175 Europeans in Kenya (Table 5.2). In 1919 about 545 families were settled under the Soldier Settlement Scheme. By 1921 the total European population in Kenya was 9,651 (Table 5.2).

A substantial number of settlers were owners of medium-sized holdings (under 1,000 acres). But most settlers aspired to accumulate larger estates and many men like Delamere,[6] Chamberlain, Flemmer and others succeeded in doing so (Tignor 1976: 23). By 1915 more than five millions acres of land had been granted to the settlers throughout the East Africa Protectorate (Sorrenson 1968: 297). Of this land about 20 per cent was held by just five individuals and consortia: Delamere; his brothers-in-law, the Coles; Grogan; the East Africa Syndicate and the East African Estates Ltd. (Sorrenson 1968: 145-46; van Zwanenberg 1975; 37). Much of this land was held idle at first and later was sold to speculators and other settlers at inflated prices.[7]

In spite of substantial alienation of land to European settlers, the operation of the Uganda railway and the increased role of Indian merchant capital, Kenya's was still not a self-sufficient colonial economy until after the First World War. Until then it kept receiving imperial grants-in-aid from London (Wolff 1974: 49). One of the reasons for the initial economic failure in Kenya lay in the indecision of settlers regarding the type of farming (English style or plantation) and the choice of crops (Wrigley 1965: 215; van Zwanenberg 1975: 38). Others included heavy expenditure on the colonial administration, maintenance of the railways, and, most important of all, the pacification of the natives. Of the several native tribal groups numbering between two and a half to three millions around the turn of the century, the Maasais and the Kikuyus, whose ancestral land was usurped by the settlers, were the most antagonistic to the colonial rule. A large number of punitive military expeditions were undertaken for the pacification of these tribes. Such expenditure accounted for as much as 30 per cent of the total Imperial expenditure in the East Africa Protectorate in 1897-98 and 25 per cent in 1905-06. This figure later declined to 7 per cent in 1910-11 and 6 per cent in 1913 (Wolff 1974: 50).

After the initial failure, however, settler agriculture had soon begun to show signs of success. By 1913 the settlers had found maize, coffee and sisal to be the most successful export crops. In 1913, the three crops constituted about 16 per cent of the total domestic export. In 1920 this figure had risen to 47 per cent and in 1930 to 72 per cent (Wolff 1974: 74). The major expansion in settler agriculture occurred between 1920 and 1929. During this period the number of occupiers had almost doubled, the area cultivated had more than trebled and the value of exports had more than quadrupled.

The settlers' need for wage labour was met by increasing the Native Hut and Poll Tax, for the payment of which Africans had to seek employment, mostly on the settlers' farms. These taxes and customs duties were excessively high and together accounted for between 75 per cent and 85 per cent of the total revenues (Brett 1973: 192). As a result of this taxation policy, in conjunction with the pass system,[8] the labour supply increased and remained satisfactory to the settlers throughout the 1920s and subsequently.

The growth and prosperity of settler agriculture blocked the development of African agriculture. One major problem in the way of African agricultural development was the shortage and the poor quality of land. The reservation of the fertile highlands for the exclusive use of white settlers meant that the African peasantry was left with poor quality land which received inadequate rainfall. Some idea of the magnitude of land shortage can be gained from the fact that while 18 per cent of Kenya's best land supported between 4,000 and 14,000 non-Africans, mostly Europeans, during the colonial era, 82 per cent of poor land supported 2,500,000 natives in the period up to 1940, 5,000,000 by 1948 and 10,000,000 by 1969 (van Zwanenberg 1975: 30). Additionally, the colonial state was biased in favour of the settler agriculture. Up to 1940, with only a few exceptions, most government assistance, services, overseas loans, etc. were directed towards the settlers. In fact, African farmers who tried to grow cash crops like coffee and pyrethrum were denied licences by the government. Growing sisal, tea, wheat or sugar was also out of question as their processing required expensive machinery, which Africans could not afford.

Thus, the introduction and growth of settler agriculture generated a series of problems which seriously affected the African peasantry. The shortage of agricultural land coupled with population growth resulted in overcrowding of the reserves. At the same time the traditional tribal land tenure systems began to break down with the attendant problems of increased unemployment. A considerable number of marginal peasants sought employment as wage labourers in the urban areas, where they lived a sort of dual existence (Leakey 1952: 107).

In the white highlands and in the reserves, the agricultural labourers were to face another problem of fluctuating employment opportunities due to such factors as the depression of the early 1930s, the Second World War and the mechanisation of the European farms. This had an adverse effect on the wage level. Thus, during the depression, those who were employed "received 15 per cent to 50 per cent less in wages and salaries than those employed in 1929" (Stichter 1975: 32). In the post-depression period, although the employment situation had eased, the real wages on the average remained constant during the War and in the early fifties. Consequently, the agricultural labourers, whose wages were the lowest, suffered the most, and not surprisingly, were a strong factor behind the Mau Mau rebellion (Barnett and Njama 1966).[9]

In sum, the foundation of the racial problem in Kenya was laid in the colonial economy which had generated extreme class and racial inequalities. The European-owned plantation agriculture was maintained at the expense of the African peasantry with the result that the high rate of native hut and poll taxes, increasing proletarianisation, and the low wages of agricultural workers in conjunction with the emergent African nationalism pushed the whole situation into the Mau Mau rebellion. Although the Mau Mau was primarily directed against the Europeans, as we shall see the Indians were not spared.

II. CLASS AND RACE RELATIONS IN THE COLONIAL PERIOD

The "Indian Question" : Class and Race Relations Between the Indians and Europeans

A review of the literature leads to the conclusion that the so-called "Indian question" in Kenya which at times led to bitter conflict between the European Petty bourgeoisie and its Indian counterpart mainly involved four contentious issues: (i) reservation of the highlands for Europeans, (ii) segregation of Indians in urban areas, (iii) restrictions on Indian immigration, and (iv) the question of political representation of Indians in the legislature. Regarding all these issues, while the Indians demanded equal treatment *vis-a-vis* Europeans, the European settlers, who had considerable hold on the colonial government, attempted to maintain their privileged position.

The "Indian questions" in Kenya had begun to emerge as early as 1902 when a group of European settlers formed the Society to Promote European Immigration to discourage Indian immigration and foster white settlement in the highlands. This organisation petitioned the Commissioner for land grants and mining rights. "It asked that the Africans be made more amenable to European supervision and charged that Indian immigration was 'detrimental to the European settler in particular and to the native inhabitant generally'" (Gregory 1971: 71). The Commissioner of the Protectorate, Sir Charles Eliot, who earlier was in favour of both European and Indian settlement schemes, recommended to the Foreign Office that Indian settlement be confined to the lowlands:

> Believing as I do, that the East Africa Highlands are for the most part a white man's country and hoping that they will be taken up by white colonists in the near future, I doubt the expediency of settling large bodies of Indians in them (quoted in Gregory 1971: 72).

With this the policy of Indian exclusion from the highlands had begun to take place. The official sanction to the policy was given in 1908 when the Secretary of State for the Colonies, Lord Elgin declared:

> It is not consonant with the view of his Majesty's Government to impose legal restrictions on any section of the community, but as a matter of administrative convenience, grants in the upland area should not be made to Asiatics (quoted in Lord Hailey 1957: 406).

Through a political organisation called the Colonists' Association (formed in 1902), the Europeans campaigned for reforms beneficial to white settlement. Settlers, for example, demanded perpetual leases on land without reassessment. Consequently, the Colonial Office, which at first stipulated 21-year leases, had to agree to a 99-year lease-term in 1902 and to 999-year-term in 1915. They were also successful in pressuring the Colonial Office to agree to extend the control of the Governor to cover transfer of land between members of different races, a measure to prevent sale of land to Indians (Hailey 1957: 716). In 1903 the settlers had protested to Eliot over an Indian's purchase at public auction of a plot in the centre of Nairobi. "The Association protested against taxation without representation, the use of African police and Indian currency, and the Government's neglecting to 'maintain white prestige'" (Gregory 1971: 79).

Indian protest against European privileges took several forms. In 1906 Indians founded an Indian Association in Nairobi under the presidency of a pioneer businessman, Allidina Visram. In the same year, the Mombasa Indian Association under the presidency of another businessman, A.M. Jeevanjee, raised Rs. 20,000 at a mass meeting for the purpose of presenting Indian grievances to the local, imperial and Indian governments. Later in the year, Jeevanjee led a deputation to the Colonial Office. In 1907, on the eve of Churchill's visit to East Africa, the Indians formed a Mombasa-based British East Africa Indian Association and presented their grievances to Churchill during his tour (Gregory 1971: 83). Churchill was sympathetic to the problems faced by the Indians. He acknowledged the role of Indians in the economic development of East Africa. Regarding the settlers' attempts to oust Indians from East Africa, Churchill (1908: 50) wrote:

> Is it possible for any government with a scrap of respect for honest dealing between man and man, to embark upon a policy for

deliberately squeezing out the native of India from regions in which he has established himself under every security and public faith?

But despite such enlightened thinking, Kenya's political course became increasingly directed by European settlers. Thus, official sanction was given in 1908 to reserve highlands for exclusive European occupations. To plug any loopholes in the policy, in 1915 the Crown Lands Ordinance had empowered the governor to veto land transactions between the races which in practice closed the doors to any Indian access into the highlands.

Like the question of the highlands reservation, the question of Indian political representation also arose early in the colonial period and was a source of endless debates and disagreements between the Europeans and Indians. In Kenya's first Legislative Council which was formed in 1907 there was no Indian representation. Later following protests from Indians, one of their representatives was nominated to the Council in 1910. This member resigned in 1911 on the question of discriminatory policies against Indians. Thereafter until 1919 there was no Indian representation in the Council (Mangat 1969: 105).

After the First World War, a new generation of Indian leaders emerged on the East African scene.[10] Well educated and with training in law, they helped to organise the Indian communities throughout the Protectorate and renewed their demands for political reforms and racial equality. Already in 1914, the East Africa Indian National Congress was formed to replace the British East Africa Indian Association. Indians intensified their demands following the appointment of a pro-European military governor who after his arrival had declared that "British European preponderance in the government is essential" and that the Indians' demands for equal representation in the central and municipal governments were "untenable". "The bulk of their compatriots in this country", he explained, "are not qualified to vote, in their own, or any other country". Indians were futher outraged by the publication of the report of the Economic Commission (1919) dominated by the settlers. The report referred to Indians in abusive and defamatory language attributing to them "moral depravity" and "incurable repugnance to sanitation and hygiene", and calling them "inciters to crime and vice" – remarks which were later condemned by the Secretary of State in the House of Lords, saying that the Commission had gone "quite outside their terms of reference" (Bennett

1963: 43).[11] Regarding the economic role of Indians in East Africa, the Commission claimed that their presence "deprives the Africans of all incentives to ambition and opportunities of advancement. . . . In every direction the sphere of the Indian in this country is not complemental, but competitive with those of the European and the African" (quoted in Huxley 1967, II: 113). In no uncertain terms, the Commission recommended the Indians' exclusion from the Protectorate.

Meanwhile, the European settlers had already advanced their position by gaining major concessions with respect to land, labour and electoral representation (Bennett 1963: 29-40). Besides gaining monopoly of the highlands through the Crown Lands Ordinance of 1915, the government had passed a set of segregation rules in 1918. The segregation involved residential as well as commercial areas in towns. In the same year the Governor announced that the reconstituted Legislative Council would have eleven European members, while the Indian community would be represented by only two members. He also made it clear "that though Indian interests should not be lost sight of, European interests must be paramount throughout the Protectorate" (Mangat 1969: 117). Additionally, Europeans derived gains from the change of status of Kenya to a Crown Colony in 1920 and the abolition of the rupee currency during 1920-21.

Indians protested vigorously against some of these measures, especially against the proposed reconstitution of the Legislative Council. Their protest increased following the announcement of Milner's despatch in August 1920 which upheld the highland and segregation policies, though relenting on the restriction of free Indian immigration. Another political concession he announced was to have two elected Indian members on the Council based on communal franchise instead of being nominated. He also offered the Indians a special lowlands reserve (Gregory 1971: 190). Indians were not satisfied and decided as a protest not to elect members to the Legislative Council.

The Indian cause received sympathy and encouragement from the British Indian Government on the one hand and the nationalistic leaders in India on the other hand. On two important issues, namely, a common electoral roll and segregation, the Government of India took the following stands:

> We fear that separate representation for the different communities will perpetuate and intensify racial antagonism . . . if the

> qualification for a common franchise is properly defined, it follows that the number of Indian voters will be far less than the number of European voters . . . the fear of Indian domination is, we submit, unfounded (Mangat 1969: 121).
>
> It seems to us, indeed, almost inevitable that compulsory segregation will mean that the best sites will be allotted to the race which is politically more powerful. Further, it can be taken as almost certain that the race which controls the Municipal Council will spend an unfair proportion of the revenue of the Municipality on its own quarter, and will neglect the areas occupied by other races. The practical effect of compulsory segregation on the race which is politically weaker, can be seen in the Asiatic ghettos in the Transvaal (Mangat 1969: 121).

Similarly, Gandhi, also warned that "if ever India becomes lost to Britain and the British Empire, it will not be so much on account of questions of internal administration, . . . but on this question of treatment of Indians in the Colonies" (Gregory 1971: 196).

The Indian cause was also strengthened by the 1921 Imperial Conference which relented in its uncompromising views on Indian rights to pass the following resolution:

> This Conference, while reaffirming that each community should enjoy complete control over the composition of its own population by means of restriction of immigration from any of the other communities, recognises that there is an incongruity between the position of India as an equal member of the Empire and the existence of disabilities upon British Indians lawfully domiciled in some other parts of the Commonwealth, and that in the interests of the solidarity of the Empire it is desirable that the rights of such Indians to citizenship should be recognized (Mangat 1969: 122).

In 1921 Churchill succeeded Milner as Colonial Secretary. In the same year he outlined his 'Indian Policy in Kenya', subsequently known as the 'Montagu-Churchill Proposals', in which "the Indians were offered enfranchisement of approximately ten per cent of their population, a common electoral roll, and a guarantee of three or four seats in the Legislative Council" (Gregory 1971: 201). The highlands policy was retained but the bar on Indian immigration and the segregation in the townships were lifted. The Indians were also promised a 'reserve' in the lowlands. The proposal was a somewhat diluted form of the resolution of the 1921 Imperial Conference. These proposals were soon going to be incorporated into a new constitution. Within a few days, however, Churchill changed his position and delivered a pro-European dinner speech in which he declared:

> We do not contemplate any settlement or system which will prevent British East Africa, or Kenya, as it has now become known, becoming a characteristically and distinctively British Colony looking forward in the full fruition of time to complete responsible self-government (Bennett 1963: 48).

Churchill's vacillation aroused a storm of protest among the Indians and the whole issue was reopened. Governor Northey was abruptly recalled and replaced by Coryndon. A new agreement reached between the Colonial and India Offices known as the 'Wood-Winterton Proposal' (called after their Parliamentary Under-Secretaries) was soon announced. The agreement provided for the following:

(1) a common electoral roll for all British subjects, aged 21 years and upwards with a property qualification and an educational test so arranged as to enfranchise about 10 per cent of the Indian population, and to give Indians four seats on the Legislative Council,
(2) no restriction on immigration,
(3) abolition of segregation,
(4) adequate Indian representation in the municipal councils, and
(5) no change in the White Highlands policy, though kept open for future discussion.

Although according to Churchill, the proposal was only provisional and was "intended to meet difficulties in India", the European settlers felt bitterly frustrated and dissatisfied. A militant solution to the whole problem was contemplated. In fact arrangements were made for a *coup d'etat*–kidnapping of the Governor, taking over of the railways, postal and telegraphic systems, acquisition of more arms and ammunition, etc. (MacPhee 1968: 73; Ross 1927: 375-76). "No physical violence was contemplated against the Indian population, but it was decided to remove them by rail to Mombasa, whence they could be shipped back to India" (Hollingsworth 1960: 95).

The Imperial Government, alarmed by the settler insurgency, invited all the parties concerned (including the so far neglected natives, represented by the Rev. J. Arthur, a Church of Scotland missionary) to a conference in London. The conference lasted for three months and reached a compromise, known as the White Paper of 1923. In that White Paper, the central feature, the doctrine of native paramountcy, was expressed as follows:

> Primarily, Kenya is an African territory, and His Majesty's Government think it necessary definitely to record their considered opinion that the interests of the African natives must be paramount and that if, and when, those interests and the interests of the immigrant races should conflict, the former should prevail. Obviously the interests of the other communities, European, Indian or Arab, must severally be safeguarded. . . . In the administration of Kenya, His Majesty's Government regard themselves as exercising a trust on behalf of the African population, and they are unable to delegate or share this trust, the object of which may be defined as the protection and advancement of the native races.

As expected, there was tremendous outcry against the White Paper both in Kenya and in India. In India, "the Kenya Question" spurred the nationalist movement. Dozens of organisations and associations of various kinds passed resolutions calling for a boycott of British goods. Throughout the rest of the year the Indian Government continued to press for a revision in the paper. As a result of this pressure, the 'Immigrants Regulation and Employment Ordinance, 1923' which was to succeed the 'Immigration Restriction Ordinance' of 1906 and which was being hurriedly passed, had to be eventually postponed (see Gregory 1971: 249-63). In Kenya, in January 1924 following the passage of the Franchise Bill, all Indians resigned from the legislature. About the same time in support of a resolution of the East Africa Indian National Congress to boycott the poll tax, Indians held a mass meeting in Mombasa. Many leaders were arrested and the boycott failed in just two months (Gregory 1971: 276). Nevertheless, the Indian demand for a common roll continued. The "Indian Question" thus remained unsettled: "neither of the protagonists were satisfied with the White Paper of 1923; Europeans because it denied them the right of self-government, and the Indians, because it denied them the ideal of equality" (Mangat 1976: 479-80).

Other issues regarding the "Indian Question" in Kenya after 1923 arose in relation to the proposals for the 'Closer Union' of the three East African territories; restrictions on Indian traders; the government's fiscal policy; discrimination in public service; and renewed attempts to check Indian immigration.

The Closer Union

Notwithstanding the discomfiture with the 1923 White Paper, in the late 1920s the settlers attempted to strengthen their political power by fostering a closer union of Kenya, Uganda and Tanganyika.[12] Behind the idea of building "a new dominion" was the fear of the settlers that 'the native paramountcy' principle enshrined in the White Paper would lead to the expansion of native peasant agriculture resulting in the shortage of labour available to them. In a settler-controlled dominion, the settlers reasoned, the labour shortage could be averted by pressuring more and more natives into accepting wage labour and by bringing in more Europeans, especially Italians, as labourers (Bennett 1963: 60). However, although administratively the Union did not materialise until 1948 when the East Africa High Commission was formed, a Customs Union of the three territories was created in 1930. The Indians were opposed to the proposals for the Union on the ground that this would lead to the European settlers' dominance in East Africa (Mangat 1969: 148). The operation of the Customs Union was also opposed by the Indians. Appearing before the Moyne Commission (1932), the Indian Merchants' Chamber at Mombasa and the East Africa Indian National Congress complained that "the tariff was designed to favour the development of local European products and greatly augmented the Indians' cost of flour, sugar, timber, rice and dairy products including *ghee*" (Gregory 1971: 425). They also pointed out that the duty on cotton piece goods amounted to 42 per cent of their current value. The Commission, however, had dismissed the Indians' complaint with the remark that the tariff was just.

Restrictions on Indian Traders

In 1932 the Kenya Government had introduced the Marketing of Native Produce Bill that severely affected a large number of Indian traders.[13] Until then the Indians had traded freely with the natives, buying the latters' produce and selling them imported goods. The passage of the bill involved the establishment of special marketing facilities and provision for exclusive licences for the purchase of certain commodities. The trade licence fees were increased from 200 s. to 300 s. for import-export and from 300 s. to 450 s. for retail trade. "The government's purpose was to standardize marketing procedures, increase official supervision, and provide more security for African agriculturalists" (Gregory 1971: 449). Indians, however, opposed the legislation fearing that while the grant of exclusive licences would lead to a monopoly of a few big traders at the expense of many small traders, the establishment of separate marketing facilities for different produces would ruin the existing Indian trading centres in the interior. The Federation of Indian Chambers of Commerce and Industry in East Africa and Mr. K.P.S. Menon, who was deputed by the Government of India to report about the said legislation, made detailed criticism of the bill and pointed out that by inhibiting free competition it "would work against the interests of both of the Indian country trader and the African producer" (Mangat 1969: 157). Eventually, despite Indian complaints that the legislation would squeeze them out of the country, the bill was passed in 1935.

Similar Indian charges that the Europeans were manipulating economic forces to oust the Indians were later repeated when transport licensing legislation was introduced in 1937 in order to protect the railway from the competition of road transport, in which the indians had acquired considerable interests since the mid-1920s (Mangat 1969: 158).

The East Africa Royal Commission of 1953-55 later was critical of the undesirable results of misguided attempts to protect Africans from the more sophisticated Indian traders. According to the report of the Commission (1955: 69), the system of state-regulated trade had "undermined the ability of traders to utilise their stores and working capital fully throughout the year, and [had] reduced their opportunities and inducements to venture their capital in new enterprises." In some cases, in the opinion of the Commission, the bill had duplicated the effort and resources devoted to marketing and had thus increased the cost of distributing both imported supplies and locally manufactured goods.

The Fiscal Policy

In the early 1930s Indians also made frequent allegations "that government expenditure was weighted in favour of the Europeans, and that the fiscal policies–especially the protective customs duties and railway freight rates for agricultural products as well as subsidies to the farmers–directly favoured European agricultural interests, whereas the actual revenue derived from the different races did not justify such measures" (Mangat 1969: 154).

Discrimination in Government Service

Indian employees in both public and private services experienced various obstacles regarding appointment or promotion to top level jobs, salary scales and terms and conditions of services. Indians first articulated their concerns about these matters in 1934-35 when they protested against the establishment of separate terms of service for the European and Indian staff in the public service. At that time, the salary scales of Indian public servants were two to four times lower than those of their European counterparts (Kondapi 1951: 355; Mangat 1969: 155).

Indians were generally barred from appointment and/or promotion to higher posts in the government service or industry. In 1936 an Indian member of the Legislative Council complained about the position of Indians in the police service in the following words: "An Indian, no matter how efficient, how capable and deserving, cannot rise above the rank of a wretched sub-inspector in this Colony" (quoted in Mangat 1969: 156). This remark can be taken as indicative of the position of Indians in the public service generally.[14]

Restrictions on Indian Immigration

As pointed out earlier, the White Paper of 1923 had prohibited any control on Indian immigration in Kenya, subject to the condition that there would not be a large influx of Indian immigrants. However, when Europeans failed to check Indian immigration directly, they attempted to check it indirectly–by levying prohibitive immigration and repatriation fees. Thus, the Kenya Immigration Restriction Ordinance (Amendment) Act of 1938 had raised the deposit security from 50 pounds, which in effect had already excluded the entry of Indian labourers and artisans, to 500 pounds which was designed to exclude middle class immigrants (Kondapi 1951: 195).

Further proposals to restrict Indian immigration were made during the Second World War on the ground of scarcity of job opportunities. Despite Indian protest, these proposals were incorporated into the Revised Immigration Restriction Bill of 1949. Following the passage of this bill, the immigration of single Indians arriving for employment was significantly curtailed. During the 1949-56 period, only 6,452 Indians were allowed to enter Kenya as compared to 6,580 Europeans. During the same period, 926 Indians as opposed to only 71 Europeans were denied entry (Tinker 1977: 119). Nevertheless, Indians continued to arrive in large numbers as dependents.

From the above exposition of the "Indian Question" in Kenya it is obvious that the conflict between the European settlers and the Indians tended to be protracted and bitter. Besides economic factors discussed earlier, one major reason for this was that initially both parties had imperialist designs on Kenya.[15] While at least until the Second World War the settlers fought for self-government on the model of South Africa, the Indians after early setbacks merely kept on resisting the settlers' imperialist design. Therefore, one of the most important outcomes of this conflict was that Kenya did not become another South Africa. As one historian put it:

> That the East African territories did not consummate a closer union and that Kenya did not proceed to self-government under European control–in short, that the history of South Africa was not repeated in East Africa was to a great degree a result of Indian opposition (Gregory 1971: 496).

Additionally, in the opinion of Indian nationalist leaders, Kenya became a test case for the ideal of racial equality within the British empire. That eventually the Indians lost in the conflict was also a foregone conclusion; settler agriculture, after all, was central to the bilateral integration of the colonial and imperial economies.

In spite of unfair competition from European settlers, the growth of the Indian middle classes continued through the Second World War. Two factors–the post-war prosperity and the expansion of educational facilities–largely accounted for this (Delf 1963: 43-45). The total number of Indians in employment rose from 18,200 in 1946 to about 38,000 in 1960. Whereas in 1946, 10,400 Indians were employed in private industry and commerce and 7,300 in the public services, in 1960 the comparable figures were 25,600 and 11,800 (Delf 1963: 45). Thus, between 1946 and 1960, there was more rapid expansion of

Indian employment in trade and commerce than in public service. This can be explained by the fact that until the abolition of racial terms of service and salary scales in 1955, "European control of selection boards, together with the substantial increase in pay given to Europeans by way of inducement and expatriate allowances, made the public service unattractive to the most talented Asians" (Delf 1963: 45). Hence the Indian predominance in trade and commerce–a situation which was as much thrust upon the Indians as deliberately chosen by them.

Class and Race Relations Between Indians and Africans

The class antagonisms between Indians and Africans in Kenya can be analysed in terms of their two major components: (i) the relations between the Indian and the African peasantry as traders and producers/consumers, and (ii) the intra-class conflict between the Indian and African petty bourgeoisie fractions. From the point of view of Indian involvement, the scope of the latter was wider: whereas the first form of class and race relations involved only the Indian traders, the second form of relations additionally involved Indian public servants, a segment of the petty bourgeoisie. Before further examining their inter-relationship and their impact on race relations involving Indians in Kenya, it would be useful to discuss them separately.

Relations Between the Indian Traders and the African Peasantry

Class relations between the Indian traders and the African peasantry had both positive and negative aspects. On the positive side, the historical contribution of the Indian traders in East Africa lies in introducing and expanding the monetary economy into the predominantly non-capitalist subsistence economy.[16] Since the "opening up" of the interior in the late nineteenth century, the Indian traders introduced a wide variety of imported consumer goods, thus stimulating the natives' desire for money incomes. In the context of barter trade, they bought local produce, thus inducing the natives to produce beyond their subsistence needs (Ghai 1965: 101; Mangat 1969: 84-87; Ramchandani 1976: 32-35, 81-104). Thus, the growth of cotton cultivation in Uganda was largely due to the Indian traders who connected the export with the Bombay textile industry. In Kenya, as elsewhere in East Africa, the Indian traders were extensively involved in the purchase of ivory, sesame, chillies, groundnuts, *ghee*, beewax, grain, hides, and skins, etc. In return, the Indians sold mainly cotton cloth, kerosene oil, lamps, beads, hoes and bicycles. Such an exchange was obviously useful and profitable to both parties and to the overall development of the region. As the Nyanza Province (Kenya) Annual Report of 1910 indicated, "the people are daily finding fresh wants and the local Indian traders are endeavouring to meet them" (quoted in Mangat 1969: 86). Similar sentiments about the role of the Indian traders *vis-a-vis* African producers and consumers and in relation to their economic contribution to East Africa were echoed by a number of colonial officials. Sir John Kirk, Consul-General of Zanzibar and one of the founders of the Imperial British East Africa Company, in his evidence before the Sanderson Committee (1910), stated: "Drive away the Indians and you may shut up the (East Africa) Protectorate" (quoted in Mangat 1969: 95). Before the same Committee, Colonel Grogan, a wealthy settler who was bitterly opposed to the presence of Indians in East Africa, conceded that without the Indians' intermediate role, the Protectorate would "collapse like a puff ball" (Mangat 1969: 95). Perhaps the best testimonial to the Indian traders' contribution to East African economic development was given by the Hilton Young Commission of 1927 which in its report said:

> The Indian trader has been a potent factor in the process of civilising. . . . The 'dukawala', or petty shopkeeper, has carried his wares far and wide into remote areas. . . . By increasing their (Africans) wants he has created an incentive to effort and thus shown the first seeds of economic progress. The Indian dealer has performed another useful function in marketing the products of native agriculture . . . their activities have undoubtedly stimulated the spread of cotton civilisation in Uganda (Mangat 1969: 96).

The negative aspect of Indian-African relations in Kenya generally involved the widespread criticism of Indian traders for their alleged dishonest practices in business transactions–mainly in respect of the use of short or false weights, hoarding and bargaining. "It is perhaps also true that many Asian traders have shown themselves more interested in quick profits rather than in steady, long-term gains, and have not hesitated to exploit temporary scarcities to make windfall gains" (Ghai 1965: 104).

To put these charges of exploitation of Africans by the Indian traders into perspective, it must be pointed out that such malpractices in business were not peculiar to Indian traders in East Africa. As the Hilton Young Commission Report (1929) rightly noted, such charges "are brought against middlemen all the world over, and no doubt the ignorance of the African offers special opportunities to the unscrupulous" (Mangat 1969: 95). Peasants, however, were not always that "ignorant" as the Commission implied; they had devised their own tricks to match those of the traders. About the Ugandan farmers, for example, it was observed:

> Up to the early 1920s there were no fixed weights or prices and producers believed that the weighing scales would be fixed against them, or that a lesser weight would be written on the slip of paper taken to the accountant. Peasants retaliated by bribing the man who weighted the cotton by wetting the crop to increase its weight or even by putting stones in the bag covered by cotton (van Zwanenberg 1975: 203).

Such malpractices on the part of producers as well as traders are indeed common in all peasant and/or less developed capitalist economies, especially in rural areas. These malpractices are derived from the fact that in such economies, profits/earnings of both parties are usually small and therefore each of them acts to maximise them. It is for this reason that the small producers/consumers, who have no easy access to a competitive market, are exploited the most. Conversely, the exploiters generally happen to be the small traders who have small turn-over and therefore resort to unfair practices in order to raise their income.[17] It must also be stressed that in this class conflict between small peasants and traders, the traders are usually the winners, because they control the terms of exchange at the local levels. The peasants compensate their loss at the ideological level–through sharing negative stereotypes of traders, which invariabily centre around their exploitative role. In the light of the above discussion it is understandable that the exploitation of Africans took place at the hands of Indian traders, which tended to generate racial feelings and distrust. However, it was not the African peasantry but the African petty bourgeoisie which articulated these racial feelings as an ideological weapon and used them against its competitor, the Indian petty bourgeoisie.

Intra-class Conflict Between the Indian and African Fractions of Petty Bourgeoisie

This form of class conflict had begun to emerge as early as the 1930s, but was not fully crystallised until after the Second World War. The reason for this was that prior to the post-World War II period, the African fraction of Kenyan petty bourgeoisie was still in its infancy. The dominance of settler agriculture had inhibited the growth of the African petty bourgeoisie. Similarly, the African trading class was handicapped by the dominance of Indian and European traders and the European monopoly buyers and the marketing boards. At the same time, lack of education among Africans prevented any significant growth of middle class. After the Second World War, some of these disabilities were removed resulting from the development of political and economic conditions which partially changed the course of colonial policies in favour of the African middle class in Kenya.

The emergent political conditions involved the growth of African nationalism and its impact on the various aspects of colonial economy and society. African nationalism in Kenya had begun to emerge as early in 1922 with the formation of the Kikuyu Central Association whose objective was to recover the "lost land" from the white settlers (Leakey 1952: 86). The Kikuyu Central Association (K.C.A.) and its various sister organisations such as Baluya (Kavirondo) Taxpayers Welfare Association, Wakamba (Ukamba) Members Association and Wateita (Teita Hills) Association subsequently demanded political representation, removal of Hut Tax and the *kipande* (pass) system, provision for education, payment of full wages for all work performed by the native for the government in the reserves, and the grant of title deeds to the people for their lands as security against confiscation by the settlers (Nabudere 1981: 75). Such demands were presented by the natives before the Hilton Young Commission (1927) and the Kenya Land Commission (1931) among others.

Besides the above issues, one issue which greatly fuelled African nationalism in Kenya was the objections by some missionary societies to the Kikuyu custom of clitoridectomy, linked with the initiation of young girls from childhood to womanhood. The majority of Kikuyu took this to be a violent attack on an age-old custom and turned to form independent churches (i.e. independent of the Church of Scotland) and independent schools that became centres of Kikuyu nationalism (Bennett 1963: 77; Leakey 1952: 89-90).

By the 1930s, the K.C.A. had widened its support among other tribes and in the urban areas, culminating in the 1939 dock-workers' strike in Mombasa. Subsequently, during the war the K.C.A. was banned and its leaders arrested. In the post-war period as the K.C.A. was not allowed to be revived by the colonial government, a new political organisation called the Kenya African Union (K.A.U.) was formed in 1944. During the early 1950s, this became the vanguard of the Mau Mau rebellion, which was brewing among the Kikuyu squatters in the highlands over the agrarian issue (Barnett and Njama 1966; Rosberg and Nottingham 1966). Thus, by the mid-1940s, Africans in Kenya were fully prepared to launch their struggle against colonialism.

An allied political factor in the immediate post-war years was the increasing Indian participation in African nationalism. In 1929, an Indian leader, Isher Dass, accompanied Jomo Kenyatta, then an emerging African leader, to London to present Kikuyu problems before the imperial government. The 1939 Mombasa dock-workers' strike was led by another Indian leader, Makhan Singh, who was the founder of the Labour Trade Union of East Africa in 1936 (Mangat 1969: 169). Earlier in 1932-33, six prominent Indian leaders appeared before the Kenya Land Commission and highlighted the African grievances regarding land, arguing that no more land should be alienated to non-natives, irrespective of race–Indian or European. Dass in his evidence said:

> Out here everyone depends upon the African for manual work. The European supervises only. The time is coming when the sons of the soil (the Africans) will resent this. . . . We want a healthy and prosperous African peasantry, who will be able to compete with the world (quoted in Gregory 1971: 436).

Further impetus to the Indian-African collaboration was provided by India's Independence in 1947 and the increased support this event provided for African nationalism. In 1951 one settler writer E. Huxley described this cooperation in the following words:

> African newspapers are printed on terms of easy credit on Indian presses; Indians give money to such bodies as K.A.U.; African political leaders are made welcome in Indian houses; one of the K.A.U. officials (James Beauttah) is now touring India as a guest.

> The latest move, which has aroused great African enthusiasm, is the award of five scholarships to take Kenya Africans to Indian universities (Mangat 1969: 176).

During the emergency in Kenya (1952-60) four Indian lawyers participated in the defence of Jomo Kenyatta at the Kapenguria trial in 1952-53. Nehru strongly criticised the handling of the Mau Mau rebellion by the British Government,[19] and because of his friendship with Kenyatta the Indian High Commission to Kenya, Apa Pant, became very unpopular with the colonial authorities.

On the whole, however, it must be said that the Indian participation in African nationalism was limited both quantitatively and qualitatively. Their somewhat privileged class position did not allow them to fully identify with African nationalism (Tandon 1965: 75-81), and therefore did not earn them any significant degree of political legitimacy and respect in the eyes of Africans. During the post-colonial period this became one of the points of friction between the Indians and Africans. In any case, even this limited Indian political participation in African nationalism had become a cause for concern for the colonial authorities in Kenya during the 1940s and thereafter.

The post-war economic situation in Britian also compelled the British to adopt a new colonial development policy. As a result of the War, Britain was indebted to the U.S. to the tune of $311 million in 1948 (Swainson 1980: 105). Additionally, during and after the War there was an increased demand for food and raw material in the U.K. Consequently, the changed imperial policy was to raise the production of raw material in the colonies (Nabudere 1981: 63). Besides increasing agricultural production, a limited degree of industrialisation was also encouraged. In the 1950s, these measures were supplemented by the agrarian reforms which had become necessary in the wake of Mau Mau and the resultant 'politics of accommodation' (Harbeson 1973: 25-53).

It was against this back-drop that the African petty bourgeoisie in Kenya had begun to consolidate its position after the Second World War. The changed colonial policy was primarily concentrated on the economic development of native reserves, especially in the Kikuyu areas where the Mau Mau movement was strong. To assist African agriculture, in 1953 the government provided 7 million pounds. At the same time a number of land reform measures such as land consolidation, better credit facilities to farmers, grant of individual titles, and permission to grow cash crops were adopted, which facilitated the polarisation of peasantry into landed and landless classes (Harbeson 1973: 35). The landed class became the African agricultural petty bourgeoisie. Not surprisingly, this class was also the target of the Mau Mau rebellion in its later phase (Harbeson 1973: 22-23). The African landed class was further strengthened following the land transfer programme initiated in 1961. By 1970 about 53,400 families (involving nearly half a million people) had been resettled at the cost of 29 million pounds, of which 14 million pounds were borrowed from abroad (Leys 1975: 74).

After the Second World War, the African trading class which had emerged in the 1920s and was subjected to various restrictions, also received encouragement from the government through various loan schemes and other forms of assistance. Consequently, the African trading class had begun to expand rather rapidly. For example, in 1946, out of 749 new trading licences issued in Central Kavirondo, 632 were held by Africans. In the Nyanza province in 1945-46, about 3,000 applications were received for trading licences. This was a countrywide phenomenon (Swainson 1980: 177). In fact, due to a large number of applications in the rural areas, the government had to limit the number of traders.

Loans to African traders during the 1950s were administered by the Joint Boards consisting of colonial bureaucrats and African representatives. Between 1958 and 1963 further loans were dispensed through the Industrial Development Corporation. In one such scheme, loans totalling 121,000 pounds were made available to 820 traders (Swainson 1980: 180). More important than these government schemes for the growth of African commercial class, however, was the initiative taken by some foreign firms, which in the 1950s "extended wholesale facilities to African traders in the reserves for distribution of their products" (Swainson 1980: 180). These manufactured products included tobacco, cigarettes, shoes, beer, mobile oil, etc. By the end of the colonial period, some African merchants had also begun to move into small-scale manufacturing. There was thus a substantial growth in the size of the African petty bourgeoisie in the late colonial period.

The growth of the African petty bourgeoisie meant the development of a certain amount of conflict with its Indian counterpart. But it appears that this conflict was not fully crystallised until after Kenya's independence. In 1932 the Moyne Commission noted some complaints by certain African groups based in Nairobi and

Mombasa against Indians regarding discrimination in the government:

> The gradual attainment of a higher level of education and civilization by the African is being accompanied by a claim to equal treatment with the Asian in the matter of employment, pay, and conditions in the public services (quoted in Gregory 1971: 245).

However, at that time the competition was not sharp, though the Commission saw such a possibility in the near future:

> The time will surely come in Kenya, as it has already come in Uganda, when a considerable number of Africans will be available who will be just as well qualified as Asians, to man the lower ranks of the Government services (quoted in Gregory 1971: 426).

That time in Kenya did not come until after independence when under the Africanisation policy the Indian share in the civil service was significantly reduced (Ghai and Ghai 1971: 19).

A somewhat similar situation existed regarding the competition between the African and Indian trading class. Owing to the restricted government credit policy regarding Africans, typified in such measures as the Credit to Natives Ordinance of 1926, the African enterprises though larger in number remained smaller in size. However, the 1932 Marketing of Native Produce Bill was more detrimental to the Indian traders' interests than to their African counterparts. It was from then on that the competition between the Indian and African traders began to intensify. In the 1930s and subsequently, while the Indians demanded the removal of marketing restrictions in favour of free trade, the African traders demanded the removal of Indian traders from the reserves, and government assistance including better credit facilities for the expansion of African trade. Thus there was a considerable amount of competition between the two fractions of the petty bourgeoisie. As one observer noted, some Indian traders attempted to avoid such competition by moving out of the reserves and the small towns into the larger cities (Kondapi 1951: 339). In the late 1950s the African traders were still petitioning the colonial government to restrict the Indian traders who were importing commodities into the reserves (Swainson 1980: 179).

By the 1950s, the class-based African grievances against the

Indians had merged into broader national consciousness, i.e. racially exclusive African nationalism, which subsequently became the basis of the Africanisation policy in the post-independence period.

III. CLASS AND RACE RELATIONS IN THE POST-COLONIAL PERIOD

During the post-colonial period, the first priority of the new ruling class, consisting largely of the African petty bourgeoisie, was to consolidate its own economic base. Three key sectors of the economy where Africanisation could easily be implemented were agriculture, commerce and bureaucracy. During the process of decolonisation a section of the European settler agricultural bourgeoisie had already moved out of agriculture. Heavily subsidised by the British Government, the land settlement schemes coupled with political independence tended to generate a sense of goodwill between the Kenyan Europeans and Africans. The displaced Europeans had moved to the manufacturing sector of the economy where foreign capital was openly welcome by the new regime represented by the ruling party, the Kenya African National Union (K.A.N.U.),[18] as part of its developmental strategy (Nabudere 1981: 118-28).

Amongst Indians, the civil servants were the first to be affected by the process of Africanisation. According to one estimate, in the first year of independence alone, the number of Indian civil servants was reduced by over 3,000 from 11,900 in 1963 to 8,800 in 1964 (Ghai and Ghai 1971: 19). Although in the wake of rapid expansion of the bureaucracy in the post-colonial period, the number of Indian civil servants had risen to 10,600 in 1966, by 1968 it had again declined to 8,000 (Ghai and Ghai 1971: 19). Thus within this five-year period of independence, the number of Indian civil servants had declined by about 4,000. It is believed that the majority of Indians thus affected were non-citizens. In this connection, the 1967 Immigration Act played the key role in that it made it obligatory for non-citizens in certain categories of occupations to obtain work permits. In early 1968, some 8,000 work permits were issued. These work permits were valid for periods from one to two years in the case of secretaries, artisans, masons and carpenters, and from six months to one year in the case of salesmen, shop assistants, etc. (Rothchild 1973: 265). It was expected that in due course, local staff would be trained to take over from non-citizens (Tandon 1973: 16; Tinker 1977: 129). At the same time, the act also controlled further immigration of Indians into Kenya.

If the 1967 Immigration Act promoted Africanisation at the expense of Indian Government servants and other wage earners in the private sector, the Trading Licensing Act of 1967 fulfilled the same function in the commercial sector of the economy. Under this act, which did not come into effect until January 1969, the non-citizens without licences were barred from trading in certain areas (mostly rural) and in most of the consumer goods. This move virtually forced the non-citizen Indian traders to go to five major cities and towns declared as "general business areas" where all traders irrespective of their citizenship status were required to obtain new trading licences. In 1969 and 1970, about 3,000 traders were refused licences in Kenya (Ghai and Ghai 1971: 21; Rothchild 1973: 266-70; Tinker 1977: 130). Although a majority of affected Indians were non-citizens, some citizen businessmen of Indian origin were also affected.

The 1967 Immigration and Trading Licences Acts had introduced a mood of near-panic in the Kenya Indian community. Many feared that they would be deported. Indian emigration, which had begun to offset immigration as early as 1962, continued to rise during the late sixties. As a large majority of Indians were British passport holders (between 52,000 to 67,000 out of their estimated total population of 140,000 in 1969; see Rothchild 1973: 408, fn 13), they increasingly emigrated to Britain. A total of about 13,000 Kenya Indians emigrated to Britain in 1965 and 1966 (Tinker 1977: 130). Amidst speculation that the U.K. was considering closing the door against British citizens of Asian origin, 13,600 Asians emigrated to Britain in 1967 and probably another 10,000 in the first two months of 1968 (Tandon 1973: 19). Consequently, Indian population in Kenya declined from 176,613 in 1962 to 139,037 in 1969 (Table 5.2). Following the mass expulsion of about 50,000 Indians from Uganda in 1972 (Twadle 1975), the Kenyan Indian population further declined to 78,600 in 1979, of whom only 32,554 were citizens (*Statistical Abstract* 1981: 14).

Finally, in spite of the fact that the Indian entrepreneurial class had the financial potential of incorporating itself into the indigenous industrial bourgeoisie, it was not allowed to expand into the manufacturing sector. Already in 1961, over 67 per cent of all locally owned industrial enterprises with fifty or more employees were Indian-owned (Leys 1975: 45). In 1971 about two-thirds of the non-farm private assets were in Indian hands (Table 5.3). About half of their capital was in real estate (Table 5.3; also Bharati 1972: 150). But

Kenyan officials preferred Western transnational capital in alliance with an African auxiliary bourgeoisie. These multinationals whose investment in Kenya in 1968 accounted for 60 per cent of the total investment in the manufacturing sector, made huge profits and reptriated them abroad (for example, 1,600 million pounds in 1964-70 period; see Leys 1975: 137-38). Although the negative implications of this externally-oriented economy in terms of unemployment, balance of payment, drainage of resources, uneven development, exploitation of labour and the suppression of the labour movement were not apparent until the 1970s, it was obvious that without the partnership of foreign capital, the African bourgeoisie would not have been able to compete with and undermine its Indian counterpart. In this connection the neo-colonial state in which Indians have little say and whose relationship with foreign capital has been characterised as a "symbiotic one" played an increasingly active role (Godfrey and Langdon 1976; Swainson 1980: 16-18).

TABLE 5.3 **Approximate Distribution of Private Non-Farm Assets (but including Plantations), 1971 (in million Pounds)**

	Asians	Non-Asians
Industry or plantations	70	120
Shares in public companies	20	30
Real estate	200	15
Trade	100	25
Cash	35	35
Total	425	225

Source: Leys (1975: 120).

Devoid of political power in Kenya, the Indian petty bourgeoisie (especially non-citizens) resisted Africanisation by resorting to tactics that would amount to "economic sabotage" (Mamdani 1976: 262). This primarily included the illegal transfer of assets abroad. No definite estimates of such transfers are available, but the alleged means used for the purpose were widely known, even to the government. According to the Attorney-General of Kenya, Indians sent money abroad by

> smuggling currency or gold, purchasing air passage tickets at

> inflated prices and receiving back the balance, subsidizing the passage of poor Asians in order to utilize their emigration allowance, underpricing goods sold abroad and crediting the difference between the actual selling price and the declared price, inflating the price of imports, collecting travellers checks (*sic*) or convertible currencies and sending them abroad, leaving tourist payment in overseas banks, and having commissions owed to Kenya manufacturers' agents retained abroad (Rothchild 1973: 415, fn 135).

However, as a contemporary observer pointed out, "not all Asians indulged, or could afford to indulge, in these practices, nor indeed were these practices confined to the Asian only, for Europeans and African ministers were often as conversant with these practices as the wealthiest and the shrewdest Asians" (Tandon 1973: 18).

Besides illegal transfer of money, the legal transfer of assets allowed to the emigrants (5,000 pounds until 1968 and 2,500 pounds subsequently *plus* minor allowances to children) was itself becoming a drain on the economy. Thus, according to one estimate based on withdrawals from the Nairobi Bank, "capital transfers to Britain comprised 25 million pounds in the late 1967 to early 1968 period" (Rothchild 1973: 404). Obviously, this scale of capital transfer may not all have been due to the Indian emigrants; as already mentioned, profit transfer by multinationals must have been a major factor. The Indians were nevertheless blamed.

In addition to their role in the capital drain, another charge against Indians, which tended to undermine the spirit of Africanisation, was the lack of business collaboration between Indians and Africans. In 1967, the Trading Licensing Act required increasing trade partnership between Africans and non-Africans. Very few Indians, however, responded to this call. In a survey of the Indian businesses in Kenya in 1967 it was found that "a large number of respondents simply did not deem such associations to be practicable" (Rothchild 1973: 349). Most of the Indian businesses were either owned singly, or were joint family affairs and therefore preferred not to enter into partnership with Africans. A few of them who took in Africans complained that the latter lacked business "ethic" and skills–they expected to receive profits without first making any contribution to earnings (Bhatia 1973: 88).[19]

Some non-citizen Indians had entered into fake joint partnerships registering the businesses in the name of Africans or inactive (e.g. minors) citizen Indians. African leaders were naturally resentful of such "window dressing" Africanisation, and consequently tightened up the Trade Lincensing Act as it was applied to partnership procedures.

Indian reaction to Africanisation in terms of remittances, emigration, etc., also generated a fair amount of corruption in the bureaucracy. As Tandon (1973: 17) put it, in the late 1960s, a constant subject of conversation among the Indians was as to "which officials in the local Immigration Department, Ministry of Commerce, or British High Commission were open to corruption. . . . The situation gave rise to a whole new breed of entrepreneurs, called simply 'agents' who would perform services, such as securing a passport or a work permit or a British quota voucher, with or without bribes, for what sometimes were extortionate fees."

Indian exodus from East Africa was itself considered by Africans as proof of the lack of commitment among Indians to Kenya. On the eve of independence, African leaders warned Indians to take up citizenship of Kenya as a proof that they were serious about staying in Africa (Mboya 1963: 109-13). Non-citizen Indians, however, remained ambivalent about taking up Kenyan citizenship for two important reasons: (i) a large majority of them held British passports and as their destination of exodus showed, they eventually wanted to settle in Britain, and (ii) the political events in neighbouring countries (e.g. the 1957 Indian trade boycott in Uganda, civil wars in Congo, Rwanda and Burundi, and the 1964 revolution in Zanzibar) had unsettling effect on Indians, who tended to think that the neo-colonial regimes might be a threat to their position of privilege and security.[20] Not surprisingly, in 1960 the Indian National Congress in Kenya and its counterpart in Uganda, the Central Council of Indian Association, advocated the communal franchise for Indians–ironically, the very proposal against which Indians had fought throughout the colonial period. The proposal was not only rejected by the African leaders, but it was also unacceptable to the new generation of Indian leaders, who recognised it as providing only a false sense of security.

The only event involving racial violence against Indians occurred during the August 1982 attempted coup, which was masterminded by Kenya's now disbanded Air Force. The attempted coup resulted in at least 145 deaths (all Africans) and about $120 million worth of damages (mostly to Indian business and property). According to press reports, more than a hundred women were raped (about 40 being

Indians) during the anarchy on 1 August, or later by government troops conducting house to house searches for rebels.

The coup enjoyed wide support among the people, including university students. The reasons behind the coup were mainly economic: growing poverty and unemployment, persisting inequalities and increasing corruption in the government and bureaucracy. During the first half of the Kenyatta era (1963-78), Kenya had achieved some measure of economic success: an average annual GDP growth of 6.5 per cent between 1964 and 1973, agricultural growth of 6.0 per cent, which in the 1970s declined to about 2.0 per cent. By the early 1970s, Kenya's land settlement schemes assisted by the British were also completed, creating a rich African agricultural bourgeoisie in the process. At the same time, Africanisation of the civil service also provided employment to the educated Africans and the civil service grew by more than 40 per cent during the same period. In spite of all these figures, and in spite of the 1976 coffee and tea boom, Kenya's economy had begun to decline in the early 1970s. Agricultural production fell by about 4 per cent annually. Falling commodity prices and rising import costs have deteriorated the country's international terms of trade by more than 27 per cent since 1976. Moreover, Kenya's population is increasing at the rate of 4 per cent annually–the fastest rate in Africa. All this contributed to the unsuccessful coup and continue to breed popular discontent in Kenya.

Although the coup was promptly averted, its more immediate impact was felt by the 80,000 strong Indian community, whose fragile sense of security in Kenya had again been shaken. Shortly after the coup, on 4 September, 1982, President Daniel Arap Moi made a statement, apparently aimed at reassuring Indians. He urged insurance companies to reverse their decision against compensating businessmen whose properties were looted during the averted coup. Three days later, Mr. John Keen, a junior minister appealed to Indians to remain in Kenya by maintaining that Nairobi's looting was not as grave as that experienced during the 1982 police strike in Bombay or during the rioting the year before in Liverpool. He said:

> If Asian shops were looted, so were African shops. If Asian women were raped, the number of African women raped was bigger. The only difference here is that while 159 Africans were lying dead in the mortuary, there was not one member of the Asian community killed. I see no reason therefore, why they should

> panic, because Kenya has afforded them, and will continue to afford them, a paradise of peace (*African Recorder* 1982: 6017).

In another statement he emphasised the fact that the Indian community had been more exposed because of its location in the centre of the city: "Since they happened to have more shops in the city centre they suffered most because they became victims, not because of religion, background or creed" (*Africa Diary* 1983: 11343).

Such reassuring statements generally reflect the current policy of the Kenyan ruling class towards the minorities–Europeans, Indians and Arabs. These minorities in Kenya generally represent foreign capital and skill in coalition with indigenous capital, and as such the ruling class greatly benefits from this class-coalition. This is so because the neo-colonial economy of Kenya characteristically generates limited economic growth at the expense of distributive justice. Those who potentially oppose this class-coalition are the African masses–peasantry, working class and a fraction of the commercial petty bourgeoisie, the latter being particularly frustrated by the entrenched position of its Indian counterpart in the economy. As Kenya has been a one-party state from independence,[21] the African masses do not find the legitimate expression of their grievances. One form of expression, of course, was the averted coup, which was primarily directed at changing the regime, but whose convenient target was the Indians. Occasionally, however, Indians are criticised for unscrupulous commercial practices (e.g. hoarding, blackmarketing, remittances, bribery etc.) by some KANU back-benchers or a few junior ministers in the parliament. It is during these debates in the parliament that the social exclusiveness of Indians is highlighted and their lack of integration ("inter-racial marriage") along with their "sojourning" attitude are pointed out. On the whole, since the late 1970s, Indians in Kenya appear to be better placed than before. Their position in the given class structure of Kenya, however, continue to remain the source of their vulnerability as well as their strength.

IV. SUMMARY AND CONCLUSIONS

In Kenya the initial situation of racial discrimination against Indians arose in relation to European settlers. This involved several issues. One major issue was the European merchants' inability to compete with their Indian counterparts. Indian merchants were successful in undercutting European merchants mainly because the former seemed satisfied with a lower standards of living *vis-a-vis* Europeans. Another issue which generated a bitter controversy was the government scheme to colonise Kenya through the settlement of Indian peasantry, and the European settlers' opposition to the scheme. A related issue in this regard was the exclusive reservation of the Highlands for the white settlers. Other issues in the "Indian Question", involved Indian opposition to various colonial policies regarding immigration, segregation, education and political representation. Whereas the European settlers wanted to advance and retain their privileged position in the colony, the Indians demanded racial equality in such matters as land ownership, immigration, accessibility to higher posts in the government, etc.

With the adoption of the principle of native paramountcy and at the same time with the rejection of the settlers' goal of self-government, the 1923 White Paper had appeared to "settle" the "Indian Question". Indian leaders derived some satisfaction from the fact that Kenya did not follow the political course of South Africa. After the great depression the conflict between the settlers and Indians tended to be more economic in nature than political. This renewed conflict represented the Indian petty bourgeoisie's resistance to monopoly capitalism. The 1932 Marketing of Native Produce Bill was the water-shed in this regard. Additionally, there were discriminatory tariff and customs duties on goods imported by Indians (Gregory 1971: 425). During the 1930s the Indians often complained of these policies saying that they were designed to squeeze them out of the country (Mangat 1969: 157). *The East Africa Royal Commission Report* (1955: 69) had also noted with concern the detrimental effects of the state-regulated trade system on small traders. The government, however, was too preoccupied with the emergency situation resulting from the Mau Mau rebellion to address the concerns of Indians.

Race relations between Indians and Africans in Kenya are analysed in terms of their two components: (i) relations between the Indian traders and the African peasantry, and (ii) the intra-class conflict between the Indian and African petty bourgeois fractions. The first is the classic conflict between traders and peasantry that attaches a stigma of "the exploiter" of the poor masses on any trading community. In Kenya, this tended to generate defencive feelings and distrust against the Indians. However, it was left to the African petty bourgeoisie to articulate feelings of racial exclusiveness and use them against its Indian competitor. The African petty bourgeoisie had begun to emerge in the 1920s and was consolidated after the Second World War. Although in the 1930s, conflict between the two class fractions had begun to arise with the result that the Indian traders in the rural areas (where the class conflict first developed) left for the cities, serious class conflict occurred only after independence.

During the post-colonial period, while the settler bourgeoisie had moved out of plantation agriculture giving way to its African counterpart, the Indian commercial bourgeoisie was left in a visibly affluent position in the major Kenyan cities. The burden of Africanisation therefore fell mainly on the non-citizen Indians belonging to this class, especially the small traders and the lower-grade government servants. Africanisation resulted in the exodus of about 100,000 Indians between 1962 and 1979, with most having gone to Britian and other western countries. Simultaneously, it also generated a sense of insecurity which prompted Indians to send their wealth abroad.

In Kenya's context, Africanisation represents an ideological answer to colonial racialism. However, so far as the Indians are concerned, Africanisation represents a continuity of discriminatory economic policies. Just as colonial racialism confined them to a class fraction of the petty bourgeoisie, Africanisation served the same function. It is this seemingly unchanged and privileged class position of Indians since the colonial days *vis-a-vis* the impoverished masses that explains the persistence of middleman minority status of Indians.

NOTES

1. Kenya was known as the East African mainland or interior until its take-over by the Foreign Office in 1895, whence it became the British East Africa Protectorate. This situation continued for the next 25 years. In 1920 the protectorate was declared a Crown Colony and was named Kenya.
2. After the partition of the Indian subcontinent in 1947, Indian population in East and Central Africa are generally referred to as "Asians". In this study the term Indian is retained for two important reasons: (i) a large majority of Indians in Kenya (over 90%) originated and continue to have some affinity with India, and (ii) the term "Indian" provides uniformity of terminology throughout the work.
3. Customs collection was done on a rental basis. Therefore the customs master was able to collect much more in duties than he could for the privilege. Jairam Sewji's was the first firm to be involved in customs collection, followed in

1876 by Tharia Topan's. According to one historian (Cooper 1977: 140), "Jairam Sewji and his agent Ludda Damji realized a fortune of between 1 and 2 million pounds and invested 434,000 pounds in loans and mortgages to Arabs, Indians and Europeans. Tharia Topan was probably the wealthiest man in all of East Africa when he died in 1891".

4. Earlier unsuccessful attempts were made for a Jewish settlement scheme in East Africa, which was supposed to rehabilitate Russian Jews, who were being persecuted. At first the offer was accepted by the Jewish leadership in 1903, but later, following protests from the white Kenyan settlers, and because of a number of other factors, the scheme did not materialise. Under the leadership of Lord Lugard, the white settlers opposed the scheme saying the Jews were paupers, spoke a foreign language and were not skilled in agriculture. Later on with the advent of white settlers from Europe and South Africa, the administration itself changed its mind about the whole idea. Jews themselves were divided, and some of them were not content with having merely "an antechamber to the holy land". They wanted *the* "holy land" (see Huxley 1967: 117-25; also Eliot 177-78).
5. Indian indentured immigration in the East Africa did not cease with the completion of the Uganda railway; it continued until 1922 when the system was finally abolished by the Indian Government. These later immigrants numbering about 5,500 were contracted for the building of new branches and the maintenance of the old lines, and for the construction of roads. They were employed by the Public Works Department (Gregory 1971: 53).
6. In the early colonial period in Kenya, Lord Delamere played an important role as a prominent settler. He was the president of a prominent European association called the Colonists' Association. In 1910 he resigned his post suggesting the formation of a new association. In the same year the Convention of Associations was formed. This was regarded as "the unofficial parliament", and was recognised by the Government as an organ of general settler opinion (see the biography of Lord Delamere by Huxley 1967: 262).
7. Regarding the land kept idle by the white settlers, Kondapi (1951: 305-06) wrote: "The area actually under European occupation was 5,138,324 acres in 1936, of which only 556,182 acres or 10.82 per cent was cultivated. Even if 2,302,293 acres were added as an estimated area utilized by Europeans for their livestock, the total area developed in the highlands would only amount to 2,858,475 acres. Thus less than 38 per cent of the land allotted long before had not been used either for cultivation or for raising stock."
8. The pass was a certificate of registration (*kipande*) required to be carried by every African adult male in which each of his employers recorded such information as the kind of work performed, the time worked, the wages earned, and general comments on the holder's ability, character, etc. (Kuczynski 1949: 140-43).
9. There is no generally accepted meaning or origin of the term "Mau Mau" which refers to about a decade-long underground peasant movement in Kenya in the 1950s. The movement was direct lineal descendent of the banned Kikuyu Central Association. Apparently, there was a connection between the only African political organisation after the Second World War, the Kenya

African Union, and the Mau Mau. The Mau Mau was rather a well organised movement with sacrificial oath ceremonies of a religious cult nature to foster a sense of unity and purpose among its members. The movement, whose primary objective was to recover the "stolen land" from "the enemy, the white men", did not spare those Africans who betrayed it or were government sympathisers and informers. The organised violence, including assassination and arson, was the basic means adopted by the movement in order to achieve its objective. This became more pronounced after the declaration of the state of emergency in October 1952. About 100,000 Kikuyu squatters, who were sympathisers of the movement, were evicted from the highlands. Almost 200 African leaders, including Jomo Kenyatta, were arrested and detained. In response to government repression, several thousand Kikuyu and others retreated to the forests in 1953 to launch a full-fledged offensive. In the end, although the movement was controlled by the late 1950s, it also expedited Kenya's independence. According to one estimate (Majdalany 1963: 221), 10,527 rebels were killed and 2,633 were captured. Other casualties were as follows: *Security Forces*: (i) killed: 534 Africans, 63 Europeans, 3 Asians, (ii) wounded: 465 Africans, 102 Europeans, 12 Asians; *Civilians*: (i) killed: 1,826 Africans, 32 Europeans, 26 Asians, (ii) wounded: 918 Africans, 265 Europeans, 36 Asians. In all 38,449 arrests were made. The estimated cost amounted to 55.5 million pounds, half of it borne by the Kenya Government.

10. Among the new Indian leaders in Kenya the following were prominent: A. Desai, a businessman and lawyer turned to politics and journalism; Hussein Suleman Virjee, an Ismaili businessman; Govind Bhimrao Tadwalker, an accountant; Kalyanji Narshibhai Jani, a businessman; Cowasjee Manakji Dalal, a barrister and Legislative Councilor; J.B. Pandya, the founder and printer of the *Kenya Daily Mail*; V.V. Phadke, a lawyer and the first Indian Executive Councilor in Kenya; and Shams-ud-Deen, a railway clerk and later Legislative Councilor (see Shanti Pandit 1961).
11. These stereotypes were based on the experience of "coolie" labourers who were brought from India in connection with the construction of the Uganda Railway and who worked and lived in degrading conditions.
12. There was even a proposal by the Kenyan settlers in 1945 for a still larger union comprising South Africa, East Africa and Central African territories (Kondapi 1951: 395).
13. Similar legislations were passed in Uganda, Tanganyika and Zanzibar. In fact, in Zanzibar the government's attempt to monopolise the clove trade through a parastatal, the Clove Growers Association, and thereby curb the activities of the Indian traders led to a major crisis in the 1930s. The local Indian traders and the major buyers in India jointly boycotted the Zanzibar clove industry resulting in considerable financial loss to the government revenues. Finally, following the intervention of the Indian Government, a satisfactory settlement was reached between the Indian traders and the new British Resident in 1938 (Hollingsworth 1960: 109-19).
14. Racial terms of service and salary scales remained effective until 1955 when, following the recommendations of the Lidbury Report of 1954, such discriminatory practices were removed. However, Indians did not enjoy the

beneficial effects of the new policy as the Africanisation of the civil service began to be implemented in the early 1960s.

15. While settlers' unsuccessful attempt to gain self-government in Kenya is well documented, references to Indians' imperial aspirations in Kenya are few and far between. The following two statements by the Kenya Indian leaders shed some light on this aspect. In one statement Mr. Mangal Dass said: "It might be asked why Indians wanted land so particularly. India has an overcrowded population. She wants room for expansion in the British Empire, as she has every right to do .... Europeans can go to Canada, to Australia and to South Africa, and for Europeans to claim this colony their special preserve is grossly unfair. We have been promised time after time that his country should be an Indian colony" (quoted in Huxley 1967: 121). In another statement Mr. A.M. Jeevanjee said: "I would go so far as to advocate the annexation of this African territory (Kenya) to the Indian Empire, with provincial government under the Indian Viceroy, and let it be opened to us, and in a very few years it will be a second Indian" (quoted in Huxley 1967: 121).

16. Regarding the role of trade in economic development Lewis (1954: 70) observed: "Trade stimulates demand, but introducing new goods to a community, and in doing so, it may stimulate the desire to work more, or more effectively. Since limited wants, due to limited horizons, keep effort low in many primitive communities, the opening the trade may effect a revolutionary change in the attitude towards the value of work."

17. In this connection one settler writer observed: "The lower class Asian trader stoops to many petty-trickeries in his business methods and search for profits, ... the better class Asian merchant generally provides a high standard of service and efficiency in dealing with his customers" (Thurnwald 1935: 131).

18. The Kenya African National Union has been the only ruling party since 1961. It was formed in 1960. At that time the party represented the economic interests of two major tribal groups, the Kikuyu and Luo. In order to represent the interests of other, tribal groups and regions, another political party the Kenya African Democratic Union was formed in 1960. Following the 1961 general elections based on universal suffrage, these parties formed a coalition government which lasted until independence in 1963. Following appeal for a one party system from the KANU party leader and the then President of Kenya, Jomo Kenyatta, in August 1964, the opposition party K.A.D.U. was voluntarily dissolved and its leaders had joined the KANU government. In 1966 there was a split in the KANU, but the break-away party, the Kenya People's Union lasted only for three years; in 1969 the party was banned by the government. Kenya remained a *de facto* one party state until 9 June 1982, on which date the parliament unanimously approved a bill amending the constitution so as to enable the country to become *de jure* one party state.

19. The following can be taken as an example, though an extreme one, of the difficulties in the joint ventures between the Indian and African traders in the '60s. According to the then Indian High Commissioner to Kenya, Mr. Prem Bhatia (1973: 88), "a wealthy and cooperative businessman of Indian origin in Nairobi who had been advised by me to take an African in partnership told me the following story: 'I took Joseph Kamau as a partner under your advice. He

knew nothing about business but I thought he would learn because he is an intelligent person. When we closed the shop on the first day of our association Joseph Kamau asked me to hand over to him his share of the profits for the day'".

20. About 35 per cent of the Kenya Indians had received Kenya citizenship automatically or applied for within the legal delay of two years following independence. Most of the remainder chose to become British subject, and some 3 or 4 per cent were Indian or Pakistani citizens. "The Kenya Government has been dilatory in granting citizenship to Asian applicants, and, as of Jan. 1968, there were still some 10,000 unprocessed cases" (van den Berghe 1970: 302, fn 15). There is reason to believe that this may have been an additional factor in Indians' ambivalence towards taking up or waiting for Kenyan citizenship.
21. A brief exception, as noted earlier (fn 18 above) was the existence of the Kenya People's Union during the late '60s. Apparently, K.P.U. was more sympathetic towards the African masses–small peasantry, unemployed, landless workers and traders. As such it was opposed to Kenya's increasing dependence on Western capital. It wanted the government to increase the pace of Africanisation in all sectors of the economy (see Odinga 1967: 253-315).

6

Summary and Conclusions

I

The present study is a theoretical reinterpretation of the race relations situations of overseas Indian communities from a class perspective and as such takes issue with two major theories of race relations, i.e. pluralism and the middleman minority theory. While the pluralists view the problem of race relations of overseas Indians in terms of their political subordination as a minority in different societies (Despres 1967; H. Kuper 1969; Tinker 1977; van den Berghe 1970; 1981), the middleman minority theory explains it in terms of their economic success resulting from certain culturally determined characteristics such as a sojourning orientation, preference for liquidable occupations, and cultural unassimilability (Bonacich 1973; Blalock 1967). In both approaches Indians are viewed as "strangers" in their respective host societies (Bonacich 1973; H. Kuper 1969). Both also agree on the total autonomy and non-reductiveness of race or ethnicity of Indians.

The major objection to such theories emerges from the fact that they ignore the critical fact that race relations involving Indians are directly linked with historical economic processes within the wider reality of colonialism–as a result of which the overseas Indian communities were formed in the first place. Pluralism and the middleman minority theories not only ignore this important aspect of overseas Indian communities, their conceptualisation of the colonial societies is also misleading. Whereas the pluralists define such societies in terms of their political boundaries, the middleman minority theorists characterise them as agricultural or peasant-feudal societies. Thus both theories are conspicuously silent about the emergent peripheral capitalism and its implications for the emergence of class and race relations situations in colonial societies. Therefore, for the study of racial discrimination against the overseas Indian communities from class perspective, it is useful to begin with the conceptualisation of colonial societies as peripheral capitalist social formations.

Peripheral capitalism is characterised by uneven development, which in turn implies marked social inequalities of which class inequality is of fundamental importance. From this assumption, then, it becomes possible to ask how the processes of class formation and class conflict shape race relations.

II

Colonialism was instrumental both for the formation of overseas Indian communities and for the development of socio-economic and political conditions in the colonies which fuelled the varied manifestations of racial and class antagonisms directed against the overseas Indians. Both structural and ideological elements present in a race relations situation are derived from the historical processes and labour demands associated with colonialism, and its derivative neo-colonialism. The structural elements are conceptualised in terms of peripheral capitalism, class conflict and/or intra-class conflict (e.g., split labour market), and the ideological elements, that rationalise the above conflicts, in terms of such ideologies of ethnic differences as racism, *apartheid*, "somatic norm image", etc.

Colonialism in the tropical countries, with which this study is concerned, involved not so much of European settlement as the extraction of economic surplus from the colonies by means of compulsion and its transfer to the metropolis. The need for raw materials for the metropolitan economy largely determined the nature of the colonial economies which were mainly based on plantation agriculture and mining. Thus, in the case of the British Empire, the production of sugar in the Caribbean, Fiji and Mauritius, rubber and tin in Malaysia, rice in Burma, tea in Ceylon, tea and cotton in India, coffee and cotton in East Africa–all fulfilled the vital needs of the metropolitan economy. The heavy emphasis on the plantation and mining enterprises tended to distort and undermine peasant production with the result that food needed to be imported. At the same time, the processing of raw material in the factories located in the metropolitan country precluded any significant growth of the manufacturing sector in the colonial economy. Consequently, the colonial economies were prevented from achieving economic self-sufficiency and well-rounded economic development. In this way the colonial economies remained dependent on and peripheral to the metropolitan economy. The concept of "peripheral capitalism", derived from the Marxist critique of the current economic situation in the Third World countries, captures the economic reality of the colonial as well as post colonial societies.

Class formation in colonial societies was dependent on the peripheral capitalist nature of their economies and more specifically, the degree of penetration of the capitalist mode of production in different sectors of these economies. In colonial economies, where plantation and/or mining were central to colonial enterprises, the major class conflict occurred between the two primary classes relating to these forms of production: the plantation/mining bourgeoisie and the proletariat. These economic sectors were generally owned by the white metropolitan absentee bourgeoisie and/or expatriates. On the other hand, forced labour (slave, indenture, compound, etc.) employed on these enterprises mostly involved non-white populations. Where native populations did not provide adequate supplies of labour, employers imported foreign (e.g., Indian) non-white labour. Thus the relations of production in the plantation and mining sectors of the colonial economy directly contributed to the emergence of a class structure which coincided with and created new racial divisions.

Given the economic and political dominance of the planters and mine owners in the colonial societies and their racist world views, which considered non-white populations as subhuman, the oppression of the working class inevitably carried racist overtones. The working class was effectively exploited through several means: the suppression of labour movements until the Second World War, the regimentation of workers on the estates or in mining compounds, treatment of labour offences as criminal offences, and the deliberate creation of split labour market situations through the promotion of ethnic/racial divisions.

The operation of the plantation system generated further contradictions which accounted for the emergence of antagonisms between non-white populations in the colonial societies. Planter's preference for cheaper immigrant labour meant the lessening of employment opportunities for the ex-slave native labourers, who were otherwise struggling to survive as small peasants. The latter were virtually helpless against the plantocracy; but their anger was often directed against the Indians, who were regarded as stealing their jobs. In additions, the government-sponsored land settlement schemes for immigrant labourers further outraged the African peasantry. It is significant to note in this connection that such communal conflicts within the working classes were understood by the contending parties not in ethnic or racial terms but in terms of "natives" (as the Africans called themselves) versus "immigrants" (Rodney 1981; 183).

Race relations in Kenya and Malaysia involving the Indian petty bourgeoisie can best be understood in relation to the growth of merchant capital and the commodity export sector of the colonial economy. The analysis was carried out in terms of two major forms of class conflict: (i) the conflict between the Indian petty bourgeoisie (merchants, traders, money-lenders, etc.) and peasantry (major producers and consumers of commodities), and (ii) the intra-class conflict between the Indian petty bourgeoisie and its native and white European counterparts. The first form of class conflict is endemic to peripheral capitalist economies. A large majority of peasants lack easy accessibility to competitive markets in selling their produce and have therefore to rely on the traders to perform this function. The nature of this class conflict, which involves profiteering on the part of traders, is such that it inevitably places the latter in the role of "exploiters". In situations where traders are distinguishable by "race" or ethnicity (as in the case of overseas Indians), the conflict takes on racist dimensions.

Intra-class conflict between different class fractions of the petty bourgeosie involves the use by each class fraction of its resources such as cultural traditions, kinship ties and political power to undercut the other. Thus in East Africa and South Africa, the Indian traders obtained competitive advantage against their European counterparts by turning to such ethnic resources and adaptive behaviour as working long hours, using business premises as residential quarters, hiring Indians as shop assistants, accepting a lower standard of living and thereby selling goods for low profit. The European traders, on the other hand, relied on the favours of the colonial government which frequently introduced a number of policies favourable to Europeans, such as restrictions on immigration, land ownership, trade licensing, political representation and various segregation rules. In independent Kenya, the policy of Africanisation, which was intended to undermine the Indian petty bourgeoisie, amounted to similar exclusionary practices. The Malay *versus* non-Malay conflict over several issues of an exclusionary nature provide another example of the class conflict between different fractions of the petty bourgeoisie.

The three case studies of Guyana, Malaysia and Kenya examined here demonstrate the analytical strength of a class analysis of race relations. The three cases represent different conjunctures of class, race and colonialism with respect to the overseas Indian communities.

Whereas in Guyana the Indian community was formed as a result of the immigration of indentured labourers, in Kenya it was the middle classes which constituted the core of the Indian community. The Malaysian case represents the mixture of the two: estate-bound *kangani* labourers and segments of the petty bourgeoisie.

III

Historically, in Guyana, the racial subordination of Indians emerged in relation to the operation of the sugar plantation economy. In the post-emancipation period, the planters in Guyana saw the salvation of the economy in the importation of subsidised, cheap Indian 'coolie' labour and its reproduction through various means (e.g., denial of education, land settlement schemes and legal repression). Thus, racial discrimination and exploitation of Indian indentured labourers at the hands of the white plantocracy represented an aspect of their class relations.

Another dimension of race relations involving the Indian labourers in Guyana emerged in relation to Africans, the majority of whom during the middle of the nineteenth century were struggling to survive as small peasants and/or plantation labourers. The continuous importation of Indian immigrant labour and its cheap reproduction not only created a surplus labour force but also tended to generate clearcut instances of a split labour market. Racial stratification on the estates, mutual strike-breaking, the deployment of the predominantly African police force by the colonial government to supress strikes by the Indians, and the land settlement schemes involving Indians at the expense of African farmers further tended to engender hostilities between the Indians and Africans.

In spite of racial problems, the nationalist movement based on the unity of the working class and peasantry had emerged in Guyana after the Second World War and in 1953 led to representative self-government. Soon, however, Anglo-American capital interests were successful in exploiting rifts between the two major racial fractions of the ruling party and eventually in 1964 in removing from office the Jagan government which had received a mandate in the 1957 and 1961 elections, and which stood for socialist economic policies. It was during the process of discrediting this government that widespread racial violence broke out during the early 1960s. The opposition parties accused the government of bringing about the dominance of Indians as well as promoting communism.

The post-colonial economy of Guyana, in spite of the radical decolonisation policies, continued to be dependent and underdeveloped with all its inherent contradictions. The emergence of state capitalism following the nationalisation of major industries, co-operativism and militarisation has created a sharp division between the ruling class (African-dominated state petty bourgeoisie) and the masses, mainly consisting of Indian peasantry and working class. The self-serving policies of the ruling class (reflected in the conspicuous growth of the civil service and the security forces and the disarray of the peasantry) have increasingly antagonised the masses. With the growing discontent of the masses, state repression has considerably increased resulting in serious human rights violations. In this situation of intensified class conflict and racial pluralism, the Indians feel themselves both politically as well as economically oppressed.

The colonial economy of Malaysia was based on tin mining and rubber plantation. Indian *kangani* labourers migrated to Malaysia in order to work on rubber plantations. The simultaneous growth of merchant capital, commodity export and service sectors also created opportunities for the immigration of Indian middle classes consisting of such diverse occupational groups as money-lenders and bankers, merchants and shopkeepers, teachers. policemen, clerks and lower-grade civil servants. The Indian working classes and the petty bourgeoisie, however, remained politically and socially isolated from each other. Characteristically, race relations involving Indians in Malaysia followed two different patterns: one resulted from the class exploitation of estate workers and the other emerged from intra-class conflict within the petty bourgeoisie.

Racialised as a "peaceable and easily governed race" by the plantation interests, the Indian estate workers were exploited to the full. Low wages, indebtedness, migratory status, illiteracy, legal repression and isolated existence on the estates made it possible for the planters to exploit them thoroughly. Thus racial categorisation and class exploitation went hand in hand. Despite the politically free nature of *kangani* migrants, in comparison with the indentured labourers in Guyana, the *kangani* labourers were more exploited. As was observed earlier, this occurred for several reasons: (a) the private organisation of the *kangani* labour recruitment and consequently the emergence of the situation of a surplus labour force, (b) the immobility and marginalisation of the *kangani* labourers due to lack of any land settlement schemes, and (c) the demise of radical trade unionism resulting from the legal repression during the prolonged emergency in Malaysia.

During both the colonial and post-colonial periods, the Indian petty bourgeoisie gained from the presence of its Chinese counterpart, which was far more numerous and prosperous. Thus, although in the colonial period the resentment of the emergent Malay petty bourgeoisie was directed against non-Malays (both Indians and Chinese), during the post-colonial period (e.g., the 1969 riots) the Chinese rather than Indians have been the target of hostility of the relatively impoverished Malay masses as well as the Malay petty bourgeoisie. In spite of the policy of elite accommodation being followed by the Malay ruling party, the potential for racial conflict exists in Malaysia. Under the New Economic Policy, the Malay petty bourgeoisie and bourgeosie are being strengthened as the expense of their Chinese counterparts. There exists a legitimacy crisis in that the government's effectiveness in removing Malay poverty paradoxically depends, among other things, on the full participation of the Chinese and foreign business interests in the economy. In this "tripartite race relations situation" the Indian petty bourgeosie remains auxiliary–both in terms of size as well as class strength. However, the Indian petty bourgeoisie has also begun to feel the impact of the New Economic Policy. Thus, during the 1970s, the proportion of Indians in professional, administrative, technical, sales and clerical occupations has declined, mainly in favour of the Malays. At the same time, they are experiencing hardships regarding promotions in employment, scholarships for children and new business opportunities.

In Kenya, the majority of Indians have occupied a middleman minority position and have formed an important fraction of the foreign petty bourgeoisie. Initially, conflicts emerged between Indians and European traders. At the same time, Indians demanded the right to own land in the fertile Highlands which was reserved for Europeans only. Later on this conflict became broader incorporating such issues as proportional political representation at the various levels of government, repeal of the segregation laws, the removal of undue restriction on Indian immigration, accessibility of the higher ranks of the civil service to Indians, and adequate provision for the education of Indian children. On several occasions both imperial and Indian Governments intervened in the conflict.

During the inter-war period Indians were involved in two forms of class conflict: (i) class conflict between the Indian traders and the African peasantry, and (ii) the intra-class conflict between the emergent African petty bourgeoisie and its Indian counterpart. The second form of class conflict was especially sharp during and after the decolonisation process in the early 1960s. In the post-independence period, while the politically dominant African petty bourgeoisie followed the exclusionary policy of Africanisation, the Indians, insecure and powerless, resorted to emigration and "economic sabotage": remittance, corruption, hoarding, black-marketeering, etc. In contrast to the middleman minority theory which seeks to explain this behaviour in terms of such imponderables as "sojourning", and the middleman minority's preference for liquidable occupations and its non-commital orientation towards the host society, the class perspective adopted in this study viewed it as the logical outcome of the pursuit of class interests.

The approach adopted in this study can be fruitfully applied to the race relations situations of other overseas Indian communities. This point is illustrated by briefly reviewing the race relations situations of three additional overseas Indian communities in Uganda, South Africa and Burma. In all these countries, the Indian migrants formed part of the petty bourgeoisie. In Burma and South Africa, the Indians also formed part of the working class.

The colonial economy of Uganda was mainly based on the production of cotton by the native peasantry and to a lesser extent by non-African (European and Indian) planters. There was simultaneously the development of trade in a wide variety of commodities. It was in relation to this latter sector of the colonial economy that the Indian community was formed in Uganda. Characteristically, the pattern of race relations involving Indians in Uganda closely followed the Kenyan pattern. As in Kenya, the majority of gainfully employed Indians in Uganda belonged to the commercial classes (Ramchandani 1972). Although in Uganda there was no significant degree of European settlement and therefore the "Indian Question" did not emerge as in Kenya, the class conflict between the Indian and African petty bourgeois fractions was sharper than in Kenya. One major expression of this intra-class conflict was the 1959 Asian trade boycott which "was led by the aspiring Buganda businessman, Augustine Kamya. Predictably it was the emerging Baganda petty bourgeoisie that benefited from the boycott, for in the seven months that it lasted, they took over small trading centres and transport services from

Asians" (Tandon 1973: 15). Later in the post-independence period, the state-directed Africanisation policy was pursued in order to eliminate non-citizen Indians from the economy. Following the Immigration and Trading Licensing Acts of 1969, over 20,000 Indians left Uganda within two years, travelling mostly to Britain (Tinker 1977: 156). In an atmosphere of economic uncertainty, as in Kenya, the emigrating Indian petty bourgeoisie also resorted to economic sabotage through hoarding, remittance, and other means. The culmination of this intra-class conflict was the expulsion of almost 50,000 Indians by 1972 by President Idi Amin whose newly recruited army as well as the Baganda petty bourgeoisie profitted from the expulsion (Mamdani 1976: 302-12).

Unlike Uganda where the Indians exclusively belonged to the commercial classes, in South Africa the Indian community consisted of both working class as well as petty bourgeoisie members. The Indians were first imported as indentured labourers in relation to the sugar plantation economy. In the late nineteenth century as the sugar plantations declined, the Indian labourers began to move out of the plantations. Indians, however, did not go to work on gold and diamond mining, which by then had become the mainstay of the South African economy and which was worked by the black 'compound' labourers. Instead, they moved on to small farming, gardening and manufacturing. Today a large number of Indians belong to the skilled and semi-skilled industrial work force.

During the late nineteenth century, indentured labourers were followed by Indian traders. Their place in the society's race relations was rooted in their success as traders *vis-a-vis* European traders. As soon as the "passage" or trader Indians became entrenched in the expanding economy of Natal and began to provide competition to their European counterparts, racial discrimination began to emerge. The Indian Immigrants Commission of 1887 had noted in this ragard "the undoubted ability of Arab (*sic*) traders to compete with European merchants" (Pachai 1971: 7). Consequently, the exclusionary policies that followed involved a series of legislations aimed at weakening the Indian position: revocation of the equal civic status of Indians in Natal in the 1880s, introduction of various segregation rules, disenfranchisement of Indians in 1896, restriction on Indian immigration by a test in one of the European languages, and introduction of a highly discretionary municipal trading licensing system which was beyond the jurisdiction of any court, including the

Supreme Court of Natal (Narain 1962). In the Transvaal Province, the Indians were denied any mining rights. The Orange Free State was absolutely closed for the Indians and remains so even today. It was against such anti-Indian legislations that Mahatma Ghandhi, himself an immigrant lawyer, had first raised the so-called "Indian Question" in South Africa in the late nineteenth century (Gandhi 1940).

The *apartheid* and the Group Areas Act (first introduced in 1950 and subsequently revised several times) again represent the same exclusionary policies which have generally impeded the graduation of the Indian commercial and petty bourgeoisie into a segment of the industrial bourgeoisie. Under the Group Areas Act, Indian firms can operate only in designated Indian areas. There also exist inter-provincial barriers against the movement of Indian capital, skill and labour. Moreover, a large number of Indian traders have been affected by the policy of discretionary trade licensing.

The class and race relations situations of Indians in South Africa obviously cannot be studied in isolation from the broader issue of *apartheid* which is instrumental in "maintaining a high rate of capitalistic exploitation through a system which guarantees a cheap and controlled labour-force, . . ." (Wolpe 1972: 433; Jain 1986). Historically, *apartheid* has fostered a social system whereby a large number of urban blacks have to live in slum conditions and in Bantustans and compete with the Indians and Coloured minorities for living space, jobs and services (Magubane 1979). The 1949 Durban riots between Indians and Africans were the extreme expression of this situation. African aggression was mainly directed against the Indian traders and landlords. While most of the fifty Indians who lost their lives in the riots were killed by Africans, most of the eighty-seven Africans killed were the victims of police and military action.

For the past four decades or so, apartheid in South Africa has been continuing unabated. However, in recent years some concessions have been made to the Indians as well as the Coloureds. These pertain to trade, recreation, sports and religious activities–all cosmetic changes, so to say. Politically, a section of the Indian community has been coopted by the racist regime through the tricameral parliamentary system. This has further distanced the Indians from the African masses who generally tend to view the former as cheeky traders out to exploit their customers. Moreover, a significant proportion of the Indian population is fencesitter or simply apolitical. These Indians are afraid of black militancy and are reluctant to commit to African nationalist movements. Such mutual fears between the Indians and the Africans prevent the two groups from putting up a united fight against the apartheid regime. The 1986 Phoenix riots only confirm these observations, and remind one of the 1949 Durban riots. In sum, it seems reasonable to conclude that given their population size and class positions in South Africa, the Indians would continue to work for limited concessions rather than radical reforms.

The Burmese colonial economy was based mainly on the peasant production of rice. As the Burmese peasantry remained confined to rice cultivation, Indian emigrants filled the role of industrial workers and segments of petty bourgeoisie, and the racial conflict involved both these class fractions.

In Burma much of the Burmese resentment against Indians originated from the commercial and banking activities of the Chettiars who were organised into a closed business network called the *Nattakkottai Chettiar Association* (N.C.A.). In the 1920s the N.C.A. represented about 1,500 member banks in Burma. The Chettiars provided credit to Burmese paddy farmers. Everything went well until the great depression of the 1930s when the world price of rice fell by one-fourth and by default the Chettiars became landlords of a substantial amount of land in Lower Burma (Tinker 1977: 144). Subsequently, absentee landlordism became a major political issue and remained so until the early 1950s when, through a number of legislative measures, the Chettiars were compelled to surrender land without adequate compensation. The final blow to the Indian petty bourgeoisie came in 1962 when General Ne Win seized power and implemented his "Burmese Way to Socialism". "As private trading was replaced by state marketing, the Indian shops were forced out of business, except in remote areas where the government writ did not run" (Tinker 1977: 149). Forced repatriation or deportation followed and by 1964 over 300,000 Indians had arrived in India as refugees.

In 1930 there were communal riots between Burmese and Indians. The riots originated in strike-breaking by the Burmese labourers on the Rangoon dockyard where about 2,000 Indian labourers had gone on strike for a wage increase. Within two weeks, however, the strike was settled and the Indian labourers were rehired, but the employers failed to come to terms with the Burmese labourers, who were to be retrenched. In the ensuing riots some 2,000 rickshaws owned by Indians were destroyed and over 25,000 Indians were scared out of their homes (Mahajani 1960: 73). "The resentment of the Burmese was not vented upon the European employers, who had made use of them, but upon the Indians" (Tinker 1977: 144).

Further anti-Indian riots occurred in 1938. These were triggered by a book in which a few derogatory remarks were made against Buddhism, the majority religion of Burma. The book was written by a Burmese Muslim, but "a rabble-rousing Burmese politician saw this as a means of toppling a political rival" (Tinker 1977: 144). The attacks by the Burmese Buddhists were first directed against the Burmese Muslims, then against the Indian Muslims. Soon however the whole situation developed into a Burmese-Indians conflict.

Such a development of the situation should not be surprising given the fact that in the 1920s and thirties the Burmese and Indians were locked in a class and intra-class conflict on several fronts, involving the Burmese peasants and the Indian money-lenders and the Burmese and Indian labourers. The Indians were not only demographically dominant in the capital city of Rangoon, they also monopolised commercial and banking activities, services in transport, posts and telegraphs, police and armed forces, and various professions, including medicine (Mahajani 1960: 7; Tinker 1977: 142). In 1933, of the total labour force (skilled and unskilled), the Indians constituted about 69 per cent, and the Burmese only 26 per cent. The Burmese politicians as well as intelligentsia naturally resented this dominance. This was further complicated by the growth of Burmese nationalism and the demand for separation of Burma from India, which eventually happened in 1937.

The foregoing discussion suggests that while the particular forms of race relations experienced by overseas Indians communities are influenced by a variety of demographic, socio-political, and cultural factors, they are invariably linked to the position of Indians in the class structure of a given society. Indians migrating to colonial societies have been incorporated either as part of the labouring class and/or petty bourgeoisie. In societies where Indians were incorporated as a segment of the working class, they found themselves in situations in which racial antagonism against them was directed from two major sources: (1) the employer–the estate bourgeoisie and its subordinate bureaucracy, and (ii) the other fraction(s) of the working class. The first was the classic situation of class exploitation coupled with white racism which tended to super-exploit Indian labour. It is in this context, as Hall (1980: 341) has rightly observed, that race acquires "the modality in which class is 'lived', the medium through which class relations are experienced, the form in which it is appropriated and 'fought through'". The second form of racial antagonism directed against Indian labourers emerged from such situations of intra-class conflict as the split-labour market and strike-breaking. Here, as the Guyanese case clearly shows, racial antagonism often tended to be mutually directed and consequently advantageous to the employers.

The types of racial antagonisms and forms of discrimination encountered by the petty bourgeois or middleman segments of overseas Indian communities were somewhat different. In both Kenya and Uganda, this group was involved in intra-class conflict with its native or white counterparts; aided by the state, the latter groups attempted to dominate the former by such exclusionary policies as residential and business segregation, discretionary policies of trade licensing, restrictions on immigration, and the denial of political power. Our study of Indians in Kenya indicate that exclusionary race policies and behaviour tend to intensify during the post-colonial period, resulting in involuntary emigration, repatriation, expulsion, or continued subordination of the communities involved.

What emerges from these various case studies is the fact that race relations involving Indians in different colonial and post-colonial societies were dependent on their economic position and the class dynamics specific to each social formation. In all the cases discussed above, racial antogonism directed against the Indian petty bourgeoisie appears to be particularly intense. Thus, this class was the victim of violent riots in Kenya, South Africa and Burma, and the target of expulsion in Burma and Uganda.

IV

The class analysis of race relations situations of overseas Indian communities presented in this study clearly shows that race relations do not involve monolithic situations as the theory and methodology of pluralism implies. This is clear in countries such as Malaysia where the Indian community has been historically divided into estate workers and the middle classes. In such instances, one cannot even speak of a "community" without reference to its class composition. Race relations therefore need to be conceptualised in terms of their class components, and analysed in terms of class conflicts. In its complex form, class analysis requires not only an understanding of class interests and class competition but also of the nature of the ideological struggle between the classes and the form of state intervention. Thus race relations are not amorphous relationships between groups but, "for the most part, a series of specific class relations that vary by place and over time and that change as a consequence of changing material conditions" (Greenberg 1980: 406).

A class analysis of colonial societies reveals the inadequacy of the pluralist perspective. It shows that the plural character of the colonial societies, which the pluralists assume as a given condition, was acquired as part of the process of capital accumulation by the dominant classes. It was for this reason alone that various forms of migrant labour and middleman minorities were introduced in the colonies.

A class perspective also reveals the limitations of the middleman minority model which oversimplifies the class bases for the development of this minority. According to this formulation the middleman minority are sojourners, preferring liquidable occupations, retaining a strong orientation to the home country of origin and only a weak commitment to their host countries. Among indications of this middleman minority orientation would be their ultimate intentions to return home and the sending of remittances there, and their refusal to change their citizenship status. In contrast to such a pattern, this study found that Indians in East Africa had invested heavily in real estate, acquiring the kinds of holdings which were not very liquidable in East African countries; that a majority of non-citizen Indians in East Africa were British subjects rather than Indian citizens; that most of their remittances were directed to British and European banks rather than to India; that following the launching of the policy of Africanisation the majority of them migrated to the metropolitan countries of Europe and North America. These facts serve to support the argument that the conduct of members of a middleman minority should be viewed in terms of their rational class behaviour rather than in terms of their cultural predispositions.

A class analysis of middleman minority race relations situations nevertheless raises questions about the relationship between class conflict and race relations. How is an intra-class conflict between fractions of the petty bourgeoisie transformed into a wider conflict between the masses and the middleman minority? Why is the class conflict seen in terms of racial/ethnic categories? The answers lie in the complex nature of class struggle which is carried on in both material and ideological realms. A clearer understanding of the ideological aspect of class conflict and the various forms it takes in specific social formations would need to supplement the class analysis presented here which focuses on conflicting material interests. Recent neo-Marxist explorations into such interrelated fields as hegemony, state power and ideological discourse suggest how competing classes or class fractions articulate their respective ideologies from a pluralistic universe of ideological elements (Hall 1980; Laclau 1977). Because of its indigenous origin, the native petty bourgeoisie is better placed to legitimately articulate the 'national-popular' ideology. In some situations, this ideology become part of state power whose expression we find in Africanisation and *bumiputerisation* (Malaysia). These national-popular ideologies serve to mask the underlying class conflict and discredit the middleman minority's economic, political and socio-cultural roles and indeed their very existence.

Racist ideologies not only distort class conflict, they also dehistoricise them. Anti-Indian sentiments in Uganda and the subsequent expulsion of Indians were articulated in terms of removing the exploiters of the masses from the scene. The expulsion not only revealed the historically determined neo-colonial and peripheral character of the Ugandan economy, but also showed the futility of the action. In expelling the Indians the ruling classes were not changing the capitalist character of the economy and its dependence on the metropolitan countries. Thus as August Bebel pointed out in relation to anti-Semitism in Europe, the anti-Indian sentiments and the expulsion of Indians contained elements of a genuine social protest, but with the wrong solutions (cited in van Arkel 1982: 16). Far from removing the poverty and discontent of the masses, the expulsion of the Indians from Uganda was followed by the country's worst economic and political crises of its turbulent history.

In sum, the relationship between class and race is complex. From a class perspective, race relations would appear to be emergent phenomena rather than given relationships. Race relations do not exist naturally or essentially by virtue of the existence of phenotypical differences. As Leo Kuper (1975: 196) pointed out:

> Racial difference has no intrinsic significance. Even when it is present in a society, as an objective fact, it may not be relevant in social relationships; and where it is recognized as relevant, its significance is highly variable, depending entirely on the way in which it is socially elaborated.

To assume the existence of race relations naturally is to confuse the difference between appearance and reality. Race and race relations should be treated as descriptive, rather than analytical categories. Neither of these terms has equal explanatory significance *vis-a-vis* class. To argue for a class analysis, however, is not to suggest that class analysis is without contradictions, or that it is fully developed. As Hall (1980) has pointed out, with the recent paradigmatic shift, the current class analysis of race relations is locked in internal debate. Nevertheless, the approach looks promising. This study is a small contribution in that direction.

Bibliography

Adamson, A.H. (1972) *Sugar Without Slaves: The Political Economy of British Guiana, 1883-1904*. New Haven and London: Yale University Press.

Africa Diary. New Delhi: Africa Publications.

African Recorder. New Delhi: The Recorder Press.

Allen, J. (1967) *The Malayan Union*. Yale Southeast Asian Monograph Series, No. 10.

Amin, M. (1977) "British "Intervention" and Malay Resistance", in Mohamed Amin and Malcolm Caldwell (eds.), *Malaya: The Making of a Neo-Colony*. Nottingham: Spokesman Books.

Amin, S. (1974) *Accumulation on a World Scale*, 2 Vols. New York: Monthly Review Press.

Andrew, E.J.L. (1933) *Indian Labour in Rangoon*. Calcutta: Oxford University Press.

Arasaratnam, Sinnappah (1970) *Indians in Malaysia and Singapore*. London: Oxford University Press.

Area Handbook for Malaysia (1977). Washington, D.C.: Foreign Area Studies, The American Universities.

Aziz, M. (1981) "The Indian Community in West Malaysia", *Journal of Contemporary Asia* 11 (3): 366-74.

Bacchus, M.K. (1980) *Education for Development or Underdevelopment?: Guyana's Educational System and its Implications for the Third World*. Waterloo, Ont.: Wilfrid Laurier University Press.

Banton, M. (1967) *Race Relations*. London: Tavistock.

Barnett, D.L. and Karari Njama (1966) *Mau Mau from Within: Autobiography and Analysis of Kenya's Peasant Revolt*. London: MacGibbon & Kee Ltd.

Barth, F. (ed.) (1969) *Ethnic Groups and Boundaries: The Social Organization of Culture Difference*. London: George Allen and Unwin.

Beckford, G.L. (1972) *Persistent Poverty: Underdevelopment in*

Plantation Economies of the Third World. Oxford: Oxford University Press.

Bennett, G. (1963) *Kenya: A Political History.* London: Oxford University Press.

Bharati, A. (1972) *The Asians in East Africa: Jayhind and Uhuru.* Chicago: Nelson-Hall Company.

Bhatia, B.M. (1967) *Famines in India: A Study in Some Aspects of the Economic History of India (1860-1965).* London: Asia Publishing House.

Bhatia, Prem (1973) *Indian Ordeal in Africa.* Delhi: Vikas Publishing House.

Blalock, H.M. (1967) *Toward a Theory of Minority-Group Relations.* New York: John Wiley & Sons, Inc.

Bonacich, E. (1972) "A Theory of Ethnic Antagonism: The Split Labour Market", *American Sociological Reveiw* 37 (5): 547-59.

Bonacich, E. (1973) "A Theoty of Middleman Minorities", *American Sociological Review* 38 (October): 583-94.

Bonacich, E. (1980) "Class Approaches to Ethnicity and Race", *Insurgent Sociologist* X(2): 9-23.

Bradley, P. (1961) "The Party System in British Guiana and the General Election of 1961", *Caribbean Studies* (October).

Breman, Jan (1974) *Patronage and Exploitation: Changing Agrarian Relations in South Gujarat, India.* Los Angeles and Berkeley: University of California Press.

Brett, E.A. (1973) *Colonialism and Underdevelopment in East Africa: The Politics of Economic Change, 1919-1939.* London and Nairobi: Heinemann.

Buchanan, D.H. (1966) *The Development of Capitalist Enterprise in India.* Oxford: Oxford University Press.

Burawoy, M. (1974) "Race, Class and Colonialism", *Social and Economic Studies* 23 (4): 521-50.

Burnham, Forbes (1970) *A Destiny to Mould: Selected Discourses by the Prime Minister of Guyana.* London: Longman Caribean Ltd.

Caldwell, M. (1977a) "The British "Forward Movement", 1874-1914", in Mohamed Amin and Malcolm Caldwell (eds) *Malaya: The Making of a Neo-Colony.* Nottingham: Spokesman Books.

Caldwell, M. (1977b) "War, Boom and Depression", in Mohamed Amin And Malcolm Caldwell (eds) *Malaya: The Making of a Neo-Colony.* Nottingham: Spokesman Books.

Caldwell, M. (1977c) "From 'Emergency' to 'Independence', 1948-57" in Mohamed Amin and Malcolm Caldwell (eds) *Malaya: The Making of a Neo-Colony*. Nottingham: Spokesman Books.

Campbell, P.C. (1969) *Chinese Coolie Emigration to Countries Within the British Empire*. London: Frank Cass.

Chakravarti, N.R. (1971) *The Indian Minority in Burma: The Rise and Decline of an Immigrant Community*. London: Oxford University Press.

Cham, B.N. (1975) "Class and Communal Conflict in Malaysia", *Journal of Contemporary Asia* 7(4): 178-99.

Charlesworth, N. (1982) *British Rule and the Indian Economy, 1800-1914*. London: The Macmillan Press.

Chase, A. (1964) *A History of Trade Unionism in Guyana, 1900 to 1961*. Ruimveldt, Guyana: New Guyana Co.

Churchill, Winston (1908) *My African Journey*. London: Hodder and Stoughton.

Clayton, Anthony (1976) *Counter-Insurgency in Kenya: A Study of Military Operations against Mau Mau*. Nairobi: Transafrican Publishers Ltd.

Clementi, Sir Cecil (1937) *A Constitutional History of British Guiana*. London: Macmillan and Company Ltd.

Colletta, N.J. (1975) "Malaysia's Forgotten People: Education, Cultural Identity and Socio-economic Mobility among South Indian Plantation Workers", *Contributions to Asian Studies* 7: 87-112.

Collins, B.A.N. (1966) "Racial Imbalance in Public Service and Security Forces", *Race* 7(3): 235-53.

Cooper, F. (1977) *Plantation Slavery in the East Coast of Africa*. New Haven & London: Yale University Press.

Cooperative Republic of Guyana (1971) *Land Use Study*, 3 vols. Georgetown: Government Printers.

Coupland, R. (1939) *The Exploitation of East Africa, 1856-1890: The Slave Trade and the Scramble*. London: Faber and Faber Ltd.

Courtenay, P.P. (1972) *A Geography of Trade and Development in Malaya*. London: G. Bell and Sons.

Cowan, C.D. (1961) *Nineteenth-Century Malaya: The Origins of British Political Control*. London: Oxford University Press.

Cox, O.C. (1948) *Caste, Class and Race*. Garden City, New York: Doubleday.

Cross, Malcolm (1968) "Cultural Pluralism and Sociological Theory", *Social and Economic Studies* 17(4): 381-97.

Cross, M. (1971) "On Conflict, Race Relations, and the Theory of the Plural Society", *Race* 12(4): 477-94.

Cross, M. (1978) "Colonialism and Ethnicity: A Theory and Comparative Case Study", *Ethnic and Racial Studies* 1(1): 37-59.

Cumpston, I.M. (1969) *Indians Overseas in British Territories, 1834-1854*. London: Oxford University Press.

Daly, V.T. (1966) *A Short History of the Guyanese People*. Georgetown: The Daily Cronicle Ltd.

Danns, G.K. (1978) "Militarization and Development: An Experiment in Nation–Building and Transition", *Journal of the Faculty of Social Sciences and the Institute of Development Studies*, 1(1): 23-44, University of Guyana.

Davis, K. (1968) *The Population of India and Pakistan*. New York: Russell & Russell.

Delf, G. (1963) *Asians in East Africa*. London: Oxford University Press.

Despres, Leo A. (1967) *Cultural Pluralism and Nationalist Politics in British Guiana*. Chicago: Rand McNally and Company.

Dilley, M.R. (1966) *British Policy in Kenya Colony*. London: Frank Cass.

Dodge, Peter (1967) "Comparative Racial Systems in the Greater Caribbean", *Social and Economic Studies* 16(3): 249-61.

Dollard, J. (1939) *Caste and Class in a Southern Town*. New York: Doubleday Anchor Books.

Dumont, L. (1961) "Caste, Racism and 'Stratification': Reflections of a Social Anthropologist", *Contributions to Indian Sociology*, No. 5, 20-43.

East African Royal Commission 1953-55 Report (1955). London: H.M.S.O.

Eliot, C. (1905) *The East Africa Protectorate*. London: E. Arnold.

Emerson, R. (1964) *Malaysia: A Study in Direct and Indirect Rule*. Kuala Lumpur: University of Malaya Press.

Enloe, Cynthia (1973) *Ethnic Conflict and Political Development*. Boston: Little Brown & Co.

Epstein. A.L. (1978) *Ethos and Identity*. London: Tavistock.

Farley, R. (1954) "The Rise of the Peasantry in British Guiana", *Social and Economic Studies* 2(4): 87-103.

Firth, R. et al. (1957) "Factions in India and Overseas Indian Societies", *British Journal of Sociology* VIII(4): 291-342.

Fitgerald, F. (1981) "Sociologies of Development", *Journal of Contemporary Asia*, 11(1): 5-18.

Fitzgerald, W.W.A. (1898) *Travels in the Coastlands of British East Africa and the Islands of Zanzibar and Pemba*. London: Chapman and Hall.

Foster-Carter, A. (1973) "Neo-Marxist Approaches to Development and Underdevelopment", *Journal of Contemporary Asia* 3(1): 7-33.

Frank, A.G. (1967) *Capitalism and Underdevelopment in Latin America: Historical Studies of Chile and Brazil*. New York: Monthly Review Press.

Freedman, M. (1960) "Growth of a Plural Society of Malaya", *Pacific Affairs* 33: 158-68.

Furnivall, J.S. (1944) *Netherlands India*. London: Cambridge University Press.

Furnivall, J.S. (1948) *Colonial Policy and Practice: A Comparative Study of Burma and Netherlands India*. London: Cambridge University Press.

Gadgil, D.R. (1971) *The Industrial Evolution of India in Recent Times, 1860-1939*. Bombay: Oxford University Press.

Gagliano, F.V. (1971) *Communal Violance in Malaysia, 1969: The Political Aftermath*. Ohio University: The Centre for Infternational Studies.

Gandhi, M.K. (1940) *An Autobiography, or the Story of My Experiments with Truth*. Ahmedabad: Navajivan Publishing House.

Ghai, D.P. (1965) "An Economic Survey", in Dharam P. Ghai (ed.), *Portrait of a Minority: Asians in East Africa*. Nairobi: Oxford University Press.

Ghai, Y.P. (1965) "The Future Prospects", in Dharam P. Ghai (ed.), *Portrait of a Minority: Asians in East Africa*. Nairobi: Oxford University Press.

Ghai, Y and D. Ghai (1971) *The Asian Minorities of East and Central Africa*. London: Minority Rights Group.

Gillion, K.L.O. (1956) "The Sources of Indian Emigration to Fiji", *Population Studies* X(2): 139-157.

Girvan, N. (1976) *Corporate Imperialism: Conflict and Expropriation*. New York and London: Monthly Review Press.

Glasgow, R.A. (1970) *Guyana: Race and Politics among Africans and East Indians*. The Hague: Martinus Nijhoff.

Glazer, N. and D.P. Moynihan (1975) *Ethnicity: Theory and Experience*. Cambridge, Mass.: Harvard University Press.

Godfrey, M. and S. Langdon (1976) "Partners in Underdevelopment: The Transnationalisation Thesis in a Kenya Context", *Journal of Commonwealth and Comparative Politics* 14(1): 42-63.

Gray, J.M. (1963) "Zanzibar and the Coastal Belt, 1840-1884", in R. Oliver and G. Matthews (eds.), *History of East Africa*, vol. 1. Oxford: Clarendon Press.

Green, J.E. (1974) *Race vs. Politics in Guyana: Political Cleavages and Political Mobilisation in the 1968 General Election*. Institute of Social and Economic Research, University of the West Indies.

Greenberg, S.B. (1980) *Race and State in Capitalist Development*. New Haven and London: Yale University Press.

Gregory, R.G. (1971) *India and East Africa*. Oxford: Clarendon Press.

Grossholtz, J. (1968) "The Rise and Demise of Konfrontasi: Impact of Politics in Malaysia", *Asain Studies* 6(3): 338.

Gullick, J.M. (1969) *Malaysia*. New York: Frederick A. Praeger, Publishers.

Gullick, J.M. (1981) *Malaysia: Economic Expansion and National Unity*. Boulder, Colorado: Westview Press.

Gupta, A. (ed.) (1971) *Indians Abroad: Report of an International Seminar*. New Delhi.

Gupta, V. (1981) *Kenya: Politics of Independence*. New Delhi: People's Publishing House

Halim, F. (1981) "Rural Labour Force and Industrial Conflict", *Journal of Contemporary Asia* 11(3): 271-96.

Hall, S. (1977) "Pluralism, Race and Class in Caribbean Societies", in *Race and Class in Post-Colonial Society*. Paris. UNESCO, 150-83.

Hall, S. (1980) "Race, Articulation and Societies Structured in Dominance", in *Sociological Theories: Race and Colonialism*. Paris: UNESCO, 305-46.

Hancock, J. (1840) *Observations on the Climate, Soil and Products of British Guiana*. London.

Harbeson, J.W. (1973) *Nation-Building in Kenya: The Role of Land Reform*. Evanston: Narthwestern University Press.

Harris, M. (1964) *Patterns of Race in the Americas*. New York: Walker.

Hazlewood, A. (1979) *The Economy of Kenya: The Kenyatta Era*. New York: Oxford University Press.

Heussler, R. (1981) *British Rule in Malaya: The Malayan Civil Service and its Predecessors, 1867-1942*. Westport, Conn.: Greenwood Press.

Hoetink, H. (1967) *Two Variants in Caribbean Race Relations*. London: Institute of Race Relations.

Hoffmann, L. and T. Siew E.E. (1980) *Industrial Growth, Employment and Foreign Investment in Peninsular Malaysia*. Kuala Lumpur: Oxford University Press.

Hollingsworth, L.W. (1960) *The Asians of East Africa*. London: Macmillan & Co. Ltd.

Horwitz, R. (1967) *The Political Economy of South Africa*. New York: Frederick A. Praeger.

Howard, R. (1978) *Colonialism and Underdevelopment in Ghana*. London: Croom Helm.

Hua, W.Y. (1983) *Class and Communalism in Malaysia*. London: Zed Books Ltd.

Husin Ali, S. (1975) *Malay Peasant Society and Leadership*. Kuala Lumpur: Oxford University Press.

Huxley, E. (1967) *White Man's Country: Lord Delamere and the Making of Kenya*. New York: Frederick Praeger.

International Commission of Jurists (1965) *Racial Problems in the Public Service*. Geneva.

Jackson, R.N. (1961) *Immigrant Labour and the Development of Malaya, 1786-1920*. Kuala Lumpur: Government Press.

Jagan, C. (1954) *Forbidden Freedom: The Story of British Guiana*. London: Lawrance & Wishart Ltd.

Jagan C. (1972) *The West on Trial, The Fight for Guyana's Freedom*. New York: International Publishers.

Jain, P.C. (1982) "Indians Abroad: A Current Population Estimate", *Economic and Political Weekly* XVII(8): 299-304.

Jain P.C. (1985) *Colonialism, Class and Race Relations: The Case of Overseas Indians*. Ph.D. Thesis. Carleton University, Ottawa.

Jain, P.C. (1986) "Apartheid and Indians in South Africa", *Mainstream* XXIV(47): 7-9.

Jain, P.C. (1988a) "Towards Class Analysis of Race Relations: Overseas Indians in Colonial/Post-Colonial Societies", *Economic and Political Weekly* XXIII(3): 95-103.

Jain, P.C. (1988b) "Exploitation and Reproduction of Migrant Indian Labour in Colonial Guyana and Malaysia", *Journal of Contemporary Asia* 18(2): 189-206.

Jain, P.C. (1989a) "Emigration and Settlement of Indians Abroad", *Sociological Bulletin* 38(1): 1-17.

Jain, P.C. (1989b) "A Socio-Economic History of Indians in Kenya", pp. 44-52 in Jagat K. Motwani and Jyoti Barot-Motwani (eds), *Global Migration of Indians*. New York: National Federation of Indian-American Associations.

Jain, R.K. (1970) *South Indians on the Plantation Frontier in Malaya*. New Haven: Yale University Press.

Jayawardena, C. (1963) *Conflict and Solidarity on a Guianese Plantation*. London: Athlone Press.

Jayawardena, C. (1968) "Migration and Social Change: A Survey of Indian Communities Overseas", *The Geographical Review* 58: 426-49.

Keesing's Contemporary Archives. London: Longman.

Kennedy, J. (1970) *A History of Malaya*. London: Macmillan.

Khoo, K.K. (1972) *The Western Malay States, 1850-1873*. Kuala Lumpur: Oxford University Press.

Kinloch, G.C. (1979) *The Sociology of Minority Group Relations*. Englewood Cliffs, New Jersey: Prentice-Hall.

Kirke, H. (1970) *Twenty-five Years in British Guiana*. Westport, Conn.: Negro Universities Press.

Kondapi, C. (1951) *Indians Overseas, 1838-1949*. Madras: Oxford University Press.

Kuczynski, R.R. (1949) *Demographic Survey of the British Colonial Empire*, 3 Vols. London: Oxford University Press.

Kumar, D. (1965) *Land and Caste in South India: Agricultural Labour in Madras Presidency in the Nineteenth Century*. Cambridge: Cambridge University Press.

Kundu, A. (1963) "The Economy of British Guiana, 1960-1975", *Social and Economic Studies* 12(3): 307-80.

Kuper, H. (1969) "'Strangers' in Plural Societies: Asians in South Africa and Uganda", pp.247-82, in Kuper and Smith (eds.), *Pluralism in Africa*. Berkeley and Los Angeles: University of California Press.

Kuper, L. (1975) *Race, Class, and Power: Ideology and Revolutionary Change in Plural Societies*. Chicago: Aldine Publishing Co.

Laclau, E. (1977) *Politics and Ideology in Marxist Theory*. London: New Left Books.

Lal, Brij, V. (1983) *Girmitiyas: The Origins of the Fiji Indians*. Canberra: Journal of Pacific History.

Lamb, H. (1955) "The State and Economic Development in India", Simon Kuznets, et al. (eds), *Economic Growth: Brazil, India, Japan*. Durham, N.C.: University of North Carolina Press.

Landis, J.B. (1973) "Racial Attitudes of Africans and Indians in Guyana", *Social and Economic Studies* 22 (4): 427-39.

Latham, A.J.H. (1978) *The International Economy and the Undeveloped World, 1865-1914*. London: Croom Helm.

Latham, A.J.H., (1981) *The Depression and the Developing World, 1914-1939*. London: Croom Helm.

Latiff, D. (1977) "Contradictions in Pre-War Colonialism, 1930-45" in Mohamed Amin and Malcolm Caldwell (eds), *Malaya: The Making of a Neo-Colony*. Nottingham: Spokesman Books.

Leakey, L.S.B. (1952) *Mau Mau and the Kikuyu*. London.

Lee, G. (1973) "Commodity Production and Reproduction amongst the Malayan peasantry", *Journal of Contemporary Asia* 3(4): 441-56.

Lent, J.A. (ed.) (1977) *Cultural Pluralism in Malaysia*. Special Report No. 14. Northern Illinois University: Centre for Southeast Asian Studies.

Leon, A. (1970) *The Jewish Question: A Marxist Interpretation*. New York: Pathfinders Press.

Lewis, W.A. (1954) *Theory of Economic Growth*. London: Allen and Unwin.

Leys, C. (1975) *Underdevelopment in Kenya: The Political Economy of Neo-Colonialism, 1964-1971*. Berkeley and Los Angeles: University of California Press.

Leys, C. (1977) "Underdevelopment and Dependency: Critical Notes", *Journal of Contemporary Asia* 7(1): 92-107.

Lim, D. (1973) *Economic Growth and Development in West Malaysia, 1947-1970*. Kuala Lumpur: Oxford University Press.

Lim, M.H. (1980) "Ethnic and Class Relations in Malaysia", *Journal of Contemporary Asia* 10(1-2): 130-54.

Lim, M.H. and W. Canak (1981) "The Political Economy of State Policies in Malaysia", *Journal of Contemporary Asia* 11(2): 204-24.

Lonsdale, J. and B. Berman (1979) "Coping with the Contradictions: The Development of the Colonial State in Kenya, 1895-1914", *Journal of African History* 20(4): 487-95.

Lord Hailey (1957) *An African Survey*. London: Oxford University Press.

Lugard, F.D. (1968) *The Rise of Our East African Empire*, 2 vols.

London: Frank Cass & Co. Ltd.

Lutchman, H.A. (1974) *From Colonialism to Co-operative Republic*. Rio Piedras, Puerto Rico: Institute of Caribbean Studies, University of Puerto Rico.

Lyon, M. (1972) "Race and Ethnicity in Pluralistic Societies", *New Community* 1: 256-62.

MacPhee, A.M. (1968) *Kenya*. New York: Frederick A. Praeger.

McDermott, P.L. (1893) *British East Africa*. London: Chapman and Hall.

Magubane, B. (1979) *Political Economy of Race and Class in South Africa*. New York: Monthly Review Press.

Mahajani, U. (1960) *The Role of Indian Minorities in Burma and Malaya*. Bombay: Vora & Company.

Majdalany, F. (1963) *State of Emergency: The Full Story of Mau Mau*. Boston: Houghton Miffin.

Malinowski, B. (1945) *The Dynamics of Culture Change: An Inquiry into Race Relations in Africa*. New Haven: Yale University Press.

Mamdani, M. (1976) *Politics and Class Formation in Uganda*. New York and London: Monthly Review Press.

Mandle, J.R. (1973) *The Plantation Economy: Population and Economic Change in Guyana, 1838-1960*. Philadelphia: Temple University Press.

Manley, R.H. (1979) *Guyana Emergent: The Post-Indepence Struggle for Nondependent Development*. Boston: G.K. Hall & Co.

Mangat, J.S. (1969) *A History of the Asians in East Africa, 1886 to 1945*. Oxford: Clarendon Press.

Mangat, J.S. (1976) "The Immigrant Communities (2): The Asians", in D.A. Low and Alison Smith (eds), *History of East Africa III*. Oxford: Clarendon Press.

Mars, P. (1976) "Political Violence and Ethnic Polarization in Guyana", in Harold Lutchman, et al. (eds) *Selected Issues in Guyanese Politics*. Georgetown: The Deptt. of Political Science and Law, University of Guyana.

Marshall, W.K. (1968) "Notes on Peasant Development in the West Indies", *Social and Economic Studies* 17(3): 252-63.

Marx, K. (1943) *Articles on India*. Bombay: Peoples Publishing House.

Mboya, T, (1963) *Freedom and After*. London: Andre Deutsch.

Mehra, C. (1983) "Indians in East Africa–II", *The Statesman* (Delhi), April 12, p.6.

Menezes, M.N. (1977) *British Policy Towards the Amerindian in*

British Guiana, 1803-1873. Oxford: Clarendon Press.

Miles, R. (1982) *Racism and Migrant Labour*. London: Routledge and Kegan Paul.

Milne, R.S. (1977) "Politics, Ethnicity and Class in Guyana and Malaysia", *Social and Economic Studies* 26(1): 18-37.

Mohamad, M. (1970) *The Malay Dilemma*. Singapore: Asia Pacific Press.

Moore, R.J. (1970) *East Indians and Negroes in British Guiana, 1838-1880*. D. Phil. Thesis, University of Sussex. Micro film.

Morgan, M. (1977) "The Rise and Fall of Malayan Trade Unionism, 1945-50", in Mohamed Amin and Malcolm Caldwell (eds) *Malaya: The Making of a Neo-Colony*. Nottingham: Spokesman Books.

Morris, H.S. (1956) "Indians in East Africa: A study in a Plural Society", *British Journal of Sociology* 7(3): 194-211.

Morris, H.S. (1968) *The Indians in Uganda*. Chicago: The University of Chicago Press.

Mukherjee, R. (1958) *The Rise and Fall of the East India Company: A Sociological Appraisal*. Berlin: Veb Deutscher Verlag Der Wissenschaften.

Mungeam, G.H. (1966) *British Rule in Kenya, 1895-1912*. Oxford: Clarendon Press.

Myrdal, Gunnar (1944) *An American Dilemma*. New York: Harper and Brothers.

Nabudere, D.W. (1981) *Imperialism in East Africa, vol. 1: Imperialism and Exploitation*. London: Zed Press.

Nabudere, D.W. (1982) *Imperialism in East Africa, vol. 2: Imperialism and Integration*. London: Zed Press.

Nagata, J. (1975) "Perceptions of Social Inequality in Malaysia", *Contributions to Asian Studies* 7: 113-36.

Nair, M.N. (1937) *Indians in Malaya*. Koduvayar: Koduvayar Press.

Narain, I. (1962) *The Politics of Racialism: A Study of the Indian Minority in South Africa down to the Gandhi-Smuts Agreement*. Agra: Shiva Lal Agarwala & Co. (P.) Ltd.

Nath, D. (1970) *A History of Indians in Guyana*. London: published by the Author.

National Operations Council (1969) *The May 13 Tragedy: A Report*. Kuala Lumpur.

Nehru, J. (1960) *The Discovery of India*. Garden City, N.Y.: Anchor Books.

Nehru, J. (1962) *An Autobiography*. Bombay: Allied Publishers.

Newman. P. (1962) "Racial Tension in British Guiana", *Race* 3(2): 31-45.

Newman, P. (1964) *British Guiana: Problems of Cohesion in an Immigrant Society*. London: Oxford University Press.

Neelkantha Aiyer, K.A. (1938) *Indian Problems in Malaya: A Brief Survey in Relation to Emigration*. Kuala Lumpur: Indian Office.

Nesh, G.D. (1967) *Bureaucracy and Rural Development in Malaysia*. Berkeley and Los Angeles: University of California Press.

Nkrumah, K. (1968) *Neo-Colonialism: The Last Stage of Imperialism*. London: Heinemann Educational Books Ltd.

Norton, R. (1984) "Ethnicity and Class: A Conceptual Note with Reference to the Politics of Post-Colonial Societies", *Ethnic and Racial Studies* 7(3): 426-34.

Odinga, O. (1967) *Not Yet Uhuru: An Autobiography*. New York: Hill and Wang.

O'Loughlin, C. (1959) "The Economy of British Guiana, 1952-56", *Social and Economic Studies* 8(1): 1-104.

Ooi, Jin-Bee (1963) *Land, People and Economy in Malaya*. London.

Pachai, B. (1971) *The International Aspects of the South African Indian Question, 1860-1971*. Cape Town: C. Struik Ltd.

Pandit, S. (1961) *Brief History of the Development of Indian Settlement in East Africa*. Nairobi: Pancho Publications.

Park, R.E. (1950) *Race and Culture: Essays in the Sociology of Contemporary Man*. New York: Free Press of Glencoe.

Parkinson, C.N. (1960) *British Intervention in Malaya, 1867-1877*. Singapore: University of Malaya Press.

Parmer, J.N. (1960) *Colonial Labour Policy and Administration: History of Labour in the Rubber Plantation Industry c. 1910-1941*. Locust Valley, New York: J.J. Augustin, Inc.

Pearn, B.R. (1946) *The Indians in Burma*. Ledbury, England: Le Play House Press.

Petras, J. (1978) *Critical Perspective on Imperialism and Social Class in Third World*. New York: Monthly Review Press.

Post K.W.J. (1969) Book review of *Cultural Pluralism and Nationalist Politics in British Guiana* by Leo Despres, *Social and Economic Studies* 18 (1): 90-92.

Poulantzas, N. (1975) *Classes in Capitalist Society*. London: New Left Books.

Premdas, R. (1977) "Guyana: Communal Conflict, Socialism and

Political Reconciliation", *Inter-American Economic Affairs* 30(4): 63-82.

Purcal, J.T. (1975) "Rural Economic Development and its impact on Economic and Social Integration in West Malaysia", *Contributions to Asian Studies* 7: 65-78.

Purcell, V. (1946) *Malaya, Outline of a Colony*. London: Thomas Nelson & Sons.

Purcell, V. (1948) *The Chinese in Malaya*. London: Oxford University Press.

Purcell, V. (1954) *Malaya: Communist or Free*? London: Victor Gollancz Ltd.

Ramchandani, R.R. (1976) *Uganda Asians: The End of an Enterprise*. Bombay: United Asia Publication.

Ramnarine, T. (1977) *The Growth of the East Indian Community in British Guiana, 1880-1920*. D. Phil. Thesis, University of Sussex. Micro film.

Ratnam, K.J. (1965) *Communalism and the Political Process in Malaya*. Kuala Lumpur: University of Malaya Press.

Reno, P. (1964) *The Ordeal of British Guiana*. New York: Monthly Review Press.

Rex, J. (1959) "The Plural Society in Sociological Theory", *British Journal of Sociology* 10 (June): 114:124.

Rex, J. (1970a) *Race Relations in Sociological Theory*. New York: Schocken Books.

Rex, J. (1970b) "The Concept of Race in Sociological Theory", pp. 35-56, in *Race and Racialism* edited by Sami Zubaida. London: Tavistock Publications.

Rex, J. (1978) "New Nations and Ethnic Minorities" in *Race amd Class in Post-Colonial Society*. Paris: UNESCO.

Rex, J. (1981) "A Working Paradigm for Race Relations Research", *Ethnic and Racial Studies* 4(1): 1-25.

Rex, J. (1982) "Racism and the Structure of Colonial Societies", pp. 199-218, in R. Ross (ed) *Racism and Colonialism*. The Hague: Martinus Nijhoff.

Roberts, G.W. and J.A. Byrne (1965) "Memorandum on the Racial Composition of British Guiana's Public Service" (Appendix 5), in International Commission of Jurists, *Report of the British Guiana Commission of Inquiry on Racial Problems in the Public Service*. Geneva.

Rodney, W. (1981) *A History of the Guyanese People, 1881-1905*.

Baltimore and London: The John Hopkins University Press.

Roff, W.R. (1967) *The Origins of Malay Nationalism*. New Haven and London: Yale University Press.

Rosberg, C.G. and J. Nottingham (1966) *The Myth of "Mau Mau": Nationalism in Kenya*. Nairobi: East African Publishing House.

Ross, W.M. (1968) *Kenya from Within: A Short Political History*. London: Frank Cass & Co. Ltd.

Rothchild, D. (1973) *Racial Bargaining in Independent Kenya: A Study of Minorities and Decolonization*. London: Oxford University Press.

Ruhomon, P. (1947) *Centenary History of the East Indians in British Guiana*. Georgetown: Daily Cronicle.

Sackey, J.A. (1979) "Dependence, Underdevelopment and Socialist-oriented Transformation in Guyana", *Inter-American Economic Affairs* 33(1): 29-50.

Saha, P. (1970) *Emigration of Indian Labour, 1834-1900*. Delhi: People's Publishing House.

Sandbrook, R. (1975) *Proletarians and African Capitalism: The Kenyan Case, 1960-1972*. London: Cambridge University Press.

Sandhu, K.S. (1969) *Indians in Malaya: Some Aspects of Their Immigration and Settlement, 1786-1957*. London: Cambridge University Press.

Saunders, K. (ed.) (1984) *Indentured Labour in the Caribbean, 1840-1920*. London and Canberra.

Schermerhorn, R.A. (1970) *Comparative Ethnic Relations: A Framework for Theory and Research*. New York: Random House.

Schlesinger, A.M. (1965) *A Thousand Days*. New York: Houghton.

Short, A. (1975) *The Communist Insurrection in Malaya, 1948-1960*. London: Frederick Muller Ltd.

Silcock, T.H. (1965) "The Effects of Industrialisation on Race Relations in Malaya", in Guy Hunter (ed): *Industrialisation and Race Relations: A Symposium*. London: Oxford University Press.

Singer, L. (1983) "Some Sociohistorical Perspectives on Race Relations", in Joseph Maier and C.I. Waxman (eds) *Ethnicity, Identity and History*. New Brunswick: Transaction Books, 125-46.

Singh, C. (1965) "A Historical Survey", in D.P. Ghai (ed.), *Portrait of a Minority*. Nairobi: Oxford University Press.

Smith, M.G. (1965) *The Plural Society in the British West Indies*. Berkeley: University of California Press.

Smith, M.G. (1969) "Some Developments in the Analytical

Framework of Pluralism", pp. 415-58 in *Pluralism in Africa* edited by Leo Kuper and M.G. Smith. Berkeley and Los Angeles: University of California Press.

Smith, M.G. (1974) *Corporation and Society*. London: Duckworth.

Smith, R.T. (1959) "Some Social Characterisitcs of Indian Immigrants to British Guiana", *Population Studies* XIII: 34-39.

Smith, R.T. (1962) *British Guiana*. London: Oxford University Press.

Smith, R.T. (1967) "Social Stratification, Cultural Pluralism, and Integration in West Indian Societies", in Sybil Lewis and Thomas Matthews (eds), *Caribbean Papers on Social, Political, and Economic Integration*. Rio Piedras: Institute of Caribbean Studies.

Smith, R.T. (1971) "Race and Political Conflict in Guyana", *Race* 12(4): 415-27.

Some New World Associates (1963) "Changes in the Character of the Political Situation, 1953-1962", *New World Quarterly* (March).

Sorrenson, M.P.K. (1968) *Origins of White Settlement in Kenya*. Nairobi: Oxford University Press.

Speckmann, J.D. (1965) *Marriage and Kinship Among the Indians in Surinam*. Netherlands: Van Gorcum & Co.

Spinner, T.J. (1980) "The Emperor Burnham Has Lost His Clothes: Guyana's Political Life in Disarray", *Caribbean Review* IX(4): 4-8.

Spinner, T.J. (1982) Guyana Update: Political, Economic, Moral Bankruptcy", *Caribbean Review* 10(4): 9-11 and 30-32.

Standing, G. (1978) "Basic Needs and Contrived Stagnation in Guyana", *Caribbean Issues* 4(3): 49-77.

Stasiulis, D.K. (1980) "Pluralist and Marxist Perspectives on Racial Discrimination in South Africa", *British Journal of Sociology* 31(4): 463-90.

Statistical Abstract 1981. Nairobi: Government Press.

Stenson, M. (1980) *Class, Race and Colonialism in West Malaysia: The Indian Case*. St. Lucia, Queensland: University of Queensland Press.

Stichter, S. (1975) "The Formation of a Working Class in Kenya", in Richard Sandbrook and Robin Cohen (eds), *the Development of an African Working Class*. London: Longman.

Sukdeo, F. (1976) "Political Economy of the Rice Industry", in H. Lutchman (ed) *Selected Issues in Guyanese Politics*. Georgetown: University of Georgetown Press.

Swainson, N. (1980) *The Development of Corporate Capitalism in*

Kenya, 1918-77. London: Heinemann Educational Books Ltd.

Swettenham, F. (1948) *British Malaya*. London: George Allen and Unwin Ltd.

Szymanski, A. (1981) *The Logic of Imperialism*. New York: Praeger Publishers.

Tandberg, O.G. (1963) "Duka-Wallah–The Backbone of East Africa's Early Economy", pp. 48-62, in Shanti Pandit (ed.), *Asians in East and Central Africa*. Nairobi: Pancho Publications.

Tandon, Y. (1965) "A Political Survey", pp. 65-89, in D.P. Ghai (ed), *Portrait of a Minority*. Nairobi: Oxford University Press.

Tandon, Y. (1973) *Problems of a Displaced Minority: The New Position of the Asians in East Africa*. London: Minority Rights Group.

Taylor, J. (1979) *From Modernization to Modes of Production*. London: Macmillan.

Tennassee, P.N. (1982) *Guyana: A Nation in Ruins*. Toronto: Guyanese Research and Representation Services.

Thoburn, J.T. (1977) *Primary Commodity Exports and Economic Development: Theory, Evidence and a Study of Malaysia*. London: John Wiley & Sons.

Thomas, C.Y. (1982) "Guyana: The I.M.F.–World Bank Group and the General Crisis", *Social and Economic Studies* 31(4): 16-70.

Thurnwald, R.C. (1935) *Black and White in East Africa*. London.

Tignor, R.L. (1976) *The Colonial Transformation of Kenya*. Princeton, N.J.: Princeton University Press.

Tinker, H. (1974) *A New System of Slavery: The Export of Indian Labour Overseas, 1830-1920*. London: Oxford University Press.

Tinker, H. (1976) *Separate and Unequal: India and the Indians in the British Commonwealth, 1920-1950*. Vancouver: University of British Columbia Press.

Tinker, H. (1977) *The Banyan Tree: Overseas Emigrants from India, Pakistan, and Bangladesh*. Oxford: Oxford University Press.

Turnbull, C.M. (1972) *The Straits Settlements, 1826-67: Indian Presidency to Crown Colony*. London: The Athlone Press.

Twaddle, M. (ed) (1975) *Expulsion of a Minority: Essays on Ugandan Asians*. London: The Athlone Press.

van Arkel (1982) "Racism in Europe", pp. 11-32, in R. Ross (ed.), *Racism and Colonialism*. The Hague: Martinus Nijhoff.

van den Berghe, P.L. (1967) *Race and Racism: A Comparative Perspective*. New York: John Wiley & Sons.

van den Berghe, P.L. (1970) *Race and Ethnicity: Essays in Comparative Sociology*. New York: Basic Books, Inc.

van den Berghe, P.L. (1981) *The Ethnic Phenomenon*. Amsterdam: Elsevier.

van Zwanenberg, R.M.A. with A. King (1975) *An Economic History of Kenya and Uganda, 1800-1970*. London: The Macmillan Press Ltd.

Warner, W.L. (1936) "American Caste and Class", *American Journal of Sociology* 42: 234-40.

Wasserman, G. (1976) *Politics of Decolonisation: Kenya Europeans and the Land Issue*, 1960-1965. Cambridge, Cambridge University Press.

Waters, D.J. (1980) "Jungle Politics: Guyana, The Peoples Temple, and the Affairs of State", *Caribbean Review* IX(2): 8-13.

Weber, M. (1968) *Economy and Society*, Vol 1. New York: Bedminster Press.

West Indian Royal Commission Report, 1945. London: H.M.S.O.

Wheatley, P. (1961) *The Golden Khersonese*. Westport, Conn.: Greenwood Press.

Wiebe, P.D. and S. Mariappen (1978) *Indian Malaysians: The View from the Plantation*. New Delhi: Monohar Publications.

Williams, E. (1961) *Capitalism and Slavery*. Chapel Hill: University of North Carolina Press.

Wilson, W.J. (1973) *Power, Racism, and Privilege: Race Relations in Theoretical and Sociohistorical Perspectives*. New York: The Macmillan Co.

Wolff, R.D. (1974) *The Economics of Colonialism: Britain and Kenya, 1870-1930*. New Haven and London: Yale University Press.

Wolpe, H. (1972) "Capitalism and Cheap Labour-Power in South Africa: From Segregation to Apartheid", *Economy and Society* 1(4): 425-56.

Worsley, P. (1967) *The Third World*. London: Weidenfeld and Nicolson.

Wrigley, C.C. (1965) "Kenya: The Patterns of Economic Life, 1902-1945", in Vincent Harlow and E.M. Chilver (eds.), *History of East Africa*, Vol. 2. Oxford: Clarendon Press.

Zenner, W.P. (1980) "Middleman Minority Theories: A Critical Review", pp. 413-25, in R.S. Bryce-Laporte, et al. (eds) *Source-Book on the New Immigration*. New Brunswick, N.J.: Transaction Books.

Index